D0376001

Film and Television
After DVD

Routledge Research in Cultural and Media Studies

Film and Television After DVD

Edited by James Bennett and Tom Brown

Routledge
Taylor & Francis Group
New York   London

First published 2008
by Routledge
270 Madison Ave, New York, NY 10016

Simultaneously published in the UK
by Routledge
2 Park Square, Milton Park, Abingdon, Oxon OX14 4RN

Routledge is an imprint of the Taylor & Francis Group, an informa business

© 2008 Taylor & Francis

Typeset in Sabon by IBT Global.

Library of Congress Cataloging in Publication Data

Film and television after DVD / edited by James Bennett and Tom Brown.
p. cm.
Includes bibliographical references and index.
ISBN 978-0-415-96241-4
1. DVD-Video discs—Social aspects. 2. DVD-Video discs—History. I. Bennett,
James, 1978–II. Brown, Tom, 1978–
PN1992.945.F55 2008
384.5'58—dc22
2008001577

ISBN10: 0-415-96241-2 (hbk)
ISBN10: 0-203-89429-4 (ebk)

ISBN13: 978-0-415-96241-4 (hbk)
ISBN13: 978-0-203-89429-3 (ebk)

Contents

List of Figures

Acknowledgments

This collection emerged from a conference held at the University of Warwick in April 2005. The conference would not have been possible without the generous support of the University's Humanities Research Center. We are grateful to the delegates and speakers, some of whom are contributors to this volume, who made the event so successful and inspired us to develop the project further. Special thanks must also go to the Center's secretary, Sue Dibben, who helped to organize the event.

Warwick's Department of Film and Television Studies was instrumental in the formation of the project. The department offered an intellectually stimulating but also an extremely supportive environment, one which encouraged doctoral students to develop research with an international profile. Too many people contribute to making the department what it is to single out any individual, but thanks go to them all. James Bennett would also like to thank London Metropolitan University's Research Capability Fund for support in completing the final phases of the book.

Finally, thank you to Niki and Mel, whose tireless support and encouragement made this work possible.

Introduction: Past the Boundaries of "New" and "Old" Media
Film and Television *After* DVD

James Bennett and Tom Brown

At the time of writing, late 2007, members of the Writers Guild of America (WGA) are into the seventh week of strike action demanding a pay rise to reflect monies earned by Hollywood studios through "residual" markets such as DVD sales. When DVDs (Digital Versatile Discs or Digital Video Discs) were launched in 1997 in the US and UK (having been available from late-1996 in Japan), the potential impact on the economies of film and television production was unclear, leading the WGA to agree a deal whereby writers are paid 4 cents on each $15 DVD as a residual "sell-through" of the artist's work. Yet by 2005, DVD players were in approximately 84 million homes in the US, making it the "fastest selling item in history of US consumer electronics market" (McDonald 2007: 135; In the UK, DVD players were only beaten to the same title by the phenomenally successful BBC-led digital terrestrial television platform, Freeview—cf. Iosifidis 2005.) Thus in 2007, certainly for members of the WGA, it no longer felt appropriate to describe DVD sales and rentals as a "residual" market within which film and television circulate. From some perspectives, "the cinema" (narrowly defined, that is, as the theatrical exhibition of feature films) may now be characterized as a loss-leader or as an elaborate trailer for the more profitable DVD release.[1] As Paul McDonald's study of the video and DVD industries shows, by 2004 over half of all consumer expenditure on filmed entertainment in the US came through video retail and rental, with DVD accounting for 94 per cent of this "sell-through market" (2007: 144).

However, whilst the WGA dispute has been framed in terms of a struggle for a larger share of the DVD pie, the strike simultaneously signals a potential move away from the importance of DVDs in the economics of the film and television industries. The WGA's strike is as much concerned with the Hollywood studios' attempts to extend the current residual payment structure to the new delivery methods offered by other digital platforms: from downloading or streaming online, to the distribution of content across mobile platforms such as cell phones and iPods. According to the recently published report "Do Movies Make Money?" by Global Media Intelligence, DVD sales are in rapid decline, the explosive arrival of the technology having owed as much to consumers replacing their VHS tapes with DVDs from the studios' back catalogues (Smith 2007). Indeed, a recent report in the British newspaper *The Guardian* suggested that DVD sales peaked in 2004 at $20.1 billion and will continue to fall until 2010, when it is estimated the market will "only" be worth $15.3 billion (Timms 2005). Moreover, the competition from high-definition HD-DVD/Blu-ray high-definition formats and Internet downloading seems to have already set DVD, at least as a technological format, on the road to obsoletion, just as DVD had consigned the VCR before it. Indeed, in the emergent format war between Toshiba's HD-DVD and Sony's Blu-ray standard, DVD is already cast as the inferior and "old" media technology. As proclaimed by advertisements for Blu-ray, "It only takes one look . . . one listen, to realize how far you can go beyond DVD." Similarly, Toshiba's HD-DVD advertising campaign depicts a couple as so engrossed by the technical quality of HD-DVD that they actually become immersed in an action film's diegesis, declaring the experience is "so real, you can feel it!" At the outset, it is therefore worth noting the paradox that captures this book, neatly encapsulated by the title *Film and Television After DVD*, which reflects the way in which the DVD invites us to reconsider understandings of film and television as established, "old," media forms even as we move to a mediascape that might itself be considered "after DVD."

Yet, one must reconcile this perspective with some of the bolder claims that have been made for DVD, including that it has fundamentally changed film and television culture. For example, in 2003, Philip French, one of the UK's most respected film critics commented that DVDs perhaps represented the most significant technological innovation in the movie industry since the coming of sound. French spoke as a film enthusiast who welcomed an unprecedented access to classics from cinema's past in a format of far greater fidelity than the VHS tape—an expression of DVD's impact upon what was valued by "old time cinephilia" (see Barbara Klinger's entry in this collection). However one might answer French's claim by pointing to the fact that, as with Warner Brothers' promotion of the coming of sound in *The Jazz Singer* (Crosland 1927), the emergence of DVD was not so "revolutionary" as its inventors claimed. Like DVD, the Vitaphone sound system was not so much a "new" technology as an innovative combination of "older" technologies and the result of a series of incremental developments in the synchronizing of sound to moving images. Similarly, high-definition may represent an important aesthetic shift, yet the signs are that both HD-DVD and Blu-ray will maintain the "extra" features ("making-of" documentaries, audio commentaries, elaborate animated menus) that largely define DVD textuality. Thus, despite the hyperbole of their promotion, neither HD-DVD nor Blu-ray will "revolutionize" the viewing of film and television in the home. They represent a further step in the continuous development of, for example, "home film cultures," the "political economy" of moving image consumption and the "(intra)textuality" of "digitally versatile" discs. The contributors to this collection have used DVD to assess these developments and, as such, the value of the work presented here is not tied to the shelf-life of the format. In the remainder of this introduction we use these three areas of concern, "home film cultures," "political economy" and "(intra)textuality," to structure our discussion of DVD's relationship to film, television and broader digital media. The distinctions between these categories are, to some extent, arbitrary and the point is that they are, like the technology they are used to examine, "convergent." Indeed, convergence, as an economic, textual, technological and cultural phenomenon, is one of the central themes of this collection and we return to this issue across the following discussion.

HOME FILM CULTURES

The above term is taken from the influential work by Barbara Klinger (from her 2006 book, *Beyond the Multiplex: cinema, new technologies and the home*, as well as her entry in this collection). However, "home film cultures" could also describe the nexus of technological and ideological discourses examined by Paul McDonald in his recent history of the video and DVD industries (2007). Like Klinger, McDonald reminds us that DVDs are part of a longer lineage of home video entertainment systems in which format wars such as the current one between HD-DVD and Blu-ray not only recall that between VHS and Betamax in the early 1980s (even down to some of the same players being involved), but also that such struggles have been recurrent throughout the development of the Video and DVD industries.[2] Significantly, the terms upon which such struggles are waged (one format's supposed greater "fidelity" than another's) are often set by the industry involved and may sit uneasily with the qualities, or rather limitations, of the technology that the industry seeks to elide. Thus McDonald suggests that an "aura of quality" has been attached to DVDs because of the massive improvements offered on the VCR's image resolution and DVD's apparent ability to reproduce copies of film and television without degradation from source (2007: 59). However, as McDonald goes on to argue, this aura of quality is conferred not so much by the technological qualities of DVD but rather through marketing rhetoric. Thus the aura of quality created by, for example, the designing of much DVD packaging to resemble books, or the inclusion of elaborately designed and animated menus, sits uneasily with the format's "lossy" compression, in which data and visual quality is degraded in the transfer from the original. For McDonald:

> DVD quality is therefore based on a misleading but highly marketable myth. Instead of digitization transparently and perfectly transferring data from the source to the copy, DVD mastering mediates the original, passing it through a series of intervening phases which subtly transform sound and image
>
> (2007: 61).

As a result, we can understand that the shaping of home film cultures around these concerns is affected by the vested interests of particular industries, most notably Hollywood. However, it is not solely film and television industries that impinge on the meaning and economics of DVD circulation, with computer companies and the video games industry playing an important role in the emergence of technologies like DVD. Again, McDonald's work is exemplary here, demonstrating how the computer industry played a decisive role in the adoption of a common standard for DVDs, when rival formats seemed an inevitable result of film studio maneuvering in the mid-1990s. As Robert Brookey suggests, whilst predictions as to the success of one of the emerging standards for the next generation of DVDs have highlighted the number of Hollywood studios aligned to either HD-DVD or Blu-ray, it may yet again be the computer industry that has the most decisive influence (2006: 204). Brookey notes that Sony has a ready-made catalogue of content to fill its Blu-ray discs via its ownership of Columbia Pictures and MGM, as well as exclusive distribution deals with six of the major Hollywood studios compared to Toshiba's arrangement with only four majors (Warner and Paramount having opted to supply both formats). However, he also points out that Toshiba's alliance with Microsoft might prove a powerful one that ensures HD-DVD enters the home through PCs, laptops and games consoles (2006: 204). Indeed, it is the battle between Sony's PlayStation 3 and Microsoft's Xbox 360 games console that might prove pivotal. As William Boddy's engagement with the development of second-generation DVDs attests, the association of DVD technology with these devices points to the fact that DVD is neither simply film nor television (though it provides invaluable opportunities to perceive the development of both). It is thus not only "home film cultures" that have been affected by DVD; it is also television and games cultures. Ultimately, one aspect of DVD's particular value to media scholars is in its representing the convergence of all three.

As much to do with "convergence," the format's success owes a great deal to other traditions, to more deeply embedded historical and cultural discourses. For example, the already mentioned "aura of quality" is key because it has been used to satisfy what consumers feel as the "thrill of acquisition" in the purchase of film and television (Klinger 2006: 85–90). Klinger's work charts long-standing discourses around home cinema that have stressed the ability of new technologies to replicate the experience of the movie theatre, discourses that have increasingly promoted a sense of the home as a "fortress of solitude." However, the "aura of quality" is not limited to DVD's perceived particular suitability to replicating the theatrical experience of a special effects blockbuster (something Klinger explores further in the discussion of the "perfect DVD movie" in Chapter 1), nor to the lavish packaging, both physical (DVD boxes, booklets and sleeve notes) and "digital" (menu design) that can enable a company like Criterion to talk about giving a classic work of cinema history "the Criterion treatment" (cf. Kendrick 2001). The aura of quality has been simultaneously extended to television, a medium traditionally separated from cinema for its comparative aesthetic impoverishment.[3] In this volume, James Walters notes the co-incidence of DVD with an increase in aesthetic analysis in the field of Television Studies, which as Matt Hills has noted, can re-contextualize TV series as symbolically bounded art objects that have the same "thrill of acquisition" attached to their purchase as film (2007). Moreover, whilst Walters' essay, in discussing dramatic serials, is attuned to a form of television that has increasingly attracted attention in terms of close textual analysis, the "aura of quality" associated with DVDs is less discriminating. Glyn Davis's discussion of the straight-to-DVD film *Leeches!* (DeCoteau 2003) later in this volume attests to the plethora of titles and forms of film and television available on DVD, which are not all necessarily enhanced by the fidelity of DVD technology to its source material. Whilst, as Davis shows here, a B-film such as *Leeches!* might be interesting and worthy of attention at an aesthetic level, it is less the "quality" of its aesthetics that is at stake than its place within a system of home film cultures that cherish videophilia as much as DVD's ability to replicate more established cinephilic discourses. Thus Davis explores direct-to-DVD films' destabilization of traditional hierarchies of taste and value, while, in Chapter 6, our interview with Caroline Millar (British Film Institute) and with preeminent film scholar Ginette Vincendeau discusses the role of the audio commentary and other DVD extras in the academy's formation of the canon. Both pieces explore DVD's key role in the shifting terrain of contemporary home film cultures, but are also suggestive of important issues in understanding the political economy of DVDs, which we turn to now.

POLITICAL ECONOMY

Across Davis's essay and our interview with Millar and Vincendeau, it is apparent that DVDs have not simply been associated with an aura of quality, but equally importantly, an aura of *quantity*. Their discussion of the various taste cultures catered for by the quantity of titles made available through DVDs is indicative of a wider shift in the distribution and economics of the film and television industries, in turn, speaking of new—but arguably increasingly similar—experiences of each media. Various scholars, such as McDonald (2007) and Max Dawson (2007), have drawn on Chris Anderson's book *The Long Tail* (2006) to examine how e-commerce has led to the increased ability of media industries to cater for niche markets. Thus the ability to "hunt out" *Leeches!* by the queer audience, whom Davis refers to in his chapter, is as much what John Caldwell terms a "second shift aesthetic" practice of the media industries as it is part of a wider destabilization of traditional hierarchies of taste and value (2003). As Anderson explains, "all those niches, when aggregated, can make up a significant market" (2006: 10).

However, quantity also functions in another way, apparent in the title of the conference from which this collection emerges. Inspired by an observation made by Victor Perkins, the conference's extended title "Some people are disappointed to *only* get the film," indicated the way in which the film or television program is but one part of the DVD "intratext"—"extras," such as "making-of" documentaries and "audio commentaries" are now equally defining characteristics of the format. This crucially impacts how one conceives the textuality of film and television texts on DVD and the particular textuality of DVD itself (more of which below). Across the essays in this volume, readers will find that such critical attention to the textuality of DVDs is also inevitably concerned with the kinds of activity DVD textuality seems to presuppose: the way they fit within wider industrial and economic practices and longer histories of film and television. The political economy of DVD has therefore animated many of the entrants in this collection, examining the changing formations of what "film" and "television" mean in terms of their texts, industries and audiences.

As a number of the chapters in this volume note, DVDs reconfigure the spatial and temporal dimensions of both cinema and television. As others have argued elsewhere, cinema is increasingly becoming a "distributed" phenomenon. Films no longer end with the "closing credits" but rather continue "beyond the theatre to the DVD, the videogame, the soundtrack, the website and so forth" (Grusin 2007: 214). More radically, Boddy has proposed elsewhere that, in the digital landscape, both cinema and television are "platform-indifferent," circulated as much across cell phones, computer screens, digital billboards as they are on the traditional "big" and "small" screens (2007). Similarly, work by John Caldwell (2003), Niki Strange (2007) and others has demonstrated that television's production, its texts and audiences are increasingly dispersed across multi-platform strategies that no longer take the individual broadcast program as the primary site of importance.

In the case of television, the DVD both replicates and extends existing practices of "time-shifting" derived from the VCR, and the removing of such programs from the "dirtiness" of television's flow. However, DVD also poses a challenge to how one conceives the political economy of the viewer/user's[4] interactions with the television or film text as DVD presents it. Whilst Rob Cover's work (2005) argues that DVDs are representative of a fundamental shift of power from centralized forms of media distribution to increasing power and control experienced at the point of consumption, or periphery as he terms it, the scholars in this volume strike a more cautionary tone. In Chapter 8, John Caldwell's historicizing of DVD extras as an extension of pre-existing marketing practices of the film and television industries suggests that the "disciplined" structure of DVDs actually functions to remove critical voices and power away from the periphery, disciplining the "unruly crowd" through pervasive marketing discourses. Similarly Jo Smith's discussion of DVD's political economy of attention positions its consumption as a form of "ludic labor," which blurs the boundaries between workplace media and leisure-time activities.

Whilst DVDs dislocate our experience of television from the ontology of flow and live-ness that has marked understanding of television, they simultaneously "bundle" together the film or television text with a range of secondary, often promotional texts. In this sense, DVDs are already in some ways part of an "old" media economy of "bundling" at odds with what Max Dawson's work convincingly describes as the emerging "itemized economy" of "unbundling" (2007). Dawson's examination of iTunes and other download services, which dislocate TV from the television screen, suggests that the unit of exchange is increasingly no longer the album or series, but rather the individual song or episode. Yet, just as Dawson's argument demonstrates that such "unbundling" does not suggest a fundamental or radical shift in the form of television itself, McDonald's analysis of the video industries suggests that the move to downloading services for film and television is perhaps not as inevitable and certain as at first glance. As McDonald argues, whilst DVD may have signaled the death knell of the VCR, media forms rarely totally supplant each other, with the co-existence of film and television for over half a century demonstrating that "new" forms multiply and co-exist with older media forms. Further, as Barbara Klinger's work attests, the "thrill of acquisition" has deep historical roots and it would be technologically determinist to suggest that, because "unbundling" is increasingly pervasive in our consumption of contemporary media, we will cease to enjoy films and even television series as relatively unified texts. The DVD (or the high-definition version that succeeds it) will also likely persist alongside more pervasive download and pay-per-view film and television services because, as suggested by an otherwise largely unreflective account of "the DVD revolution," "Americans are more comfortable with things than with access" (Barlow 2005: 27). In terms of DVD technology's potential longevity, McDonald usefully reminds us of the vested interests at stake in the development of new technologies:

> [T]here is every reason that hard carrier media in some form or other will still exist for video entertainment. Not least among the reasons for [their survival] are copyright concerns regarding the use of the Internet as a platform for the distribution of the major Hollywood and television studio's work
>
> (2007: 204).

Indeed, Jo Smith's essay in this volume implies that this very *physicality* of the DVD is what makes it so productive a site for unpicking some of the complexities of digital culture and the seemingly inexorable rush to dematerialization, an issue that William Boddy's essay returns to in this collection's final entry.

(INTRA)TEXTUALITY

> Primary and secondary texts are usually physically distinct from one another and are often read at different times, creating an intertextual relationship that is marked by both temporal and spatial distance. However, by including such distinct but interrelated texts in a self-contained package, the DVD turns this intertextual relationship into an intratextual relationship. Thus the DVD is perhaps the ultimate example of media-industry synergy, in which the promotion of the media product is collapsed into the product itself
>
> (Brookey and Westerfelhaus 2002: 23).

The above is an extract from perhaps the most cited work in the (admittedly small) field of scholarship devoted directly to DVD. The authors note a shift from traditional forms of film promotion that remained materially separate from the primary film text (for example, a magazine article detailing the making of some blockbuster) to the incorporation of promotional discourses into the exhibition of the film in the home (with for example, the access to a making-of featurette from a DVD menu, or by selecting a filmmaker audio commentary)—the promotional function of so many DVD "extra" features is noted at various points in this collection. As well as affording a useful vocabulary for understanding the relationship between primary texts and the ancillary materials on DVDs, Brookey and Westerfelhaus's model has proved useful to scholars interested in the close analysis of particular DVD texts. Their notion of the DVD "intratext" suggests a textual form more susceptible to discussions of coherent meaning than is often associated with the more commonly used "intertext." However, the apparent unity of "intratext" has been the focus of objections by other scholars. For example, in this volume, Catherine Grant suggests that Brookey and Westerfelhaus's analysis of the DVD release of David Fincher's 1999 *Fight Club* (whose homoeroticism, they claim, the filmmakers' audio commentary denies) falls into the auteurist discourse it purports to resist. Thus, identifying an intratext's "voice" may negate the indeterminacy of the texts' meanings and neglect the import of the variety of home film cultures into which such meanings are received.

Grant's objections to Brookey and Westerfelhaus's model of the DVD "intratext" are, in many respects, mirrored in Craig Hight's writing on "special edition" DVDs (2005: 8–10). Hight is interested in the alternative offered by the concept of "database," and particularly new media theorist Lev Manovich's discussion of the term. In *The Language of New Media* (2001), Manovich discusses the "database" as one of the defining forms of the new media age and as the natural enemy to narrative (the cinema is Manovich's recurrent representative of narrative): "As a cultural form, the database represents the world as a list of items, and refuses to order this list. In contrast, a narrative creates a cause-and-effect trajectory of seemingly unordered items (events)" (225). Already, objections may be raised concerning this simple dichotomy. However, one should acknowledge that the complexities of Manovich's argument are beyond the scope available in this introduction. Moreover, Manovich's discussion of the importance of the "interface," the system through which we access a database and through which a semblance of order is inevitably imposed, is useful for understanding DVD. Menus are the interface that helps define DVD textuality, requiring of the viewer a more complexly reactive (if not, more problematically, "interactive"[5]) relationship with the text than was the case with, for example, VHS. Hight adds further nuance to Manovich's model of the database, stressing the significance of a hierarchy and, in many cases, an overarching meaning to the organization of material on special edition DVDs. He also notes (quoting Downes and McMillan [2000: 173]) that "as users, we 'interact' with DVDs but only to a limited extent, and certainly not in the sense of creating a new experience each time we engage with the text" (Hight 2005: 10). Such assertions are useful in warning against any naïve associations of database with a new and radically democratic indeterminacy of meaning and fluidity in the user-text relationship. For example, in Chapter 4, Brown notes that the organization of material on the special edition of *The Lion King* (Allers and Minkoff 1994) is far more carefully managed than the text itself claims: a voiceover commentary on one of the menus tells the user, "your exploration . . . is different each time you visit."

One of the disadvantages of the concept of "database" is its potential to dehistoricize the forms it describes. Though Brookey and Westerfelhaus might be criticized for aspects of their argument, their examination of DVD's intratextual reformation of traditional intertextual forms of marketing relates the presentation of films on DVD to important historical antecedents. The discussion of "database," if not modified in careful ways such as in Hight's piece, may go too far in suggesting the openness of the format. John Caldwell's essay in this volume should remind us that DVD is a much more carefully controlled platform than, for example, the Internet. Indeed, Caldwell's use of the EPK (the electronic press kit) to understand the organization of data on a DVD answers the plea to historicize, implicit in the "after" in the title of this collection. So too, Jo Smith's analysis of the DVD as a hybrid technology locates DVD as database (or rather "its rather awkward manifestation as TV, as database *and* as cinema") in a particular moment in time; the "clunkiness" of DVD reveals its position in relation to both "old" and "new" media: "It points to the 'not yet' of digital technologies and the industrial drive towards newer and improved forms of audiovisual culture even as it demonstrates the refashioning of older versions of cinema."

Each essay in this volume is highly conscious of the need to historicize. Each contribution is also conscious of the significance of questions of disciplinarity that DVD throws up. We have noted how DVD asks important questions of the related but often unfortunately segregated disciplines of Film, Television and (New) Media studies. This is not indicative of mere academic navel gazing, but an important meta-critical project concerned to assess the place and impact of DVD in contemporary visual culture. The key theme of the book is to move beyond simply assessing the relationship between film and television and the DVD as a cultural object and think about the way in which DVDs invite us to *converge* scholarly fields. As Jo Smith suggests in her essay in this volume, the "DVD is not strictly cinema, nor is it a computer, television or computer game," yet it is often all of these things at once. Indeed, the book's genesis from a conference held at the University of Warwick in 2005 is worth noting in this context. As Charlotte Brunsdon noted there, the crucial lesson is that contemporary media studies must "converge its disciplines" if it is to understand a convergent object like the DVD. By treating DVD as a cultural object in its own right, with particular relationships to film, television and digital media industries, audiences, aesthetics and debates, this collection marks an attempt to engage with such a scholarly form of convergence. The interdisciplinarity of *Film and Television After DVD* provides the ideal forum for such a project. The variety of complementary, sometimes conflicting paradigms for understanding DVD textuality offered here attest to the richness of the object of study. Moreover, whilst "old-time" DVDs may increasingly be supplanted by HD-DVD and Blu-ray hard storage media forms, or by digital downloading, the convergence of media forms and scholarship will continue to be of central importance in understanding the developing digital mediascape. In the section that follows we provide a short summary and assessment of what each individual essay in this volume contributes to these debates and the fields of Film, Television and New Media scholarship.

CHAPTER SUMMARIES

In Chapter 1, "DVD and Home Film Cultures," Barbara Klinger provides the ideal opening to this collection, offering detailed context for the meteoric rise of DVD and outlining a set of interlocking discourses through which we can understand DVD's impact upon home film cultures. Klinger explores home film cultures as "arenas of meaning that shape the exhibition and reception of movies in domestic space," and she focuses on two particular manifestations that have developed in relation to DVD: reformulations of "old-time cinephilia" and "the perfect DVD movie." For Klinger, "old-time cinephilia . . . operates discursively as a means of establishing a familiar, experiential register for a later technological phenomenon." Thus, like its "old-time" predecessor, the cinephilia associated with DVD values a culture of film exhibition distinct from the limited range represented by "studio Hollywood": independent, eclectic "art house" cinemas find their latter-day equivalent in classic and esoteric DVD selections ordered over the internet and perhaps played on multi-region players. However, Klinger does not represent this historical narrative as a static one, noting DVD's encouragement of "home film cultures" centered around modern equivalents of B-movies and exploitation genres—something explored further in Glyn Davis's contribution to this volume. As Klinger writes, "along with its more aristocratic associations, DVD appears to have assumed the democratic mantle from television and VHS."

If Klinger's discussion of "old-time cinephilia" shows there is a kind of synergy between pre-video cinephilia and home film cultures after DVD, "the perfect DVD movie" she goes on to explore represents a different, more technophilic kind of synergy. Klinger notes the elevation of a certain kind of filmmaking (special effects and action-based Hollywood blockbusters, primarily) in fan discourses circulating around what DVD is best suited for. A set of criteria concerning the "perfect DVD movie" sees Woody Allen, whose films are rarely released with much in the way of "extra features," become digital persona non-grata, whilst *Lord of the Rings* (2001–2003) director Peter Jackson is exalted as the greatest DVD auteur, and *Star Wars* impresario George Lucas find himself in an interestingly conflicted position (see also Derek Johnson's 2005 interview with Will Brooker). The democratizing tendencies of DVD home cultures are highly contingent in this context, the discourses circulating "around the perfect DVD movie" being predominantly "masculine."

In Chapter 2, Glyn Davis's discussion of direct-to-DVD features (designated by "DTV" to note their relationship to "direct-to-video" films) examines a genre (in its loosest sense) often untouched by Film Studies. For Davis, films like the soft-core, homoerotic horror *Leeches!*—which, in a highly suggestive coda, he links to recent mainstream, theatrical cinema— represent a destabilization of previous filmmaking categories. The DTV thus follows on from what Adrian Martin (quoted by Barbara Klinger in chapter one) had noted regarding the impact of VHS on film culture: "[the videocassette opened up] new intensities, new streams for the circulation and appreciation of cinema" (Martin 2003: 6—7). Drawing on Derrida's notion of "undecidability" (cf. Derrida 2004), Davis uses the hybrid text *Leeches!* to explore the DVD realm, which, "like the bloodsuckers in DeCoteau's film," he writes, is "endlessly shifting [its] shape." In his theoretical explorations, Davis examines the importance of marketing (both in its "viral" and more traditional forms), analyzing the circulation of *Leeches!* and its relatives in online DVD rental stores. A fundamental characteristic of the format often neglected by those writing on DVD is the compact, light-weight design that has enabled online companies like netflix.com, lovefilm.com (in the UK and Europe) and amazon.co.uk to redefine the terrain of home movie rental. By close attention to interactions between DVD consumers on discussion boards and through other systems of peer-to-peer recommendation (something also addressed by Barbara Klinger), Davis shows how a film like *Leeches!* can find a market and, moreover, can contribute to a bleeding across traditional generic and taste demarcations. While being skeptical of any ultimately utopian outcome of the developments in contemporary DVD cultures, Davis detects "the seeds of a new ethics and politics of consumption and audience malleability."

In Chapter 3 James Walters's essay introduces the volume's concern with the way in which DVDs might inform practices within Film, Television and New Media scholarship. Taking his cue from Bart Simpson's adroit analysis of television from within the diegesis of *The Simpsons* (Fox 1987–ongoing), Walters focuses on the relationship between DVD technology and Television Studies, particularly the way in which DVDs might interconnect with the emerging interest in television aesthetics. Through the use of close textual analysis, Walters's essay effectively suggests the convergence of academic fields that the analysis of DVDs invites. On one level, by engaging with the way in which DVDs invite new temporal relations with the texts of film and television, Walters's work touches on a field of emerging work that treats television as new media (cf. Bennett 2006, 2008; Cover 2005; Dawson 2007; Kompare 2006). However, Walters' aims differ significantly from much of this work. Whilst Kompare deals with the way in which DVDs represent a removal of particular programmes from television's "flow," as part of an industrial switch to a model of "publishing," and Cover's work suggests that the new temporal control afforded by DVDs enables a restructuring of narrative according to viewer preferences, Walters's concern is an enriched understanding of the long-arcs of serial television. Drawing on Jason Jacobs's (2001) influential work on television aesthetics, Walters examines key moments in a recent series of *Doctor Who* (BBC Television 1963–ongoing) and season six of *24* (Fox 2001–ongoing) to suggest that the DVD, through its position as a "technology of choice," can reward critics by enabling close attention to scenes that draw "together broader themes that have developed throughout a run of episodes." Walters approach to television is therefore one very much informed by Film Studies approaches to film style, particularly in his focus upon detail, composition and the tone of particular moments of a text "in order to better understand the whole." What is of course also interesting in this context, is that it is the "new media" features of DVDs—enabling access to films or television programmes as a "technology of choice," a facet most often associated with new media (Kerr et al. 2006)—that enable this mode of analysis.

The question of the applicability of Film Studies' approaches to understanding DVDs as a new media technology is returned to in Tom Brown's essay "'The DVD of Attractions?' *The Lion King* and the Digital Theme Park." Brown's essay contributes to a growing body of work that links the "remediation" of cinema and television by new media technologies with the introduction of cinema at the turn of the nineteenth century.[6] Drawing on Tom Gunning's influential work on the "cinema of attractions," Brown uses this heuristic to move beyond the by now familiar arguments about the need to historicize the seemingly "revolutionary" nature of digital technologies such as DVD. In so doing, his essay is expressly engaged with issues of academic disciplinarity—the question in his essay's title inviting a closer examination of the applicability of particular forms of film scholarship to DVDs as a "new media" technology. Similar to Walters' work in this volume, Brown's essay adopts a deeply textual approach to analyzing the aesthetic make-up of the *Lion King* DVD as an example of the way in which DVD "intratexts" frame a film's exhibition context and, in turn, shape our understanding of the textuality of the film and the DVD itself. Paying particular attention to the way in which *The Lion King*'s DVD's menus and extras set up the experience of using the DVD as one akin to the theme park (indeed, linked explicitly to the possibility of attending one of Disney's actual theme parks), Brown demonstrates how this exhibition context has its own important historical antecedents. By considering the limitations of particular forms of scholarship, Brown's essay offers an importantly different critical insight into DVDs as an aesthetic "remediation" of Gunning's "cinema of attractions" to Richard Grusin's recent mobilization of this heuristic to understand DVDs as part of a wider mediascape he calls the "cinema of interactions" (2007). By recognizing the way in which *The Lion King* DVD "tames" the park, Brown avoids merely distinguishing the aesthetics of a DVD's intratextual form from understanding the intratext as simply a part of a multiplatform marketing strategy. Thus, whilst Grusin's notion of the "cinema of interactions" focuses only on the socio-technical and aesthetic forms of DVDs, Brown is able to draw our attention to the way in which such elements are always already embedded in corporate ownership and production strategies.

In Chapter 5 Catherine Grant relates her research on authorship in contemporary film cultures to DVD, identifying the latter as something akin to an "auteur machine." Grant explores DVD's "paratextual" (cf. Genette 1997) forms of auteurist discourse, the purest embodiment of which is one of the most ubiquitous DVD "extra features," the director's commentary. In this, Grant both draws on and distinguishes her work from Brookey and Westerfelhaus's discussion of the DVD as "intratext" (2002). She points out that Brookey and Westerfelhaus's critique of the restrictive authorial discourses performed by the *Fight Club* DVD audio commentary is itself highly restrictive. Brookey and Westerfelhaus assume that the narrative (one of the areas of filmmaking over which the director does have a *relatively* high degree of control) is the primary site of the film's meaning and that the audio commentary's redirecting of viewer interpretation of the narrative therefore fully achieves its apparently oppressive aims. Grant also points out that, in their over-reliance on narrative-oriented models of film interpretation, Brookey and Westerfelhaus crucially neglect the documentary quality of director's audio commentary. One of Grant's most fascinating insights is that "the act of selecting the director's commentary turns the 'original' (theatrical) experience of watching the film *as fiction* into one of watching it 're-directed,' or literally re-performed, *as a documentary*." Like many of the contributors to this book, Grant also uses close analysis to illustrate her arguments about film culture after DVD. Her consideration of the functions of director's commentary on the DVD of *Timecode* (Figgis 2000) shows how the text's narrative and documentary discourses "interpellate a connoisseur community." More broadly, Grant's analysis of the convergence of documentary with narrative film through DVD is related to a film culture in which the "auteur" has become so commodified (and so emptied out of what the *Cahiers du cinema* critics invested in the term in the 1950s) that a film like *King Arthur* (Fuqua 2004) can be released almost immediately on DVD in two versions, one of which is advertised as a "director's cut."

Chapter 6 takes the form of an interview with British Film Institute (BFI) DVD producer, Caroline Millar and film scholar, Ginette Vincendeau, conducted by this volume's editors in June 2007. Vincendeau has provided audio commentaries and a range of "extra" features for Millar and producers of DVDs at a number of other companies. The interview is focused primarily on the practice and purpose of academic audio commentaries, through which are broached the issues of canonicity, author-oriented readings and DVD's discursive role within the academy. The interview has an introduction in which these issues are sketched more fully.

The following two chapters of this volume historicize the interactive, digital media aspects of DVDs. Firstly, in Chapter 7, Jo Smith's essay thinks "across the gaps between Film, Television and New Media scholarship," considering how its status as the latter might impact on our relationship to film and television. Drawing on Gilles Deleuze's work and its newly championed status within New Media scholarship, Smith situates DVDs within a wider discursive understanding of media technologies' place in "societies of control." Moving beyond a simple Marxist account of the way in which such technologies mine the consumer's "time, attention and labor" in order to discipline and regulate audience behavior, Smith introduces the notion of the "clunk affect" of DVDs to profitably examine DVD's hybrid and physical status. Her essay argues that whilst DVD menus and bonus features might increasingly extend the look and aesthetic world of a film in order to promote a seamless experience of the DVD package, the numerous delays and interruptions involved in accessing DVD content "suggests a kind of interruption or time lag in new media's drive towards dematerialization." Whilst Smith might therefore be accused of a "technological determinism" in her analysis, her argument is more nuanced than this, suggesting that this "clunky" dimension of the DVD offers us up time and space for thought. As with Zizek's arguments regarding the shattering of the "fantasmatic screen" by the events of 9/11 (2001), the frozen and delayed screens rendered by DVD technology become a way of challenging and interrogating "new media's promises of more efficient and immediate media consumption." In so doing, similarly to McDonald's notion of the "aura of quality," Smith pays attention to the way in which DVD's aesthetic appeal is "harnessed" by database structures which, when thought of in relationship to this experience of delay, deferral and "clunkiness," can be understood as both "optimistic and pessimistic dimensions of emerging control systems."

If Smith's essay points to the possibility of understanding DVD as a new media form, as part of a wider era of emerging "control societies" in the digital age, the next essay in this volume reminds us that it is one that is dominated and disciplined by "old media" industrial practices. In Chapter 8 John Caldwell argues that "viewed in terms of institutional logic, rather than via 'new media' theory, the hard distinctions . . . between analog (or old media) . . . and digital (or new media)" are far from immutable or certain. Discussing the way in which DVDs function as part of a wider mode of "second shift" business practices, Caldwell outlines five intimately connected variants of "viral" marketing and programming strategies used by contemporary Hollywood and US television industries. Termed, "deep," "negotiated," "stunted," "value added" and "disciplined" variants, his chapter argues that it is this final variant that best encapsulates the DVD, restricting audiences to "locked-down" modes of interactivity. Against more celebratory arguments of the potential for DVDs to be used in fans' and audiences' critical exchanges, reading practices (Hight 2005) or as a kind of "peer-to-peer" network that challenges the hegemony of centralized media industries such as Hollywood (Cover 2005), Caldwell argues that DVDs actually intentionally harvest and monetize such user-generated content or user activity, positioning the audience as "faux-gatekeepers" and "quasi-critics" for this purpose. Indeed, such a view chimes well with fears raised in Vincendeau's interview about the use of DVD extras by students of Film, Television and Media studies. Together, their insights suggest we would do well, as part of teaching film and television aesthetic analysis, to make students critically aware of the way in which such extras function to actually cut out other critical readings as a way of managing and rationalizing the unruly crowds of the digital mediascape.

In the volume's final chapter, William Boddy explicitly engages in the film and television landscape *after* DVD. His chapter highlights how entwined these industries, and indeed the future fate of hard carrier media formats, have become with those of the IT and games industries. Chapter 9 offers a fitting conclusion to the book by historicizing not only the current move towards second-generation, high-definition DVD formats, but in so doing, also offering a valuable account of the rise of DVD technology, itself piggy-backing on the success of VHS. Importantly, however, Boddy's essay refuses the now well-established position of simply asserting that what's "new" about "new" media is never revolutionary and goes on to discuss the very real possibility that the battle between Blu-ray and HD-DVD may indeed be the "last format war" of hard carrier media for film, television and software industries.

A final note should be made at this point, concerning the issue of referencing in this volume. It has become the convention in Film, Television, and Media Studies to provide the year of release when citing film and television programmes, adding details of directors and production companies where appropriate. In *Film & Television After DVD*, we have stuck with this convention, but as many of the essays here implicitly note, one needs to make a distinction between discussing the film or television programme and the DVD itself, both of which, of course, share the same title. As Tom Brown's essay demonstrates, this is a question of examining the film (or television program) in relationship to its exhibition context, whereby the film exists as but one element in a series of texts that viewers might select from within the DVD. To this end, we've supplied an additional date for references where authors are referring to a particular DVD, rather than simply the "original" film or television programme. Thus, on first citation of a film or television text, readers will find the normal referencing details, such as "*The Lion King* (Allers and Minkoff 1994)." However, where authors are discussing the DVD of the same title, we also provide the year of the DVD's release: "*The Lion King* (1994[2003])." Where the film and DVD were released in the same year, we provide only one date, so too when the text being referred to is a direct-to-DVD film (as in the case of Glyn Davis's essay). In profound as well as ordinary, un-revolutionary and even banal ways, the DVD asks us to re-examine taken-for-granted concepts in Film, Television, and Media Studies.

NOTES

1. In this volume, John Caldwell makes this very point, also noting that DVD's importance and relationship to the television industry has been neglected by media scholars (cf. Caldwell 2005).
2. He suggests that these format wars are but one of three key factors in the development of DVD, its successor and antecedents, the second being competition between both forms of hard carrier media and between various forms of delivery media. Finally, struggles between copyright holders and industrialized piracy are also important to the development of a particular technology.
3. Barbara Klinger discusses how high-definition television (or HDTV) is further destabilizing these kinds of cinema-television distinctions (2006: 49). Similarly Pavel Skopal (2007) has suggested that DVDs represent a further convergence of the cinematic and the televisual, equally proclaiming their ability to recreate the spectacle of the theatrical blockbuster at the same time as offering the intimacy, authenticity and "imperfection" more associated with the domestic medium.
4. James Bennett's use of the term "viewser" (2006) to describe the role played by the audience of interactive television is useful in this context.
5. Manovich examines new media's "myth of interactivity" (Manovich 2001: 55–61). Also, John Caldwell's discussion, in chapter eight, of DVD as an intensely disciplined and disciplining medium is instructive here.
6. Aside from those works referenced by Brown, see also Hansen (1995), Boddy (2004), Bennett (2007) and Grusin (2007). The range of work perhaps illustrates Rick Altman's suggestion that "the cinema of attractions" may be "this Film Studies generation's most quoted watchword" (2004: 9).

BIBLIOGRAPHY

Altman, R. (2004) *Silent Film Sound*, New York: Columbia University Press.

Anderson, C. (2006) *The Long Tail: how endless choice is creating unlimited demand*, New York: Hyperion Books.

Barlow, A. (2005) *The DVD Revolution: movies, culture, and technology*, Westport: Praeger Publishers.

Bennett, J. (2006) "The Public Service Value of Interactive Television," *New Review of Film and Television Studies*, 4(3): 263–285.

Bennett, J. (2007) "From Museum to Interactive Television: Organizing the Navigable Space of Natural History Display," in J. Lyons and J. Plunkett (eds), *Multimedia Histories: from the magic lantern to the internet*, Exeter: University of Exeter Press: 148–162.

———. (2008) "'*Your* Window-On-The-World: The Emergence of Red Button Interactive Television in the UK," *Convergence*, 14(3): forthcoming.

Boddy, W. (2004) *New Media and Popular Imagination: launching radio, television, and digital media in the United States*, Oxford: Oxford University Press.

Boddy, W. (2007) "Dislocated Screens: The Place of Television in a Mobile Digital Culture," paper presented at "Television (Studies) Goes Digital Conference," London Metropolitan University, 14th September 2007.

Bolter, J.D. and Grusin, R. (1999) *Remediation: understanding new media*, London: The MIT Press.

Brookey, R. (2007) "The Format Wars: Drawing the Battle Lines for the Next DVD," *Convergence*, 13(2): 199–211.

Brookey, R. A. and Westerfelhaus, R. (2002) "Hiding Homoeroticism in Plain View: The *Fight Club* DVD as Digital Closet," *Critical Studies in Mass Communication*, 19(1): 21–43.

Caldwell, J. (2003) "Second Shift Aesthetics: Programming, Interactivity and User Flows," in A. Everett and J.T. Caldwell (eds), *New media: theories and practices of digitextuality*, New York: Routledge: 127–144.

———. (2005) "Welcome to the Viral Future of Cinema (Television)," *Cinema Journal*, 45(1): 90–97.

Cover, R. (2005) "DVD Time: Temporality, Audience Engagement and the New TV Culture of Digital Video," *Media International Australia Incorporating Culture and Policy*, 117: 137–147.

Dawson, M. (2007) "Little Players, Big Shows: Television's New Smaller Screens and the Aesthetics of Convergence," *Convergence*, 13(3): 231–250.

Derrida, J. (2004) *Positions*, London and New York: Continuum.

Downes, E. and McMillan, S. (2000) "Defining Interactivity: A Qualitative Identification of Key Dimensions," *New Media & Society* 2(2): 157–79.

French, P. (2003, 26 October) "The Best Thing Since the Talkies," *The Observer*. Online. Available: <http://film.guardian.co.uk/features/featurepages/0,,1071169,00.html> (accessed 15 December 2007).

Genette, G. (1997) *Paratexts: thresholds of interpretation*, trans. by J. E. Lewin, foreword by R. Macksey, Cambridge: Cambridge University Press.

Grusin, R. (2007) "DVDs, Video Games and the Cinema of Interactions," in J. Lyons & J. Plunkett (eds), *Multimedia Histories: from the magic lantern to the internet*, London: Exeter University Press: 209–221.

Hansen, M. (1995) "Early Cinema, Late Cinema: Transformations of the Public Sphere," in L. Williams (ed.), *Viewing Positions: ways of seeing film*, New Brunswick, NJ: Rutgers University Press: 134–154.

Hight, C. (2005) "Making-of documentaries on DVD: *The Lord of the Rings* trilogy and special editions," *The Velvet Light Trap*, 56: 4–17.

Hills, M. (2007) "From the Box in the Corner to the Box Set on the Shelf: "TVIII" and the Cultural/Textual Valorisations of DVD," *New Review of Film and Television Studies*, 5(1): 41–60.

Iosifidis, P. (2005) "Digital Switchover and the Role of the New BBC Services in Digital television Take-Up," *Convergence*, 11(3): 58–74.

Jacobs, J. (2001) "Issues of Judgement and Value in Television Studies," *International Journal of Cultural Studies*, 4(4): 427–447.

Johnson, D. (2005) "Star Wars Fans, DVD, and Cultural Ownership: An Interview with Will Brooker," *The Velvet Light Trap*, 56: 36–44.

Kendrick, J. (2001) "What Is the Criterion? The Criterion Collection as an Archive of Film as Culture," *Journal of Film and Video*, 53(2–3): 124–39.

Kerr, A., Kücklich, J. and Brereton, P. (2006) "New Media—New Pleasure?," *International Journal of Cultural Studies*, 9(1): 63–82.

Klinger, B. (2006) *Beyond the Multiplex: cinema, new technologies, and the home*, Berkeley: University of California Press.

Kompare, D. (2006). "Publishing Flow: DVD Box-Sets and the Reconception of Television," *Television & New Media*, 7(4): 335–360.

Manovich, L. (2001) *The Language of New Media*, London: MIT Press.

Martin, A. (2003) "Movie Mutations: Letters from (and to) Some Children of 1960," in J. Rosenbaum and A. Martin (eds), *Movie Mutations: the changing face of world cinephilia*, London: BFI Publishing: 1–34.

McDonald, P. (2007) *Video and DVD Industries*, London: BFI Publishing.

Skopal, P. (2007) "'The Adventure Continues on DVD:' Franchise Movies as Home Video," *Convergence: the international journal of research into new media technologies*, 13(2): 185–198.

Smith, R. (2007, October) *Do Movies Make Money?*, New York: Global Media Intelligence.

Strange, N. (2007) "'The Days of Commissioning Programmes are over . . . ': The BBC's Bundled Project," paper presented at "Television (Studies) Goes Digital Conference," London Metropolitan University, 14th September 2007.

Timms, D. (2005, 1 August) "Fox's Choice Hots Up DVD Wars," *The Guardian*. Online. Available HTTP: <http://www.guardian.co.uk/technology/2005/aug/01/comment.newmedia> (Accessed 15 December 2007).

Zizek, S. (2001) "Welcome to the Desert of the Real—10/7/01—Reflections on WTC." Online. Available HTTP: <http://lacan.com/reflections.htm> (accessed 17 December).

1 The DVD Cinephile
Viewing Heritages and Home Film Cultures

Barbara Klinger

Given the current DVD-saturated media landscape, it is hard to imagine that this new entertainment technology made its debut in the consumer market little more than ten years ago. DVD's meteoric rise owes to a powerful combination of economic, marketing, and technological trends. Motivated by the possibility of new and improved profits, by the end of the 1990s, the major studios were involved in releasing recent films, as well as their libraries, on DVD. Even more than VHS, DVD represented a windfall for the studios. Costing about $2 per disc to produce (Leipzig 2005: 28)—far less than the manufacturing cost of a videocassette—and identified more strongly than this older technology with the sell-through market because of its comparative quality and lack of degeneration in replay,[1] DVDs meant bigger profit margins for studios and distributors. Whereas at the height of the popularity of VHS, consumers bought approximately five videocassettes a year, by 2002 they were buying at least fifteen DVDs annually (Lyman 2002: 13). Of the 10 million copies of *Harry Potter and the Sorcerer's Stone* (Columbus 2001) sold from May to June in 2002, for instance, almost 60 per cent were DVDs, while *Lord of the Rings: Fellowship of the Rings* (Jackson 2001) sold 5.2 to 6.5 million copies in the first week, with VHS comprising only 1 to 1.5 million of these sales (Nichols 2002: 25). By 2004, sales of feature films on DVD to US audiences amounted to nearly 50 per cent of the annual feature film revenue earned by the studios (Belson 2005: sec. C, 1, 6). While film sales on DVD have slowed, causing some anxiety in the industry, this source of income still represents a tremendous boon to the media conglomerates.

Video vendors too found economic advantages to the new format. A recent release on VHS used to cost vendors $35, while the same title cost approximately $16 on DVD (Leipzig 2005: 1). Such prices had obvious benefits for consumer sales, but the lower wholesale rates also meant that vendors needed fewer rentals to make a profit. Further, while VHS degenerated and got dirty through multiple rentals and was thus less useful when it came time to sell overstocks, the more durable DVD could be easily sold after a few weeks of rental. With the economic handwriting on the wall, between 2001 and 2002, the nation's commercial video vendors began relegating their VHS stock to increasingly dustier corners of their shops, and electronics stores devoted smaller and smaller amounts of shelf space to VCRs. In the meantime, all DVD Internet rental companies, such as Netflix.com, began to achieve substantial success (beginning operations in 1998, by 2006, Netflix had 6 million subscribers and distribution rights to more than 50,000 films [Hamilton 2006]). For the public, the falling cost of DVD players, from approximately $600–$700 in 1997 to under $200 in 2001 and under $100 from 2004 on, made the devices more broadly affordable.

However, the marketing of DVD in relation to other technologies closely affiliated with the so-called "digital revolution" in the realm of personal use was particularly key to its success with consumers. Much more than VHS, a format referred to by director James Cameron as "crap vision," DVD's audio-visual quality was ideally suited to deliver the superior sound and picture promised by home theater systems and HDTV—a state of affairs that has only been more dramatically confirmed with the recent advent of DVD in HD formats. Further, from its inception, DVD equipment could also play CDs, allowing it both to capitalize on the CD's success and provide a device that could perform double entertainment duty. Along these same lines, DVD drives quickly became a fixture in desktop and laptop computers and gaming systems. Owing to such associations, DVD was advantageously positioned to become an intimate and indispensable part of a high-tech universe of home and personal technologies.

Through economic incentives and the imprimatur of digital quality, DVD has thus managed to suit the diverse interests of Hollywood studios, video vendors, electronics firms and consumers, in the process quickly becoming a synonym for the movies and the movie experience. Not surprisingly, given its pervasiveness, DVD has deeply affected the way films and other media are experienced in the home. In fact, it has created a number of what I call "home film cultures"—arenas of meaning that shape the exhibition and reception of movies in domestic space. In what follows, I will briefly explore the notion of home film cultures, moving on to focus on two prominent manifestations of such cultures that have developed in relation to DVD: what I shall refer to as "old-time cinephilia" and "the perfect DVD movie."

HOME FILM CULTURES

Although non-theatrical exhibition is little explored in the field of Film Studies, like more public spaces, the home is influenced by various social forces that exert pressure on how viewers see Hollywood films. Neither insular nor sheerly personal, home film cultures are as exposed as public film cultures to discourses related to media and media consumption. Borrowing Tom Ryall's useful definition of public film culture, we can think of the domestic version as similarly composed of "an intermingling of ideas and institutions into recognizable formations." Like its public relatives, home film cultures emerge from "the immediate contexts in which films are made and circulated such as studios, cinemas and film journals, [as well as from] the material network of the culture, the philosophies and ideologies of film" (Ryall 1996: 2). As an ensemble of discourses that coalesces into "recognizable formations," any film culture is a complex entity.

In the case of home film cultures, they exist at once in a dynamic, interactive relation with conventions of media consumption, taste formations and aesthetics linked to theatrical cinema and to other household media, as well as to past modes of film exhibition in the home. For example, in terms of audio-visual excellence, DVD is often defined as comparable to that of the motion picture theater and as far superior to that offered by VHS. DVD's identity has rested in part on the coordinates provided by these other modes of film experience. However, this indebtedness goes far deeper than such straightforward comparative dynamics would suggest. For one thing, the circulation and consumption of DVD has been substantially influenced by the more than two decades of analog "video culture" that preceded it. In this sense, as we shall later see in more detail, a film culture is not uniform or homogeneous; instead, it is a "complex non-monolithic entity containing within itself a set of practices and institutions, some of which interact in a mutually supportive fashion, some of which provide alternatives to each other, and some of which operate in a self-consciously oppositional fashion" (Ryall 1996: 2).

DVD provides particularly rich territory for considering the phenomenon of home film cultures. As I have mentioned, this new technology's economic, technological and aesthetic advantages over VHS enabled it to quickly gain a preeminent place in the home entertainment universe, so much so that it would be impossible to discuss contemporary movie watching without taking account of its impact. In addition, DVD's celebrity status in the world of entertainment has invited copious commentary that identifies its impact on many aspects of cinema, allowing a particularly vivid view of the technology's cultural circulation and meaning. Further, via the special edition, DVD acts literally as an ambassador of context, entering the home complete with its own armada of discourses meant to influence reception, including behind-the-scenes industry information and commentary tracks.

Despite its impressive ascendancy, DVD's affiliations—at the very least with TV, VHS, theatrical cinema, and digital media—suggest that both its existence and its enjoyment are intricately bound to a larger media universe. Thus, although it is tempting to say that DVD has single-handedly transfigured movie reception in the home, it is more accurate to maintain that the technology represents a unique confluence of already existing modes of media exhibition and consumption. DVD has not revolutionized, so much as reawakened, dramatically enhanced, and/or broadly disseminated ways of watching and taking pleasure in movies that came before it.[2]

Since the history of the exhibition of commercial films in US homes began in the late 1800s, shortly after Thomas Edison introduced his Kinetoscope to the public (Singer 1988), since more viewers have been watching films at home than at the motion picture theater for over twenty years (Wasko 1994: 3), and since film watching in domestic space has always relied on other media, I would argue that DVD film cultures are indebted to a series of "viewing heritages"—preceding and/or coexisting traditions of movie and media consumption—that they reanimate, and, in the process, update or otherwise transform.

As film cultures are comprised of overlapping and competing discourses, my aim is not to provide an exhaustive account of these phenomena. Rather, I hope to identify some of their central features both to engage the concept of film culture in relation to a place often ignored in Film Studies—that is, the home—and to examine the effects DVD has had on movie reception. Granting that there are other variables at play, I explore how an assembly of public discourses, including industry sources, general circulation newspapers, consumer entertainment magazines, the Internet and other venues have defined DVD spectatorship and fandom. I focus on two major home film cultures, each defined by different types of cinephilia and each indebted to different viewing heritages. The first has its roots in theatrical cinephilia, dating back at least to the post-WWII fervor for foreign film imports; the second has developed in relation to a contemporary digital aesthetic based on a sense of technologically-constituted visual and aural perfection. Together, they begin to suggest the diversity of DVD film cultures, as well as the complexity of their sources and configurations.

OLD-TIME CINEPHILIA

For some media pundits and audiences, DVD offers the closest contemporary approximation of a notable bygone public film culture—that is, post-WWII cinephilia. During this period, cultural cognoscenti and college students alike frequented art and repertory theaters to partake of the films of classic American directors, as well as foreign filmmakers such as Federico Fellini, Ingmar Bergman and Akira Kurosawa. These experiences led to a widespread heady new appreciation of film as art and of moviegoing itself as a magical and intimately engrossing activity. In her oft-quoted essay, "The Decay of Cinema," published in the *New York Times Magazine* in 1996, Susan Sontag declared that cinephilia of this kind, begun in France in the 1950s with *Cahiers du cinema* and reaching its apogee in the Western world in the 1960s and early 1970s, had been destroyed by the hegemony of the blockbuster, the rise of home viewing, and the closing of movie theaters dedicated, as she put it, to showing "original, passionate films of the highest seriousness." Meant to commemorate cinema's 100th anniversary, Sontag's article became a wake for the art form and for the kind of ecstatic cine-love she and others like her had found in darkened motion picture theaters for a fleeting moment before the 1980s (Sontag 1996: 60–61).

Although Sontag's cinephile is a denizen of the cinematheque, DVD has provided a non-theatrical forum for the cultivation of this kind of connoisseurship. Surpassing today's more sporadic theatrical offerings of foreign and independent films, DVD makes available all manner of such titles, both old and new, along with Hollywood classics. Through a DVD mail-order service such as Netflix, for example, one can find myriad art films and exercises in esoterica (from Lars von Trier's *The Five Obstructions* [2003{2004}] to Mario Bava's *Hercules in the Haunted World* [1961{2003}]) that beckon aesthetes and film buffs alike (Figure 1.1). In addition to providing access to films that are difficult or impossible to find in multiplexes or on television, for a flat monthly rate and no late fees, subscribers to this service can order as many films as they like. According to one subscriber quoted in an article on Netflix in the *New York Times*, the flat monthly fee alone encourages more frequent and more adventurous renting (*Russian Ark* [2002{2003}], why not?). This enthusiast found that Netflix not only changed his viewing routines, but, by exposing him to films that lie outside of the mainstream, "turned [him] into a different kind of movie watcher." "Culturally," he writes, "I am no longer the same person." His household too has been transformed; it "now resonates with high-toned animated discussions of directors, cinematographers, and camera angles." As a result, this viewer is reminded of his old college experiences, when moviegoing "adventure was in the air, and bright-eyed cineastes could sit through a film like *El Topo* (1970) and not demand their money back" (Grimes 2004: 24). As this testimony suggests, DVD allows certain baby-boomers to travel nostalgically back to the "good old days" of moviegoing when zealous cinephiles could discover unusual films for their viewing pleasure. Further, as such viewers experiment with arty or arcane titles, they learn something about cinema along the way, self-consciously striving to improve their cinematic IQs. Like its post-war predecessor, then, this cinephilia is associated with a kind of aristocratic cine-literacy.

To define this experience of DVD more precisely as a film culture, we can consider postwar cinephilia as providing a point of intelligibility for comprehending DVD's impact on film consumption. That is, as a historical precedent, it furnishes coordinates for explaining contemporary film pleasures based on experimentation with non-mainstream texts and educational imperatives. The two cinephilias, then, are not the same; rather, the earlier form operates discursively as a means of establishing a familiar experiential register for a later technological phenomenon. Although public coverage of DVD's impact on viewing invokes this past mode of moviegoing to suggest the rebirth of a relatively unchanged cinephilia, the differences between old and new forms of cine-love are instructive for what they reflect about broad changes in cinephilic film cultures over time that have affected DVD.

Figure 1.1 DVDs, like Mario Bava's *Hercules in the Haunted World*, beckon aesthetes and film buffs alike.

Certainly, both old and new cinephilias developed in the context of changing patterns of distribution that resulted in the greater availability of non-mainstream films. Along with other factors, the end of the studio system in the 1950s, the ensuing loss of studio control over movie theaters, and the relaxation of film censorship allowed a glut of foreign films to enter the US market. Today, the vast economic importance of the post-theatrical market to the studios has inspired the re-release of diverse films on DVD; at the same time, the existence of multiregional DVD players and Internet vendors has made films that do not circulate in US and other markets accessible to interested viewers. Between these two periods, postwar cinephilia has migrated from the motion picture theater to the home, now the most popular and profitable site of film exhibition. Further, although the class-status of this kind of cinephile appears to be similar, as we already have begun to see in the comments of the Netflix subscriber above, postwar collegiate youth and literati have aged into older enthusiasts and intellectuals engaged in nostalgia.

Other testimonials bear out the significant place nostalgia occupies in the passionate tastes of these cinephiles. For example, in *Movie Mutations* (2003), a collection dedicated to what its editors, Jonathan Rosenbaum and Adrian Martin, call "world cinephilia," Rosenbaum remarks that the availability of foreign films through new technologies, such as multiregional

DVD players, has created a "new . . . shared, international space." Here one can "easily order films from the other side of the world rather than wait for them to turn up in local cinemas" at the same time as finding and bonding with like-minded film devotees. This intimate internationalism reminds Rosenbaum of the film community he "saw being formed between . . . New York, LA, London, Paris and Rome during the early 60s," causing him "to feel nostalgic for those links" (2003: viii). Scholarly work that explores cinephilia's connections to nostalgia further suggests the centrality of this kind of affect to cine-love (De Valck and Hagener 2005).

In addition, the field of films that qualify as worthy—as exceptions to the mainstream norm—has expanded from Sontag's modernist texts "of the highest seriousness" and select American directors and films beloved by post-war cinephiles to include disreputable genres associated with bad taste (represented by Bava's peplum film).[3] This last development shows that the new articulation of old-time cinephilia, especially as it revels in the ability of DVD to deliver marginal titles, is characterized by a convergence between high- and low-brow tastes, signaling the inclusion of directors and films associated with other forms of cinephilia—particularly that of the B-film or cult-video enthusiast, as described by, among others, Jeffrey Sconce (Sconce 1995). As this convergence indicates, contemporary cinephilia is linked not only to an earlier public film culture, but also to a number of other home film cultures, particularly analog video culture.

Recognizing both the efflorescence of a new cinephilia and its differences from postwar cine-love, scholars have attempted to differentiate one from the other through periodization based on shifting exhibition technologies. Thus, for example, Thomas Elsaesser has coined the terms "cinephilia take one" and "cinephilia take two" to distinguish between these two generations of viewers. Take one refers to the original French devotees who were exposed to a potpourri of American films after WWII, as well as to their immediate comrades-in-arms, urban elites in other countries who watched large numbers of foreign films during the same era. The cinematic experiences of these groups were intimately tied to the "sacred space" of the motion picture theater. Take two is divided into two subsets of viewers: firstly, the film lovers who operate roughly in a continuum with the first generation by revering certain directors in a world cinema context, but as they materialize on the alternate public screens provided by film festivals and museum screenings; secondly, the "fan cult" viewers who came to love the cinema through its appearances on television, VHS and DVD (Elsaesser 2005).

Elsaesser does not condemn this last group of cinephiles as heralding the death of cinema because their devotion to the medium developed in relation to electronic technologies. In fact, one of the more recent scholarly views of the new cinephilia is that it has enabled a more democratic access to cine-love. As Adrian Martin remarks, while television, as it showed "the great works of cinema," inaugurated the new age of cinephilia, this age was more seriously realized through the auspices of VHS as it achieved substantial penetration of the home in the 1980s. As he writes, "Video consumption completely altered the character of film cultures all over the globe. Suddenly, there were self-cultivated specialists everywhere in previously elite areas like B cinema, exploitation cinema and so-called cult cinema." The videocassette thus opened up "new intensities, new streams for the circulation and appreciation of cinema" (Martin 2003: 6–7).

Another publication entitled, *Cinephilia: Movies, Love, and Memory*, takes the second generation of cinephilia as its main subject. Indeed, the editors reject the medium specificity of old-time cinephilia altogether, deploying the term "videosyncrasy" to describe the fact that viewers don't identify with any specific medium so much as move easily "between different technologies, platforms, and subject positions in a highly idiosyncratic fashion that nevertheless remains connective and flexible enough to allow for the intersubjective exchange of affect, objects, and memories." The big screen is not privileged in these encounters, transforming cinephilia into an "umbrella term for a number of different affective engagements with the moving image" (De Valck and Hagener 2005: 14).

Thus, along with its more aristocratic associations, DVD appears to have assumed the democratic mantle from television and VHS. Perhaps nowhere is this more visible than in the contemporary public emphasis on cine-literacy. As DVD revives films from the past, consumer entertainment magazines and other sources define it as a special archaeological tool able to dig into cinema's history, thereby offering viewers an education in the medium and, subsequently, an opportunity to display their cinematic acumen. For instance, *Entertainment Weekly,* a Time Warner publication with a subscriber base of roughly 2 million, published an issue in 2002 with cover copy that posed the question, "Do You Really Know the Movies? The 100 Must-See DVDs: How to Build the Perfect Collection." Inside the issue an article entitled, "Cinema Literacy 101: Start Your Motion Picture Education with the 100 Most Important Movies on DVD" provides readers with their "own private cinema studies program," remarking further that "homeschooling doesn't get any better." The directory to the "movies that matter" also guides readers to the most important versions, signaling the centrality of the home market to aesthetic determinations. Films included in the top 100 range from titles in silent cinema (such as D. W. Griffiths' *Intolerance* [1916]) and other canonical works of world cinema (such as Jean Renoir's *La Grand Illusion* [1938]) to recent US blockbusters. The article also offers "crash courses" in various directors seen as emblematic of particular historical moments, including Buster Keaton, Michael Powell, Alfred Hitchcock, Stanley Kubrick, Martin Scorsese and John Hughes. As a kind of film school in a box, DVD represents a mainstreaming of the educational imperative. This imperative, in turn, defines the personal library, no longer solely the possession of the eccentric, as both an archive of the past and a signifier of erudite taste (Brown 2002: 22–44).

Aided by letter-boxed special collector's editions with their streams of insider data, the growth of cine-literacy in the DVD era, such sources tell us, has brought the "esoterica of film culture, formerly consumed by a moneyed geek elite . . . [to] the broader public," meaning "everyone's a film geek now" (Mitchell 2003: 15). It is important to note, however, that not all of DVD's predecessors have been aligned with what are so often regarded as the democratizing tendencies of home media: DVD cinephiles are also related to the smaller, shorter-lived phenomenon of laser disc. Pioneered by the Criterion Collection, this breakthrough in ancillary formats in the mid-1980s catered to about 2 million US film enthusiasts and collectors (Federal Communications Commission 2000)—a true upper-crust niche market. Producing digital quality, letter-boxed, special editions of classics in world cinema, complete with director's commentary and behind-the-scenes information, laser disc helped to popularize special editions on VHS and featured items that would later become de rigueur on DVD. It was during the laser-disc era that films such as Terry Gilliam's *Brazil* (1985) and James Cameron's *Terminator 2: Judgment Day* (1991) achieved great acclaim in the home market for their extensive supplementary materials.

By this point, it is already clear that the DVD film culture I have been discussing—one devoted to a rediscovery of films that typically do not have wide distribution in the mainstream, such as art cinema, B and cult movies, and some classic American films—has a more complicated genealogy than the testimony of the Netflix enthusiast quoted earlier betrays. At the very least, this culture is indebted to a series of viewing heritages associated with the post-WWII recycling of films on network television, VHS, cable television (which should figure more prominently in accounts of take two cinephilia), and laser disc, as well as the legacy of the postwar formation of cinephilia itself. These parameters, however, still present only a part of the picture. No matter what the particular take on the new cinephilia, scholars tend to share the view that a break in exhibition contexts between public theatres and home screens represented, for better or for worse, the turning point in the history of cinephilia. At the same time, they embrace the *Cahiers du cinéma* moment as the Genesis chapter in this history. Yet, as Haidee Wasson's work has shown, there were avid cinephiles before this time who were part of a 16mm film culture and denizens of the art museum (Wasson 2005). Although there are many different kinds of cinephilia, the existence of cinema in homes and many other non-theatrical venues before the 1940s suggests that the roots of art film cinephilia and cine-literacy go deeper than the second half of the twentieth century, making an exploration of this earlier moment an essential part of the chronicle.

The DVD film culture related to old-time cinephilia is, then, defined by a radical collateralism of previous film cultures. As we can see in the case of the Netflix subscriber, whose tastes stretch from *Russian Ark*, a film with bravura sequence shots and an enigmatic narrative that fits comfortably within the high modernist tradition, to Mario Bava, the master of the

Italian splatter film and darling of cult film aficionados, and in the case of
the cinephile-colleagues contributing to Jonathan Rosenbaum and Adrian
Martin's volume on world cinephilia, *Movie Mutations*, whose tastes range
from the art films of Iranian director Abbas Kiarostami to the teenage
angst comedies of American John Hughes, this collateralism is the defining component of individual acts of taste, as well as contemporary film
cultures more generally. The old persists in the new, so much so that definitively marking the boundaries of any single film culture is a difficult, if not
impossible, enterprise (Figures 1.2 and 1.3).

Recognizing that the reinvigoration of old-time cinephilia via DVD
demonstrates the co-presence of intersecting antecedents in a film culture
is not, however, the same as saying that there is nothing new under the
entertainment sun. Just as DVD's recent hegemony has been produced by
specific economic and historical conditions, it has not simply reproduced,
but has amplified or minimized certain aspects of the film cultures that
preceded it. DVD reworks past film cultures to produce new configurations
that neither fully absorb nor duplicate these cultures. On the one hand,
the confluence of these viewing heritages guarantees a ready stock of discourses that can be used to describe emerging developments in movie spectatorship, paradoxically, as if they were new or revolutionary. On the other

Figure 1.2. DVD film cultures of "old-time cinephilia" are defined by a radical collateralism of previous film cultures, stretching taste boundaries from the art films of Iranian
director Abbas Kiarostami to . . .

Figure 1.3 . . . the teenage angst comedies of American John Hughes.

hand, the interactivity of heritages in a given film culture demonstrates the inherent volatility, even confused conglomeration, of the tastes that define any recognizable formation of viewing, even, and especially, the newest.

Perhaps this historical indebtedness and volatility is particularly visible in the case of the resurrection of old-time cinephilia. The second DVD film culture that I discuss seems less bound by such conditions. What critics hail as "the perfect DVD movie" embodies aesthetic standards more directly beholden to the technical features that seem to set DVD apart from previous ancillary exhibition formats. As we shall see, though, this type of cinephilia is as "networked" as any other.

"THE PERFECT DVD MOVIE"

With its splashy presence in special effects' blockbusters and in motion picture theater sound systems, digital technology has become synonymous in the public eye not only with quality image and sound reproduction, but with cutting-edge technological progress itself. Along with CDs, home theater, HDTV, and other developments, DVD is part of a home-based digital universe that likewise radiates the superiority of all things digital to analog counterparts, allowing consumers to marvel over the advances of computer-age wizardry. In this interplay between public and private spheres, the reputation and performance of a family of machines mutually reinforce each other's association with excellence. As a result, an all-embracing high-tech ethos pervades the promotion and consumption of these machines, crafting in its wake a shiny digital aesthetic. This aesthetic informs one of the most visible of DVD film cultures, a culture deeply invested in what commentators in the press and film enthusiasts alike refer to as the "perfect DVD movie." Linked to larger digital developments, this label sheds further light on how cinema's interface with DVD has affected ways of seeing and evaluating films as they appear in forums of ancillary exhibition.

As it emphasizes DVD as a modifier, the phrase "perfect DVD movie" suggests a shift from traditional film aesthetics. This is not just the "perfect movie," where virtue might be found in a socially-committed story, cinematically imaginative visuals, or a virtuoso performance. As deployed by newspapers, magazines and online forums, the phrase has at least two meanings which, while not totally disassociated from customary aesthetic concerns, reflect a different set of priorities. What comprises a "perfect DVD movie" is intimately tied to properties of digital technology—more pointedly, to a film's ability in its post-theatrical circulation to realize perceived digital ideals and potentials.

The first of the label's meanings targets films that appear to achieve a seamless relationship between theatrical and non-theatrical versions in the realm of the digital. That is, as films with a high quotient of computer-generated imagery (CGI) and spectacular soundtracks—most often action blockbusters such as *The Matrix* (Andy and Larry Wachowski 1999) and *Lord of the Rings: The Fellowship of the Ring*—are translated into DVD, digital playback in a home theater setting is able to approximate the magisterial illusionism and thundering sound of the film in its theatrical presentation. Although blockbusters are not the only kinds of films that transfer particularly well into DVD, public commentary depicts them as best able to attain and display the sheer capabilities of the digital. Thus, film appreciation is based on the appearance of a happy marriage between certain feature films and post-theatrical formats as they reciprocally articulate the audio-visual pleasures afforded by digital technologies.

The range of the digital aesthetic becomes particularly clear when the marriage is troubled, perhaps because the film in question had a lackluster theatrical release, fell outside of generic expectations in the age of blockbuster hegemony, and/or failed to exploit the features of DVD in ancillary reissue. In such cases, reviewers employ the aesthetic as a means of resurrecting or burying a film when it appears on DVD. For instance, in a review of Walter Hill's *Last Man Standing* (1996), the writer explains that he hadn't cared for the film in the theater. However, when he listens to the reissue in his home, "with the sound turned way up, it was a lot more appealing, regardless of the ridiculous plot." The new digital soundtrack makes the difference: Ry Cooder's score "takes on more detail and omnipresent vibrancy, while the gunfights in DTS [Dolby Theater Systems] make the Dolby Digital gunfights on earlier [versions] sound monophonic." He continues, "throughout the film, subtle touches of sound—the wind seeping through a crack or a creaking door down the street—are given more clarity, stimulating your senses and making the tough questions, like what is a sheriff doing in a town that doesn't have any people in it, not matter" (Pratt 1997: 1–2). The successful convergence of film and improved audio home technologies is enough to inspire reconsideration, even of films considered to be "duds" in their initial runs.

Conversely, the aesthetic axe falls when there is a "disconnect" between film and digital standards. Such was the fate for the DVD release of Woody Allen's *Annie Hall* (1977[2000]), a film by a director whose oeuvre, in the first place, is inimical to Hollywood's sonorous, eye-popping spectaculars. Assessing *Annie Hall*'s soundtrack, the reviewer for consumer magazine *Total DVD* writes,

> There's a great bit where a fleet of helicopter gun ships attacks the Martian invasion party with missiles, and another where the nuclear silo explodes just as Woody escapes on a jetski. No, just kidding. As we have come to expect from Allen movies, you just get mono sound, with perfectly clear dialogue and the usual smooth jazz soundtrack, but there's really nothing here to get excited about
> (*Total DVD* September 2000, 44).

As Allen's film fails to measure up in a world of multi-channel sound reproduction, it becomes vulnerable to send-up through the digital aesthetic and its association with action genres. The aesthetic thus effectively displaces aspects of Allen's previous reputation–as a cinematic artist working outside of the mainstream, a poet of New York cityscapes, a comic genius, an actor's dream, and so on. In fact, in a recent poll conducted by *Entertainment Weekly*, viewers voted Allen the director who is "phoning it in most shamelessly when it comes to DVD" (*Entertainment Weekly*, 15 April 2005: 47), suggesting that, in the context of the home movie market at the very least, he is regarded as a hopeless Luddite unable to retrofit his films for a brave new world.

The second meaning of the perfect DVD movie has less to do with the smooth fusion of theatrical and non-theatrical versions or the achievement of audio-visual excellence than with digital technology's greater storage capacity—that is, DVD's ability to contain the feature film, as well as sometimes copious supplementary materials, on one or more discs. The number and quality of these supplementary materials loom large in evaluations of films on DVD. For example, returning to *Annie Hall* for a moment, because its DVD offers only a trailer and a choice of soundtrack languages, it is judged as "pretty poor, though much what we've come to expect from Allen films" (*Total DVD* 2000: 44). Conversely, a reviewer praises the

DVD version of *The Sound of Music* (1965[2000]) as "awesome," even though he or she admits to never having seen the film. Instead the rating is based on the ingenuity of games on the disc, which the reviewer was unable to beat (Richelieu 2001: 176–177).

"Best Of" lists, so common in magazines and newspapers, demonstrate with particular clarity the preeminence of the supplement in evaluation. In an *Entertainment Weekly* article that features the "50 Best DVDs" (among them *Fight Club* [1999 {2000}], *A Bug's Life* [1998 {1999}], *Brazil* [1999], and *Terminator 2: Judgment Day* [2000]), the writer acknowledges that these are not "the greatest movies ever made." Rather, the list is a "celebration of unique-to-disc extravaganzas that best exploit DVD's massive storage capacity and multiple-choice, chapter-surfing flexibility to somehow radically enhance whatever the main event is" (Brod 2001: 22). Although the film is still considered the "main event," these other features better represent DVD's special inclusive properties. As the supplementary materials for *T2* alone demonstrate, extras can be extraordinarily broad in scope and intricately detailed. The *T2* DVD supplement boasts an intricate menu from which viewers can choose to learn about almost every aspect of the film— large and small (Figures 1.4–1.13). For example, just one category, "Core Data Sampling," offers 50 chapters of information. Here, the viewer can follow the development of the film from early conceptualization, screenplay and storyboards; pre-production, casting, location scouting and set design;

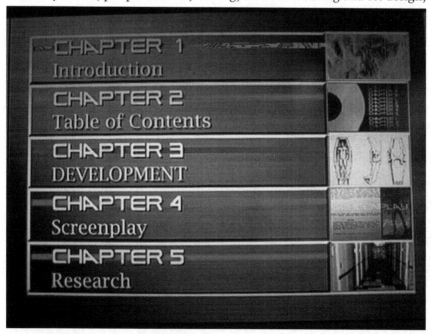

Figure 1.4. The intricate *Terminator 2* DVD menu offers viewers chances to learn about development and screenplay.

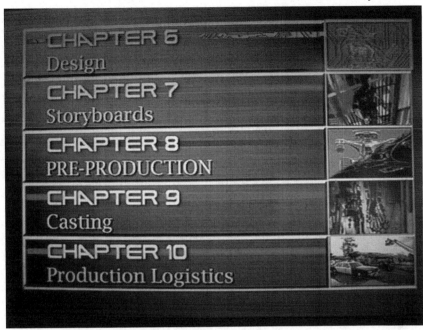

Figure 1.5 T2 DVD menu: design, storyboard and casting.

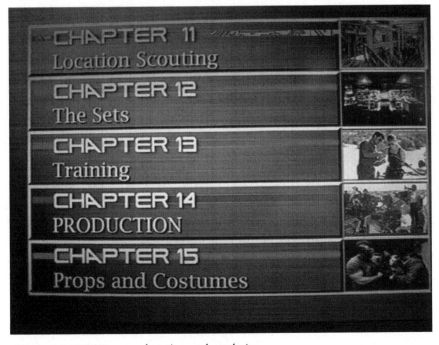

Figure 1.6 T2 DVD menu: location and set design.

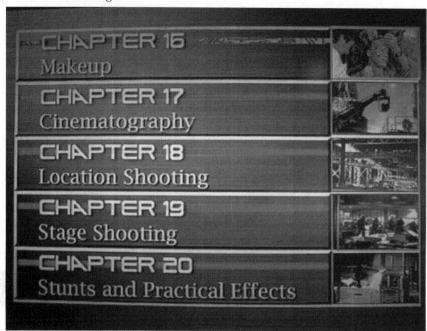

Figure 1.7 T2 DVD menu: production, make-up, cinematography and stunts.

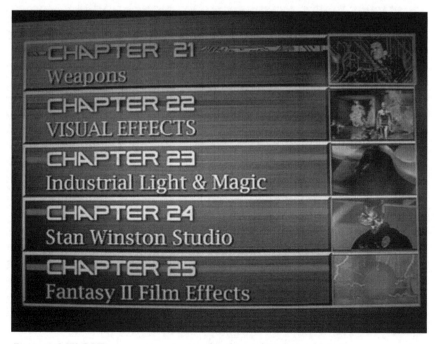

Figure 1.8 T2 DVD menu: weapons and Industrial Light and Magic.

Figure 1.9 T2 DVD menu: video image and process photography

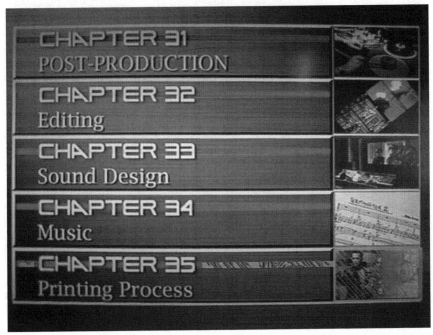

Figure 1.10 T2 DVD menu: special effects, post-production, editing and sound design.

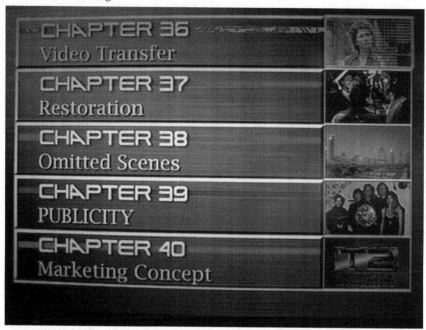

Figure 1.11 T2 DVD menu: restoration, omitted scenes and publicity.

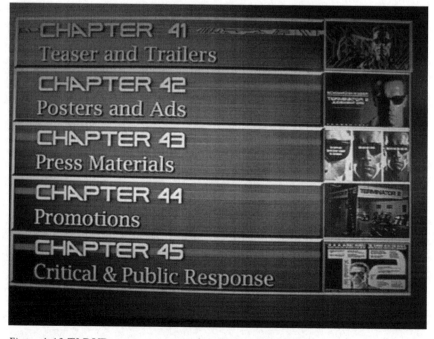

Figure 1.12 T2 DVD menu: teasers and trailers, press materials, promotions and critical response.

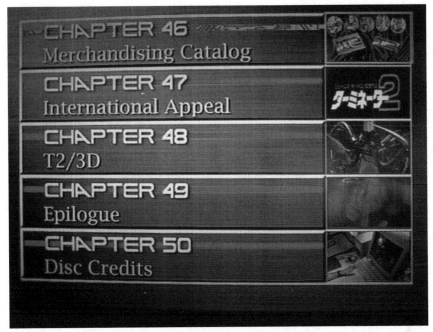

Figure 1.13. T2 DVD menu: merchandising catalog, epilogue and disc credits.

production, make-up, cinematography and stunts; special effects; post-production, editing and sound design; promotion materials and reception; to information about the "T2 in 3D" theme park. Each chapter embarks on painstaking explanations of each stage of the process, educating viewers about filmmaking, while letting them in on the secrets of the artistry and processes involved. At the same time, given the precise types of manipulation DVD technology affords, viewers attain a level of control they are accustomed to having with the computer mouse and the selection of menus available on the Internet, associating DVD with now standard modes of interactivity and the film in question with more things digital.[4]

Along with the breadth and depth of behind-the-scenes elements, the supplement's complexity and imaginativeness help further indicate the reissue's worth. As a reviewer writes of *A Bug's Life*:

> The computer-animation maestros at Pixar take the multi-gigabyte-supplement idea seriously and send it up at the same time. Thus you get golly-gee director John Lasseter and snarky Stanton [the co-director] making gag-me faces behind editor Lee Unkrich as he explains the wonders of storyboarding ... And nifty extra features just keep marching by, from effects-only audio to concept art to jokey interviews with the insect stars. The retina-rattling transfer of the main event comes directly from digital computer files, so it doesn't just outdazzle

VHS–it stomps theatrical prints, too . . . The whole package makes the DVD-movie interface feel totally, digitally organic.

(Brod 2001: 25)

Not only does this disc present extras, it self-reflexively parodies the genre of supplements, marking it as a knowing and clever addition to the DVD canon. Moreover, recalling the digital aesthetic's first meaning, as a Pixar animation *A Bug's Life* is totally digital; the reviewer depicts it as able to fuse with DVD more harmoniously than films based on live-action with CGI components. In this way, *A Bug's Life* achieves the oxymoronic ideal of organic digitality. In the process, the film on DVD represents the great digital hope of home theater: it not only surpasses VHS, but, better still, results in a film reproduction that outstrips theatrical presentation.

Supplements offer a host of other features that figure definitively in assessment. The presence and quality of "Easter eggs," for example, operate as yet another signifier of artistry in the world of DVD supplements. A term derived from a practice in computer programming, wherein the designer plants hidden features for ingenious users to discover, Easter eggs can be found in film and other media. On DVD, once uncovered, such features provide viewers with more behind-the-scenes secrets or other special information to which those less ambitious or less familiar with computer games will not be privy—in one of the editions of *The Matrix* (1999), for example, when double-clicked, a red pill sitting unobtrusively at the margins of a menu leads to a mini-documentary on bullet time. The restoration of deleted footage, the director's commentary and other features that comprise special DVD editions of films can also help a title earn the label of "perfect DVD movie." Hence, films are rated not only for how they fulfill digital standards of sound and picture, but for how their reissues realize to the fullest extent the physical capacity of the disc itself, especially when this capacity is deployed to render DVD as an autonomous art form.

As some of this commentary suggests, the film culture that has arisen around the technical features of DVD also involves a canon of directors whose work in cinema and oversight of its translation into DVD suits the digital aesthetic. As we have seen, previously lauded filmmakers like Woody Allen can become personae non grata if they fail to deploy a digital imagination in DVD versions of their films; at the same time, other directors, such as Abbas Kiarostami, are so ensconced in competing film cultures that their relationship to DVD technology hardly factors into their contemporary reputations. At the other end of the spectrum, directors known for cutting-edge experimentation with digital effects in their big-screen ventures can obtain a prominent place in this post-Sarris pantheon. This includes, of course, "King of the World" James Cameron and ruler of franchises George Lucas—although the latter's situation is interestingly vexed in ways that I will soon discuss. When an EW.com poll recently asked, "Which director is taking fullest creative advantage of the DVD format," 64 per cent of those responding named Peter Jackson, director of *The Lord of the Rings* (*LOTR*) trilogy, another wildly successful special effects franchise, as the top filmmaker in this respect (*Entertainment Weekly* 2005: 45). As this poll suggests, while the director's digital reputation theatrically can begin to generate the credibility necessary to join the canon, he or she must deliver on DVD to attain a secure position therein. With *T2* and *LOTR* faring extremely well on "Best Of" DVD lists and praised for their careful, encyclopedic disc extras, Cameron and Jackson appear to have easily navigated the divide between theatrical and non-theatrical realms.

However, particularly because DVD provides ample opportunity for affirming authorship, theatrical success is not always necessary for membership in the digital pantheon. Such features as the director's cut, the director's commentary, and the presence of imaginative supplementary materials dramatize the sense of the filmmaker's creative control, as well as his or her digital savvy; that is, their ability to make the most of what DVD has to offer. Thus, directors who have struggled in their theatrical careers have become celebrities on DVD and on its digital predecessor, laser disc. A notable case here is Terry Gilliam and his film *Brazil*, which collectors consider a hallmark in the history of digital re-release. Featuring the studio and director's versions of the film which are presented as embodiments, respectively, of crass commercialism and artistic integrity, *Brazil*'s 1996 Criterion laser disc serves as an early example of the power of post-theatrical digital venues to consecrate a director and a director's vision in the aftermath of theatrical release. Like any other aesthetic, the perfect DVD movie, then, creates a hierarchy of authors, confirmed or discovered, selected or rejected according to their perceived performance of the aesthetic's standards of value.

At the same time, this label involves a specific demographic among home audiences—as it happens the demographic most important to the blockbuster's theatrical success. According to market statistics, despite the immense popularity of DVD among families, the technology is regarded by the industry as a "man's world." A *New York Times* article entitled, "Action Hungry DVD Fans Sway Hollywood" (Kirkpatrick 2003: 1), reports that men buy the most DVDs, thus increasing their already substantial importance to Hollywood. As the author remarks, "once movies hit DVD, it's about masculinity." Men, for example, shunned the DVD re-release of high-brow literary adaptation *The Hours* (2002) in favor of other 2002 fare, such as action films *XXX*, *The Bourne Identity*, and *Die Another Day* and "sophomoric comedies" such as *Jackass: The Movie* which they consider much more re-playable than art films or romances. There were notable exceptions to this rule—e.g., the romantic comedy *My Big Fat Greek Wedding* (2002) was a sleeper hit of major proportions that appealed to both women and men. However, since DVD sales are among the largest and most lucrative aspects of industry revenue, the domination of male tastes in this market is highly influential, increasing exponentially the profits of certain films and helping to determine which projects have the green light for production.

These tastes produce a series of other markers of the home film culture associated with the perfect DVD movie, including the predominance of certain genres and stars. As we have seen, blockbusters, action films, science fiction, and certain brands of comedy are preferred genres within this digital aesthetic. Guzzlefish.com, a site with 14,000 subscribers and collectors, most of whom are men, further reflects the proclivity toward action and special effects films among its members. In the same year chronicled above, the site ranked the top collected titles on DVD among its constituency, in order of popularity, as *The LOTR: The Fellowship of the Ring*, *The LOTR: The Two Towers* (2002), *The Matrix*, *Spider-Man* (2002), *Fight Club*, *Pulp Fiction* (1994), *Reservoir Dogs* (1992), *X-Men* (2000), *Gladiator* (2000), and *Star Wars: Attack of the Clones* (2002), establishing a clear trajectory of generic tastes. Further, the site identifies action-film stars Samuel L. Jackson, Robert de Niro and Chow Yun-Fat as the most "collected" actors. In this respect, the home film culture related to the perfect DVD movie enhances the public standing of certain genres and stars, while ensuring the central place of male taste to Hollywood's cycle of production and exhibition.

This digital home film culture thus embraces films that embody audio-visual excellence on big and small screens, reissues that maximize DVD's extra features, directors with digital reputations, genres and stars associated with action blockbusters, and a male demographic. It thus presents a different world of value and a different set of viewers and viewing pleasures than that represented by contemporary old-time cinephilia, with its older, nostalgic viewers and taste formations defined by non-mainstream or historically-emblematic directors and films. Moreover, although visual and aural quality may be important to contemporary cinephiles in this tradition, they prize DVD not so much for its bells and whistles, as for its sheer ability to deliver heterogeneous titles, and to make films that might otherwise be hard or impossible to see available to the common consumer. However, while distinctions between film cultures are important to identify, these distinctions cannot ultimately be used to draw firm boundaries around these cultures.

With this in mind, thus far I have presented the film culture that surrounds the perfect DVD movie as relatively homogeneous, not, borrowing Ryall's words once more, as a "complex non-monolithic entity" composed of overlapping discourses produced by different institutions and practices. This does not diminish the fact that, particularly as they compete with one another for superiority during any given historical moment, aesthetic enterprises appear coherent; one has only to think of all of the alternative aesthetics forged worldwide in contradistinction to Hollywood narrative and style. However, whatever pitched battles may occur, a single enterprise is likely to be marked by a number of agendas, old and new, mutually supportive and oppositional. This is nowhere truer than of the digital aesthetic attached to the perfect DVD movie.

The perfect DVD movie aesthetic is clearly associated with other digital viewing and listening formations affiliated, for example, with theatrical blockbusters, computers, gaming systems, CDs and audio technologies more generally. Yet, like contemporary manifestations of old-time cinephilia, the perfect DVD movie is not simply a creation of mutually-reinforcing, cutting-edge digital technologies; it is substantially shaped by both supporting and competing viewing heritages from the past. This indebtedness to what came before can perhaps be seen most vividly in the way that DVD's reputation has rested on the ashes of VHS, how, that is, its excellence has been defined in contradistinction to the aesthetic limitations of VHS in both sound and image. The influence of preexisting viewing heritages in the world of the perfect DVD movie is realized more subtly as well. For example, while many saw Terry Gilliam's post-theatrical stardom as resulting directly from the showcasing of his cut of *Brazil* on laser disc, it also revolved significantly around a time-worn means of canonizing directors: as misunderstood geniuses or rebels who fight to achieve their artistic vision in the face of constraints imposed by the commercial studio system. Here, as often happens, the making of a digital reputation drew substantially from traditional notions of authorship. This embrace of long-established criteria for judging cinema begins to suggest the multi-vocal nature of the digital aesthetic, its deployment of a mixture of discourses as one of its primary architectural features.

The case of another director, George Lucas, provides insight into a different dimension of this aesthetic that similarly demonstrates its inevitable interactivity with other systems of value: that is, its contested place among other aesthetics. Lucas is widely recognized as a digital pioneer. Besides his stewardship of special-effects house Industrial Light and Magic, development of THX sound, and general innovations in special effects in relation to the *Star Wars* franchise, he is one of the few directors to have shot principal photography for blockbuster-sized films (that is, *Star Wars Episode II: Attack of the Clones* and *Star Wars Episode III: Revenge of the Sith* [2005]) with high-definition digital cameras and to have exhibited them in digital theaters. Although causing controversy in Hollywood, Lucas's lack of nostalgia for celluloid and muscular push for an industry totally based on digital film production and exhibition surely defines him as a digital director par excellence. However, the reception of his films demonstrates that his status in this regard is not universally embraced. Theatrically, Lucas's recent films have been lambasted for their overindulgence in special effects at the expense of what are seen as basic cinematic virtues, such as the competent directing of actors and a well-structured, engrossing storyline. DVD releases of his original trilogy (*Star Wars* [1977], *The Empire Strikes Back* [1980], and *Return of the Jedi* [1983]) have encountered further public resistance. For instance, of the trilogy's 2004 reissue, a film reviewer acknowledges that all of the films "look and sound incredible" and are "bonus-feature packed." However, along with many fans, the reviewer also laments Lucas's decision to alter aspects of the originals, including the look and outdated special effects that characterized the films when they first appeared on VHS. To recapture that experience, "Unfortunately, purists still have to dust off those old VHS tapes to visit the galaxy they fell in love with in 1977, 1980, and 1983" (Ross 2005: 38). Here the digital aesthetic comes up against a series of resistant formations, including *Star Wars* fan cultures, notions of authenticity rooted in the trilogy's earlier reissues on videocassette (interesting particularly because VHS rarely trumps DVD in relation to questions of experiential quality and authenticity), and the more general, but powerful, force of nostalgia, wherein the true experience of the films is rooted in first youthful encounters. Although critics and fans often greet the digital remastering and alteration of films with enthusiasm, in this instance they seem to regard Lucas as guilty of a form of digital excess, a single-minded pursuit of the latest and best that technology has to offer at the expense not only of his relationship to fan bases, but also of the artistic integrity of the films themselves. Thus, the digital aesthetic enters the cultural fray, where competing aesthetics question or attack its presumptions, in the process becoming an intimate part of its public identity.

As the digital aesthetic circulates culturally, we can grant that it has made an intervention in film aesthetics and reception, while reckoning with its negotiation of and place within existing aesthetics. In fact, given DVD's polyglot nature, realized through its inherent technological diversity as a visual, aural, electronic and digital medium, as well as its affiliation with numerous media in the home, from television and home theater to cinema and the computer, there is no escaping its association with multiple media, multiple aesthetics and heterogeneous audiences and fandoms. In terms of home film cultures, this means, at the very least, that appreciation of a film on DVD is not only linked to cinematic, but televisual, musical and digital pleasures. DVD, then, is the site of converging "philias"—audiophilia, telephilia, cinephilia and technophilia.[5] Because it foregrounds the interrelationship between media so vividly, it has much to tell us not only about the reception of a single medium, but about the complex choreography of pleasurable modes of media consumption that define any act of viewing or listening, whether the act in question revolves around confirmed or contested notions of technological perfection. As only two of many film cultures associated with DVD, contemporary old-time cinephilia and the perfect DVD movie cannot fully chart this new territory. Nonetheless, they strongly suggest that, despite the hype, DVD is not a revolutionary means of exhibiting films as much as a vivid reconfiguration of past and present ways of experiencing the media that has taken the media industries and the public by storm. The story each culture tells about DVD viewing reveals a family tree of media tastes and pleasures that not only helps to define the terms of this reconfiguration, but points to a potentially infinite regress in factors that have participated in the genealogies of today's film cultures. That so much of this activity has taken place and will continue to take place in the home implies that it is no longer sufficient to write about cinema's spectators without taking into account the extraordinary impact of multiple media and multiple screens on the their daily experience of the seventh art.

NOTES

1. The sell-through market refers to the studio practice of offering ancillary forms of exhibition, such as VHS and DVD, for sale at a low enough price that consumers will be tempted to buy the films (in addition to or instead of renting them). The combination of low price and superior quality, among other things, helped DVD to outstrip the earnings of VHS in this very lucrative market.
2. For more on DVD's relationship to industrial tradition (particularly in the sphere of marketing) and change (particularly in the sphere of reception), see John Caldwell's chapter in this volume.
3. Of course, post-war cinephiles lionized select "disreputable" American directors and their genre films (e.g., John Ford and the Western, Alfred Hitchcock and the thriller), meaning that a mixture of high- and low-brow tastes was not absent from this earlier articulation of cinephilia. While there is continuity in this sense, "B" and cult videophiles' later intervention into this politics of taste came in the form of focusing on "fringe" directors/genres that opened the canon further by pushing the boundaries of "good taste."
4. It must be kept in mind, however, as Caldwell points out in this volume, that DVD provides a limited, highly circumscribed or "tamed" form of interactivity, since there is little possibility for the kind of "unruly migrations" web-based forms of interactivity typically enable.
5. As I have mentioned, the co-editors of *Cinephilia* propose the term, "videosyncrasy," to circumvent the usual medium specificity that characterizes discussions of cinephilia and to acknowledge the fusion of cross-media philias that define contemporary viewing. This is an important step and one that I generally support. However, I would add that specific media philias (cinephilia, audiophilia, telephilia and so on) have individual histories worth considering in accounts of spectatorship. These histories would recognize the specificity of the philia not as some kind of "pure" entity, but as produced by a particular interplay of media and other forces that help to define it as an influential and pleasurable means of appropriating texts during certain eras.

BIBLIOGRAPHY

Belson, K. (2005, 11 July) "A DVD Standoff in Hollywood," *New York Times*: sec. C, 1, 6.

Brod, D. et al. (2001, 19 January) "The 50 Essential DVDs," *Entertainment Weekly*: 22–43.

Brown, S. et al. (2002, 11 January) "Cinema Literacy 101," *Entertainment Weekly*: 22–44.

DeValck, M. and Hagener, M. (2005) "Down with Cinephilia? Long Live Cinephilia? And Other Videosyncratic Pleasures," in M. DeValck and M. Hagener (eds) *Cinephilia: movies, love, and memory*, Amsterdam: Amsterdam University Press: 11–24.

Elsaesser, T. (2005) "Cinephilia or the Uses of Disenchantment," in M. DeValck and M. Hagener (eds), *Cinephilia: movies, love, and memory*, Amsterdam: Amsterdam University Press: 27–54.

Entertainment Weekly (2005, 15 April) "EW.com Poll": 45, 47.

Federal Communications Commission (2000, January) "Commission Adopts Sixth Annual Report on Competition in Video Markets." Online Available HTTP: http://www.fcc.gov/Bureaus/Cable/News_Releases/2000/nrcb0003. html (accessed 16 May 2007).

Grimes, W. (2004, 19 March) "Living Room Film Club, A Click Away," *New York Times*: sec. B, 24.

Hamilton, J. (2006) "Home Movies," Stanford Alumni Magazine. Online. Available HTTP: http:www.stanfordalumni.org/news/magazine/2006/janfeb/features/netflix.html (accessed 15 May 2007).

Kirkpatrick, D. (2003, 17 August) "Action Hungry Fans Sway Hollywood," *New York Times*: 1, 15.

Leipzig, A. (2005, 13 November) "How to Sell a Movie (or Fail) in Four Hours," *New York Times*: sec. 2, 1, 28.

Lyman, R. (2002, 26 August) "Revolt in the Den: DVD Has the VCR Headed to the Attic," *NewYork Times*: sec. A, 1, 13.

Martin, A. (2003) "Movie Mutations: Letters from (and to) Some Children of 1960," in J. Rosenbaum and A. Martin (eds) *Movie Mutations: the changing face of world cinephilia*, London: BFI Publishing: 1–34.

Mitchell, E. (2003, 17 August) "Everyone's a Film Geek Now," *New York Times*: sec. 2, 1, 15.

Nichols, P.M. (2002, 28 June) "DVD Has Begun to Take Over," *New York Times*: sec. B, p. 25.

Pratt, D. (1997, July) "Review of *Last Man Standing*," *The Laserdisc Newsletter*: 1–2

Richelieu, D. (2001) "Review of *The Sound of Music*," *Ultimate Widescreen DVD Movie Guide*: 176–177.

Rosenbaum, J. and Martin A. (2003) "Preface," in J. Rosenbaum and A. Martin (eds) *Movie Mutations: the changing face of world cinephilia*, London: BFI Publishing: vi–x.

Ross, D. (2005, 15 April) "*Star Wars* Trilogy," *Entertainment Weekly*: 38.

Ryall, T. (1996) *Hitchcock and the British Cinema*, London: Athlone Press Ltd.

Sconce, J. (1995) "'Trashing' the Academy: Taste, Excess, and an Emerging Politics of Cinematic Style," *Screen*, 36(4): 371–393.

Singer, B. (1988) "Early Home Cinema and the Edison Projecting Kinetoscope," *Film History*, 2(1): 37–70.

Sontag, S. (1996, 25 February) "The Decay of Cinema," *New York Times Magazine*: 60–61.

Total DVD (2000, September) "Review of *Annie Hall*": 44.

Wasko, J. (1994) *Hollywood in the Information Age: beyond the silver screen*, Austin, Texas: University of Texas Press.

Wasson, H. (2005) *Museum Movies: the museum of modern art and the birth of art cinema*, Berkeley: University of California Press.

2 A Taste for *Leeches!*
DVDs, Audience Configurations, and Generic Hybridity

Glyn Davis

The incapacity to name is a good symptom of disturbance
(Barthes 2000 [1980]: 51).

Lakecrest College: four male students dive into a swimming pool. Jeered on by a coach, they race down their segregated lanes. Alongside shots of aquatic action unfolding at a regular tempo, others are marginally slowed down to emphasize athleticism and its specular pleasures, and to match the pace of the grinding nu-metal guitars that accompany the scene. Reaching the far end, the boys (Stevo, Tony, Jason and Fish) climb out of the water, toned and muscular, all wearing goggles and the briefest of swimming trunks. They position themselves next to each other, affording the camera a clear view of their exposed, tanned and hairless bodies. The music fades into the background. The coach offers advice and praise, and leaves. Fish exits the frame. An exchange occurs between Stevo and Tony, without any cuts to close-up:

> Tony: "I've gotta say I'm impressed. I don't know what you're doing . . ."
> Stevo: "Wanna know what we're doing?"
> Tony: "Yeah man, anything that helps."
> Stevo: "Meet us in the locker room later. I'll show you the secret of my success."

The guitar surges to the foreground of the aural track again. Jason and Stevo walk back towards the other end of the pool, the shot in slow motion. As they move, they are watched by another youth (with an unreadable gaze—envious? suspicious? lustful?) preparing for his turn to dive. Cut to a different location: a communal shower room. The music turns sour, switching to eerie minor key synthesizer. Tony enters and notices several (seemingly dead) leeches on the tiled floor. He kicks these down a drain.

This sequence—which incorporates aesthetic and narrative elements recognizable from the realms of advertising, pop promos, pornography, teen movies and horror cinema—occurs around ten minutes into the film

Leeches! (2003), a direct-to-DVD homoerotic "creature feature" horror film that is indebted to both David Cronenberg's *Shivers* (1974) and Jeff Lieberman's low budget man-eating worms shocker *Squirm* (1976). *Leeches!'* narrative structure adheres to the generic format audiences may expect of the "killer creatures" horror sub-genre, familiar from such titles as *Arachnophobia* (Marshall 1990) and *Slither* (Gunn 2006); that is, the characters are picked off one by one in an episodic and gory manner, and in the final minutes, as the monsters are seemingly defeated, an explanation for their appearance is provided. But in a manner out of kilter with the horror genre as a whole, the deaths are mostly of skimpily-dressed physically attractive young men, their demises often preceded by attenuated sequences of them showering or undressing. Ultimately, the film turns out also to be an anti-drugs parable: steroids taken by the college swimming team have inadvertently been ingested by the leeches as well, causing the parasites to mutate.

Leeches! was directed by David DeCoteau, a prolific filmmaker who started his career in his late teenage years making hardcore gay pornography, directing 32 titles in around three years. Since the mid 1980s, and the beginning of his marginally more legitimate vocation, DeCoteau has made over fifty feature films often at a rate of three or four per year, many pseudonymously, almost all of which have been horror movies that have not attained theatrical distribution.[1] Despite their direct-to-video (DTV) or direct-to-DVD nature, however (and I will be using the acronym "DTV" throughout this chapter to refer to feature films debuting on video and/or DVD), some of these titles have performed well financially: *The Brotherhood* (2000), for instance, a tale of teenage Satanists, has sold more than 450,000 copies on DVD, spawning several sequels. Although examples of DeCoteau's early work featured moments of bisexuality or polymorphous perversity (see, for example, *Dreamaniac* [1986]), more recent titles—from around the time of *Voodoo Academy* (2000) onwards—have purposefully incorporated significant amounts of naked athletic male flesh. Notably, this shift occurred around the time that DeCoteau formed his own production company, Rapid Heart Pictures, which he says "was launched in late 1999 to make movies directed and produced by me and to be a closer representation of my taste in genre movie making" (Linna 2007). This queer intervention could perhaps be interpreted as providing a partial corrective to the history of horror cinema which has regularly featured naked and semi-naked women-in-peril—evident in, for instance, *The Texas Chainsaw Massacre* (Hooper 1974), *Halloween* (Carpenter 1978), and *Friday the 13th* (Cunningham 1980), parodied in *Scary Movie* (Wayans 2000), and recently experiencing a resurgence in sadistic "torture porn" titles such as *Wolf Creek* (McLean 2005), *Grindhouse* (Rodriguez/Tarantino 2007), and *Captivity* (Joffé 2007). Alternatively, it could be seen as a brazenly homoerotic contribution to a genre that, as Harry Benshoff (1995) has highlighted, has often been queerly inflected.[2]

Yet the sequence described above is a troubling one, preventing *Leeches!* from being easily subsumed within the history of the horror genre. Horror films only very rarely feature an overtly eroticized focus on male bodies. Nor does *Leeches!* identifiably belong to another generic category; for instance, it certainly isn't pornography, softcore or hardcore, as there is no sex in the film. There are, of course, significant structural and affective similarities between pornography and horror as cinematic genres, including the episodic narrative form already noted above (for more on this connection, see Williams 1991). However, *Leeches!* seems to inhabit a perverse hinterland located somewhere between gay male softcore (what exactly will be revealed when the threesome meet in the locker room?) and monster parasite film (how long until the leeches emerge from the drain?). What, in fact, would self-professed horror fans and aficionados make of the film? Indeed, who is the intended audience for *Leeches!*—is it actually produced for consumption by gay men or by women, demographics who might relish watching the frequently undressed boys? And considering the DTV nature of the film, how would any of these potential audiences even know of its existence?

In this chapter, I want to use *Leeches!* to make some observations and arguments about the culture of DVDs: their distribution, marketing, and consumption. I have chosen to focus on the DTV field—a business much larger, as James Naremore (1998: 161) has identified, than cinema produced for theatrical exhibition—partly because this realm of filmic production can, I believe, reveal a great deal about the operations of DVD culture, but also because this form of filmmaking is so sorely neglected by academic Film and Media studies. Joan Hawkins is one of the few authors to have even acknowledged the existence of DTVs, noting that "Not much has been written about the direct-to-video phenomenon" (2003: 233); as she puts it, "the rise of . . . direct-to-video films . . . has created a wide market niche for 'movies that nobody's heard of'" (2003: 230). Credit must also be paid to Linda Ruth Williams and her sustained interrogation of the aesthetics, thematics and economics of DTV movies. In her book *The Erotic Thriller in Contemporary Cinema*, Williams devotes roughly equivalent space and analysis to both mainstream and DTV incarnations of the erotic thriller, a (sub)genre that regularly features sequences of softcore sex interweaved with the standard tropes of the thriller plot (murder, duplicity, and so on). Williams identifies the tendency of film academics to focus on the canonical, the "legitimate," or on the extreme and avant-garde: as she points out, in relation to her chosen topic, film theorists would rather write about the "edgy" subject of hardcore pornography than the (arguably more ubiquitous) softcore (2005: 270). Thus, both softcore erotic thrillers and the "mainstream" realm of DTV movie production and consumption—and these two categories evidently overlap with each other to a significant extent—tend to be critically and theoretically marginalized. With both categories of films, this is (at least in part) bound up with the fact that consumption of such titles occurs largely within a domestic environment, away from the legitimizing space of the theatrical exhibition venue, and that these movies are too "popular" with mass audiences to warrant interrogation as artistically or politically experimental.

Taking *Leeches!*, then, as symptomatic of various practices and strategies associated with the DTV realm of film production, I will use DeCoteau's film as a focus for exploring audience configurations, and the relation of those groupings—what Bourdieu (1979) would perhaps have called "taste publics"—to the vast array of filmic texts that have proliferated with the advent of DVD technologies. Three main questions will be addressed. Firstly, how have audience groupings been altered and reconstituted in the era of DVD? In particular, how have cinephiles, queer movie consumers and horror audiences been reconfigured as niches (not mutually exclusive niches, of course) in the wake of DVD technologies? Secondly, how is a film like *Leeches!* distributed, marketed, and sourced? Finally, is the generic hybridity—or, to use a term from Derrida's writings, "undecidability"—of *Leeches!* (and other DeCoteau films, as well as many other DTV titles) actually *enabled* by the format and culture of DVDs, in a way that video did not, or could not, make possible? Ultimately, I want to argue that the sheer size and scope of the DVD realm—difficult to clearly map or contain and, like the bloodsuckers in DeCoteau's film, endlessly shifting shape—facilitates not only a rather wanton and perverse generic blurring in film content, but also brings previously segregated niche audience groupings into contact and discussion with each other, through their consumption of (and reflection on) specific titles. This means that there are significant political ramifications associated with the dissemination and viewing of DVD titles, which are particularly noticeable with DTV work. Although it is highly unlikely that an idealistic, socially and politically progressive utopia will be produced as an end result, the different audience members (teenagers, women, gay men, horror fans, and so on) who consume *Leeches!* (and other "undecidable" film texts that somehow find an audience on DVD formats) may at least be forced to confront and consider the diversity of movie audiences, and their disparate and complicated tastes. Films like *Leeches!* bleed their way across taste demarcations, making permeable the thin skin separating groupings, provoking screams and disgust at the mess caused. And yet located in that mess, it is possible to detect the seeds of a new ethics and politics of consumption and audience malleability.

WATCHING *LEECHES!*

Although the DVD format is only a decade old—it was launched as a system for film distribution and consumption in 1997—the uptake of the technology into homes has been fast, marked and unprecedented. As Anne Friedberg identified, "The growth curve of DVD ownership has occurred more rapidly than the growth rate of VCR households in the 1980s, a rate which had already occurred at an acceleration of the rate of television households in the 1950s" (2002: 35). As DVD players (and, marginally later, DVD recorders) have ousted VCRs as the market's—and, concomitantly, the consumer's—preferred format for audio-visual entertainment in the home, the number of DVD discs available has exploded. Again, this has been on a scale markedly larger than with the advent of VCRs as a home entertainment technology. Tim De Lisle estimated in January 2005 that there were, at that time, "29,000 titles in print, which is about five times as many as video."

Further, the appearance and swift consumer acquisition of DVD technology has enabled the DVD format to confront and challenge the cultural position and significance of cinema exhibition, in the same way that video did for over a decade. In 1992, the home video market was worth $11 billion, in comparison with $5 billion for the theatrical field (Cook and Bernink 1999: 104). Continuing this trend, the market value of the DVD field in the UK and US in 2004, for the first time, eclipsed that of cinema—an eclipse partly influenced, in relation to the DVD format, by the increased quality of home entertainment systems, and by the price of cinema admissions relative to DVD purchase or rental charges (De Lisle 2005). Indeed, a 2005 report by Tom Shone claimed that Hollywood "studios [are] now making five times as much money from home entertainment as from theatrical revenues."

These aspects of contemporary movie culture—the boom in DVD consumption, the continued overshadowing of cinema attendance by home film viewing—have been accompanied by significant shifts in audience configurations. Barbara Klinger (2001) has noted how in recent years cinephiles (usually conceived of as male) have been somewhat domesticated even though, historically, the home could have been seen as symbolically anathema to such consumers and their interests. As Klinger identifies, discussions between cinephiles who own sophisticated home entertainment systems have worked to create a canon of "great" films which are judged not according to criteria such as auteurist input, but technologically specific variables (disc transfer quality, audio channel definition, clarity of visual spectacle, letterboxing, and so on). Because DVD, as a distribution and entertainment format, has been sold to audiences on the promise of greater fidelity to source than video (no more pan-and-scan, for example), as well as on an end to the disappointments caused by videotape's deterioration (quality will supposedly remain stable however often the disc is viewed), these "canonical" variables have been picked up and replicated by a variety of publications—online and print—that assess DVD releases.

As a second example of an audience reconfiguration (and one that has important ramifications for this chapter's discussion of *Leeches!*), Mike Goodridge identified in 2004 a significant decay of the theatrical market for lesbian and gay themed cinema.[3] Goodridge acknowledged, however, that home consumption of queer movies—via mail order rentals and purchases, pay-per-view screenings, and other routes—has continued apace while cinema attendance has dropped. Indeed, although queer film festivals continue to exist around the world, still drawing in punters who want to see old and new material on the big screen in a supportive "community" environment, it is notable that the DTV market is now often where one finds queer independent, non-English language and low-budget cinema titles making their debut, from *The Safety of Objects* (Troche 2001) to *Bear Cub* (Albaladejo 2004), from *The Laramie Project* (Kaufman 2002) to *My Life with Morrissey* (Overtoom 2003). Depending on how open they are about their sexuality, some queer audience members may of course prefer to order DVDs by mail to enjoy at home, rather than risking openness, and the potential for prejudice and hostility, in a public locale—and a number of DVD distribution companies have stepped in to provide such a service. As with the cinephile's consumption, then, the queer viewing experience seems to have become increasingly solitary (or at least domesticated) rather than communal, with distribution and marketing often bypassing theatrical routes of exhibition, and the lesbian or gay film viewer sourcing their own entertainment and bringing it into the home.

Transformations in the viewing of horror cinema have been different to those affecting queer film—and less notable. Horror remains one of the US studio system's main genres, with a reliable audience, usually assumed to be of thrill-seeking teenagers and young adults (especially men), still attending cinemas to consume the latest incarnations of the genre and their sequels, whether these be remakes of already known titles, from *Dark Water* (Salles 2005) to *The Amityville Horror* (Douglas 2005), or new trends, such as the aforementioned "torture porn" cycle. As with the video market in the 1980s and 1990s, horror movies are also a staple of home entertainment consumption on DVD. (There has, as yet, been no DVD equivalent of the 1980s "video nasty" panic in the UK. Although this may be because, in contrast to some early videotapes, all DVDs are classified for consumption in the home, the worries voiced by some politicians and moral guardians during the 1980s regarding the potential psychological impact and effects of rewinding videos, and freeze-framing certain moments, have only been enhanced by DVD.) Indeed, in the UK a large number of horror titles debut on DVD, including films from East Asia—such as those on Tartan's Asia Extreme label—and low-budget genre titles that attract the avid fan rather than a larger, more general audience. This is not too different from the video scene in the 1980s and 1990s: videotapes enabled horror fans to get hold of films that were too narrow in their appeal to market to a theatrical audience (though many of these would still have had a theatrical release, however minor). The major difference with DVD, it would seem, is in the number of titles available. And within such a substantial arena of production—that is, horror cinema—DTV horror titles may need a hook, an original take, an otherness, an ineffable "something else" to draw them to the attention of an audience, whilst still being required to provide routine generic satisfactions. Horror fans, a little like the audience for lesbian and gay cinema (and it is worth reiterating that these two viewer groupings are by no means mutually exclusive), may expect to trawl through large quantities of movies, title after title, in search of something of value. Recognizing their own social marginality, the committed horror fan and the queer film viewer will partake of their exhausting (often solitary) pleasure, merely on the off-chance that perhaps, just this once, this particular film will prove to be more than mediocre. Both cinephiles in their own fashion, the queer film fan and the horror aficionado, bring their own specific markers of quality to bear on the enormous number of DVDs in circulation—and, perhaps like many movie audiences, often find the material wanting.

HUNTING OUT *LEECHES!*

The sheer volume of DVD discs available to rent or purchase is far greater in magnitude than the number of videocassettes that were on offer during the heyday of the VCR. At the time of writing, in the UK somewhere in the region of 800 new titles appear on DVD every month. The present shape of the DVD market, then, produces a key conundrum, one that has ramifications for such "taste publics" as horror fans or queer cinema audiences: that is, how does the selective film viewer negotiate and pick from the array of delights available? More particularly, how would *Leeches!* find itself an audience, or an audience know about and get hold of a copy of *Leeches!*? In this section of this chapter, I will offer brief comments on several arenas—the video rental store, online rental and purchase outlets, print publications—that may bring the movie consumer into contact with titles that have bypassed theatrical exhibition. Aside from these, there are of course other routes by which consumers may find out about or come into contact with DTV films: online (extracts from some of DeCoteau's movies can be found on YouTube, for instance), and on television (DeCoteau's production company Rapid Heart has a distribution deal with queer niche TV channels Here!TV and PrideVision, who sometimes screen his films). But as the focus of this chapter—and this book—is on the technologies, industries and audiences associated with DVD, I will focus here on the hard format of the disc itself, and how audiences will gain knowledge of its existence and availability.

Although online DVD rental companies such as Netflix and Amazon have recently boomed in popularity, the video rental store remains a key space for the sourcing of viewing pleasures. (How long this will hold true remains to be seen, especially given the rapidly diminishing costs of buying copies of DVDs to own, and the collectable appeal of the format). DeCoteau established a distribution deal with Blockbuster in the United States: "Blockbuster has been a great customer of mine. They have picked up my last 20 or so movies. Blockbuster picks up films they can make money with. My movies make money for them. I have a track record and their buying decisions are made based on that" ("Buzz" 2005). Entering any movie rental outlet the prospective customer finds, often in equal or greater volume to the known and recognizable titles, a plethora of films debuting on DVD. These movies include erotic thrillers, obvious rip-offs or cash-ins, little known or unknown sequels (such as the subsequent installments of the *Ginger Snaps* franchise, *Ginger Snaps: Unleashed* [Sullivan 2004] and *Ginger Snaps Back: The Beginning* [Harvey 2004], or the sequels to *Cruel Intentions* [Kumble 1999]), prison dramas starring model-turned-actor Boris Kodjoe (*Doing Hard Time* [Whitmore 2004]), films about bank robberies featuring Dean Cain, martial arts movies, a plethora of sport and rom-com titles specifically targeted at black audiences, movies with cameo appearances by Paris Hilton, and so on. How individual traders choose which DTV titles to stock may vary; however, the industry trade publication *Rental Home Entertainment* (formerly *Video Home Entertainment*) offers reviews and recommendations. Perhaps many individual viewers, visiting the rental store for their evening's entertainment, will ignore these films, their boxes scattered among the roster of better-known titles. However, as has already been noted, the field of DTV film production is larger than cinema which attains some form of theatrical release; therefore, these comparatively cheaply made titles—"in which," as Linda Ruth Williams puts it, "budgets are cut to the desires and limits of the living room" (2005: 8)—are evidently reaching a considerably sized audience.

Some rental stores may divide up their wares with genre headings; others may alphabetize their available titles. In either situation, for a DTV title to attain an audience, the cover of the DVD box—the title and the design—offer crucial guidance for the inquisitive. As Williams writes, "Titles are a primary part of a film's branding, and are particularly important for DTVs which will have to do a lot of selling through a few boldface words in the absence of a large marketing budget" (2005: 9). DeCoteau's films are exemplary here. He has worked on movies which are evidently titled to recall better-known studio pictures (a standard DTV strategy), such as *Witches of the Caribbean* (2005). The titles of a number of DeCoteau's other works—*Voodoo Academy*, *Young Warlocks* (2001), and so on—are rather arbitrary, and could be used to name any number of his films (indeed, some of DeCoteau's films have been released under different titles: *The Brotherhood* [2001], for example, is also available as *I've Been Watching You*). And some of his films have blunt titles—like *Leeches!*—that serve as a graphic, direct and fairly reliable indication of some of the movie's content.

Williams continues:

> Video dealers operate in a world only partly supported by mass advertising; a small proportion of DTV titles may do well because of a TV commercial campaign, but hundreds of others must stand or fall on how well they are presented in the video store. Even if we've never seen an erotic thriller, the "promise" of explicitness or the attraction of a thriller plot presented by the sleeve design informs our choice
>
> (Williams 2005: 21).

Not, of course, that the cover always accurately represents the film inside the box: scantily clad models on the cover of DTV erotic thrillers, for instance, may not actually appear in the films. The DVD packaging for *Leeches!* (Figure 2.1) depicts a screaming female face being attacked by the

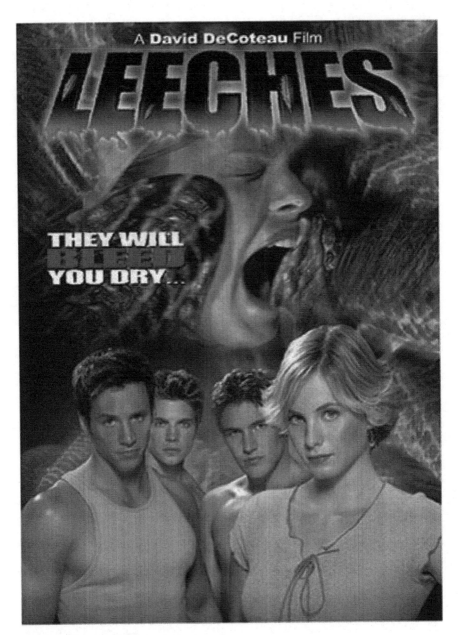

Figure 2.1 Leeches! DVD cover.

eponymous creatures, three buff male figures styled like porn stars or boy-band members, only one of whom is wearing a vest, and a foregrounded elfin actress (this prioritized position sorely out of kilter with her character's narrative prominence within the film). The overall design of this cover, from the tagline "they will bleed you dry" to the raked and oozing typographic styling of the title, situates *Leeches!* within the horror genre, although the film's homoerotics are also clearly hinted at.

Negotiating the online rental or purchase market is even more complex than the rental store. Without DVD boxes to pick up and consult—and in the absence of the delimited geography of the rental shop, whose physical restrictions make finite the number of available films—the potential for browsing movies needs to be replaced by alternative strategies. With an almost unlimited library of titles available (or at least a library whose limits are not known, as they cannot be seen), it would be possible to avoid DTV movies altogether. However, specifically targeted recommendations from the online source, clickable connections to lists of films made by other subscribers or shoppers, and "people who bought this also bought these items" links all serve to broaden the browsing field. In addition, online resources often seem to rely on their consumers being savvy and curious. Due to the size of the market, there are inevitably individual DTV titles released with little or no marketing and advertising, their success reliant on word-of-mouth, reliable recommendations, and other such impulsive and viral strategies.[4]

A useful example here is provided by the UK arm of TLA releasing, a small-scale distribution company based in Soho, London, which is staffed and run by just two people. Although this offshoot was only established in 2005, the US parent company has been around for decades, and attained reputation and status by providing product to American consumers during the first boom years of the home entertainment video industry in the 1980s. The library of titles that the London office of TLA markets to a UK audience is small, and mostly concentrated on lesbian and gay cinema, with a handful of (non-queer) American independent films also available; none of their titles have ever been released theatrically in the UK. Although some of TLA's films have been (and continue to be) available through what the industry calls "bricks-and-mortar" stores—HMV, and defunct companies SilverScreen, MVC and Music Zone—most of their sales occur through online retailers, primarily Amazon and Play. TLA spends a small sum of money on advertising in the gay press (magazines such as *Gay Times* and *Attitude*, weekly papers like *Boyz*), and an even smaller amount on adverts in film magazines such as *Sight and Sound*, but many of their roster of titles sell consistently with longevity. Robin Andrews, TLA's sales director, is honest and forthright regarding the importance of cover art: one of the company's best-selling titles, *Locked Up* (Andreas 2004), has shifted around 8000 units, at least partly on the raunchy promise of a provocative title and cover photographs; *Edge of Seventeen* (Moreton 1998) has fared well for similar reasons. TLA rely, to a significant extent, on word-of-mouth recommendations and other non-corporate viral strategies of information dissemination to attain their sales, as well as on a sizeable internet-savvy queer audience who will strategically search out niche films that may offer them a pleasurable alternative to, or some compensation for, the lack of queer characters and narratives in mainstream (theatrically-released) cinema.

In addition to rental stores and online sources, print publications may also introduce audiences to DTV titles about which they otherwise would have remained ignorant. Mainstream film magazines such as *Empire* or *DVD Review*, recognizing the size of the DTV field, make space to review movies debuting on DVD, although still tending to prioritize titles that have been screened in cinemas. Kim Newman's column "Video Dungeon" in *Empire* serves as an especially valuable guide to the highlights of the DTV rental realm. More specialist publications—such as those aimed specifically at fans of horror (*Fangoria*, *Shivers*), science fiction (*SFX*), or cult cinema and television (*Cult Times*, *Video Watchdog*), for instance—may give equal space to, or even prioritize, the DTV titles that might attract their readership, as many of these specific products will as a matter of course bypass theatrical screening venues because of their form, content and niche appeal. (Online fansites, forums and bulletin boards aimed at niche audiences can also make interested parties aware of specific directors and their DTV titles; DeCoteau interviews appear, for instance, on genre-focused www.horror-asylum.com and, more intriguingly, considering the concerns being explored by this chapter, on "homo horror" site www.campblood. org.) In all of these print publications, DVD distribution companies such as Anchor Bay may invest in full-page adverts that pitch particular DTV titles to the readership of the magazines, utilizing images and taglines that will position the film in a manner comprehensible to readers (generic markers, clear references to already existing titles, and so on). In an alternative to this fairly high risk strategy, DTV movies may be marketed among better known (that is, theatrically released) films in adverts that promote a range of titles: big budget movies will be positioned alongside both lower budget films which had a limited cinema release and DTV titles. To what extent print reviews and advertisements influence consumer behavior is, of course, very difficult to gauge. However, what seems clear from this brief overview of rental stores, internet sites and print publications is that even the casual film viewer will have some passing awareness of the DTV field.

GENRE HYBRIDITY AND THE "UNDECIDABLE" DTV

As the introduction to this chapter pointed out, *Leeches!* is a hybrid film, incorporating elements from (among other sources) gay male pornography, horror cinema, and teen movies. Indeed, classifying the content of the film is challenging. The film is dedicated in its end credits to exploitation director Doris Wishman and, in the style of DeCoteau's mentor Roger Corman, was made in just six days. Yet it is also indebted to the 1990s mainstream boom in teen movies, which included a number of horror films, such as *The Faculty* (Rodriguez 1998) and *Halloween H20* (Miner 1998). Possibly partly influenced by Paul Morrissey's *Flesh for Frankenstein* (1973) and *Blood for Dracula* (1974), *Leeches!* is much more queerly charged than the mainstream horror releases that feature beefcake sequences—one thinks of, for example, Ryan Phillippe showering in *I Know What You Did Last Summer* (Gillespie 1997), Johnny Messner's tight, wet vest in *Anacondas: The Hunt for the Blood Orchid* (Little 2004) and Ryan Reynolds, with axe, sweaty shaved chest paired with low-slung striped pajama bottoms, in the remake of *The Amityville Horror* (Douglas 2005)—and yet it still follows a standard "creature feature" format, including a conclusion involving an evil scientist. Potentially, the film could be read as camp—and here it is worth iterating Jack Babuscio's claim (1977: 50) that horror cinema is a major repository of camp pleasures—but, despite its blunt title and occasionally cheesy effects, it is not played for laughs.

Jim Collins (1993: 242–63) has argued that one of the defining characteristics of filmmaking in the 1980s and 1990s was the emergence of a new, genre-hybrid cinema whose appearance was indebted, in part, to the media-savvy cultural landscape of the postmodern era. Contrary to Collins, some film theorists have claimed that individual movies are never (and have never been) generically "pure." Christine Gledhill, for instance, suggests that all films "'participate' . . . in genres of one kind or another—and usually several at once," and argues that "Most texts, and most films, are multiply generic" (1999: 147). Whilst there have been, throughout the history of cinema, numerous films whose generic categorization has been far from straightforward (for marketers, distributors, audiences), a significant proportion of titles—the majority, I would argue—*can* be dropped into single, clear genre boxes with parameters with which most audiences are familiar. What Collins does not identify in his essay is that the proliferation of hybrid titles since the 1980s has been coterminous with the widespread dissemination of home entertainment technologies. Other authors, however, have made this connection explicit. Linda Ruth Williams has identified "the fragmentation of audiences and niche markets which followed the development of video in the 1980s, and the proliferation of digital and other imaging systems which developed later" (2005: 249); she situates the blossoming of the DTV erotic thriller in relation to this fragmentation. And Barbara Klinger, discussing the boom in home entertainment systems in the 1990s and beyond, has identified the impact of these technologies on generic product:

> The activities of both media businesses and consumers affect the identity and circulation of genres in domestic space. Each creates and popularizes

new ways of grouping films that lie outside of established formal genres, introducing "local" genres that flourish within ancillary markets
(Klinger 2006: 12).

Together, then, Collins, Klinger and Williams recognize some of the creative and unpredictable combinations of genres that have occurred in film in recent decades; Williams directly relates her arguments to those films debuting on DVD, whilst Klinger's reference to the "circulation of genres in domestic space" gestures towards this particular market. As the direct-to-video realm has given way to the much larger direct-to-DVD field, and as cheap digital technologies have made it easier to make and distribute work, directors and other creative personnel seem to have become (somewhat paradoxically) more confident in producing genre-messy movies, reliant on the possibility that, with the size of the DTV arena, any one title will always find some kind of audience. Indeed, as David DeCoteau (2007) has said, "I make the films that I want to make. My films have enjoyed a huge audience that support my type of filmmaking. There is an audience for all kinds of films, you just have to find it." The resultant "new" (or, more specifically, newly widespread) generic hybridity produces a raft of "undecidable" media texts: films which trouble classification as one thing or another, unsettling accepted orders of understanding and comprehension, bothering audiences and marketers and, indeed, a wider film culture. Rather than being inept or catastrophically bad (although some may be), the "undecidable" direct-to-DVD film is likely to be passable, workmanlike, possibly quickly made and attempting to conceal the limitations of its budget. Flying slightly below the cultural radar of critical respectability, these titles may provide multivalent pleasures and can be riven by contradictory impulses.

Rather than seeing these movies as problematic, it is worth considering their political valence. The notion of the "undecidable" object or concept, that which resists conclusive categorization or comprehension, has been engaged with by a number of philosophers and critics, all of whom have noted its political significance. Derrida, in an interview, has discussed the term, which he describes as follows:

Unities of simulacrum, "false" verbal properties (nominal or semantic) that can no longer be included within philosophical (binary) opposition, but which, however, inhabit philosophical opposition, resisting and disorganizing it, *without ever* constituting a third term, without ever leaving room for a solution in the form of speculative dialectics (the *pharmakon* is neither remedy nor poison, neither good nor evil, neither the inside nor the outside, neither speech nor writing; . . . the *gram* is neither a signifier nor a signified, neither a sign nor a thing, neither a presence nor an absence, neither a position nor a negation, etc.; . . . Neither/nor, that is, *simultaneously* either *or* . . .)
(Derrida 2004: 40).

To which one might add that *Leeches!* is neither horror nor porn, camp nor serious, B movie nor exploitation film, not exactly something else ("a third term"), but also not reducible to any known and understood categories or polarized descriptors. Conceptualizing of some things, some spaces (terms, objects, properties) that pass beyond the binary and the dialectic (or at least hint at the possibility of a beyond), Derrida reveals in this quote how key terms used throughout his writing operate as "undecidables." His frequent return to such terms, and the potential that they hold to "resist" and "disorganize," suggests the political significance and resonance of that which breaks from calcified categories. The "undecidable"—as thing, and as concept—enables the possibility of looking and thinking outside of the stable and ingrained, the habituated and restricted.

A similar prospect is discussed by Foucault in the preface to *The Order of Things.* Using an extract from Borges which outlines a complex, perverse, and impossible system for classifying animals, Foucault identifies the power of this writing to provoke laughter, and to break up "all the ordered surfaces and all the planes with which we are accustomed to tame the wild profusion of existing things;" that which problematizes classification can draw attention to "the empty space, the interstitial blanks *separating* all these entities from one another" (2002 [1970]: xvi–xvii). He goes on to suggest that Borges's list can be understood as a heterotopia:

> *Heterotopias* are disturbing, probably because they secretly undermine language, because they make it impossible to name this *and* that, because they shatter or tangle common names, because they destroy "syntax" in advance, and not only the syntax with which we construct sentences but also that less apparent syntax which causes words and things (next to and also opposite one another) to "hold together" . . . heterotopias (such as those to be found in Borges) desiccate speech, stop words in their tracks, contest the very possibility of grammar at its source; they dissolve our myths and sterilize the lyricism of our sentences
>
> (Foucault 2002[1970]: xix).

Whilst it may be far-reaching to identify *Leeches!* as a heterotopian site, Foucault's comments (like those of Derrida) hint at the possibilities afforded by that which reaches beyond the limits of the known, proffering a vision of an alternative. The substantial vista opened up by the direct-to-DVD movie may be one such realm, a heterotopia of sorts, in which the "undecidable" is enabled to flourish, to bloom.

That the DTV realm can complicate known systems of clear categorization is evidenced by the responses of audiences to some of the titles produced in recent years by David DeCoteau. Comments posted on bulletin boards, review sites, online stores and information databases demonstrate the tensions individual audience members experience when consuming his films. Grasping for recognizable generic categories with which to comprehend these cheaply-made queer fantasies, the discussions and revelations demonstrate that the affective responses produced from viewing cannot be so easily tamed or boxed. Indeed, though taking DeCoteau here as emblematic, I would argue that the boom in the DTV consumer market has—possibly temporarily, and certainly only in relation to a percentage of the available titles—afforded the possibility of unsettling taste formations associated with specific audience configurations. This has occurred via the appearance of a rash of film titles that creatively (or, possibly, haphazardly) combine elements of already existing film forms. Through direct-to-DVD movies, audiences are being confronted with films they might never have come into contact with before, films which they may take pleasure in but find difficult to square with their previous experience.

Online discussions about DeCoteau's oeuvre between markedly different audience members expose the ways in which formerly segregated niche groupings struggle to make sense of multivalent texts. To take just one example, the consumer reviews of *Leeches!* available on amazon.com are varied in their judgments, but many acknowledge (however inadvertently) the unsettling potential of the "undecidable" film. One reviewer, "socalraverboy," writes, "This is definitely a B-movie, so don't expect great acting or special effects, but boy, does it have hunky guys showing off their glistening bodies as much as possible. Imagine a movie starring Abercrombie and Fitch models . . . and imagine acting along the caliber of said models" (2005). "Ericswrongturn" wrote that "this 1 [*sic*] has a stupid plot. . . . Though with such a plot . . . it actually came out pretty decent. For straight to video and silly creature features go . . . this one definitely rates up to the top [*sic*]. The only thing that's bad is there's too many guys walking around in speedos half naked for the entire movie. Kill them leeches. Go leeches go!" (2004). Both of these authors attempt to categorize DeCoteau's film (as "B" and as a "creature feature"). At the same time, their comments draw attention to the disruptive role of the male flesh on display.

Leeches!, then—a direct-to-DVD title that is representative of the hybrid, "undecidable" texts that have proliferated with the rapid uptake of DVD technologies into the home—is evidently a provocative film for its challenges to taste boundaries and to predictable or expected generic pleasures. The monstrous bloodsuckers in DeCoteau's film are hybrids of animal and steroid. Similarly, *Leeches!* itself is a rather monstrous hybrid movie, of a form that certainly seems to be proliferating with the continued widespread dispersal of DVD technologies and the boom of the DTV market. Troubling at the categories of horror cinema, queer film, teen movies and pornography, and yet not clearly occupying any of these genres, *Leeches!* confounds its audiences, forcing them to wonder who exactly this film is for, how its pleasures operate, what is to be made of its content; in this respect, DeCoteau's film is emblematic of the unpredictable formations and appeal of the "undecidable" DTV film. It also serves as a warning, to potential audiences of DTV cinema—to you. For if as an inexperienced swimmer you should choose to dip your toes into the pool of DTV pleasures—and the waters of that pool are continuing to steadily rise—then be cautious, for you never know what is lurking in there, or how it might bleed you, infect you, mutate you. Or, indeed, what you might learn: that there are things out there that you never knew existed, gruesome things, seductive things. Meet me in the locker room, and I'll show you.

CODA

In September 2006, Renny Harlin's film *The Covenant* was released into US cinemas: it was the highest grossing movie of the week (although it had the lowest takings for a number one film for three years). Made for a rumored $20 million—a sum it had made back within three weeks of release—the movie starred a cast of virtual unknowns. Its narrative centers on a group of four teenage boys with supernatural abilities, and the threat posed to them by a rival warlock. Written by J. S. Cardone, the script seems to pilfer elements of DeCoteau's back catalogue: the four teenagers are on the swimming team, where they use their powers to win races; significant conversations take place in the school showers (again, as with *Leeches!*, the smallest swimwear available is sourced by the wardrobe department); the seductive power of the supernatural turns the boys against each other, as in DeCoteau's *Brotherhood* films. The lead character, Caleb (played by former model Steven Strait, whose astonishing moniker is not enough to ward off the film's relentless homoerotics) often wakes from bad dreams, his shaved muscular chest wet with sweat.

Slickly produced, with a large amount of computer-generated imagery overlaid in post-production, *The Covenant* is DTV material on a more mainstream budget. Although Hollywood is known for stealing from the margins, the art-house, other national cinemas, and so on, and reshaping such work for a potential mass audience, the financing and distribution of *The Covenant* marks an interesting development. For whilst some sorts of DTV product—such as the erotic thriller—have a mainstream counterpart, separated from the non-theatrical market by such variables as star power, the perverse "undecidable" media text has largely been left alone by Hollywood studios to proliferate on domestic formats. The success of *The Covenant* (a minor one, but notable nonetheless) could lead to further odd hybrids breaking free from the realm of DTV production, attracting known directors and sizeable budgets, and appearing in theatrical venues. Should this occur, it will be important to recognize that its green-lighting would never have occurred without the existence of DVD, and the astonishing range of complex and unpredictable content that the format has spawned.

NOTES

1. Arguably, the main anomaly on DeCoteau's CV is the gay indie/arthouse film *Leather Jacket Love Story* (1997).
2. See also Clover's observations (1992: 21–64) regarding the ambiguous sexuality of the predator and the "final girl" in the slasher film.
3. See also James (2005: 3), who notes the "lacklustre performance" at the box office of queer independent films *Tarnation* (Caouette 2004), and *Mysterious Skin* (Araki 2005).
4. See John Caldwell's essay in this collection for a discussion of such "viral" marketing.

BIBLIOGRAPHY

Babuscio, J. (1977) "Camp and the Gay Sensibility," in R. Dyer (ed.) *Gays and Film*, London: British Film Institute: 40–57.

Barthes, R. (2000[1980]) *Camera Lucida*, London: Vintage.

Benshoff, H. (1995) *Monsters in the Closet: homosexuality and the horror film*, Manchester: Manchester University Press.

Bourdieu, P. (1979) *La Distinction*; trans. Richard Nice (1986) *Distinction: a social critique of the judgement of taste*, London: Routledge and Kegan Paul.

"Buzz" (2005) "Interview with Homo Horror Hall-of-Famer Dave DeCoteau," CampBlood.org. Online. Available HTTP: http://campblood.org/Features/Dave%20DeCoteau.htm (accessed 12 September 2007).

Clover, C. (1992) *Men, Women and Chainsaws: gender in the modern horror film*, London: BFI.

Collins, J. (1993) "Genericity in the Nineties: Eclectic Irony and the New Sincerity," in J. Collins, H. Radner and A. P. Collins (eds) *Film Theory Goes to the Movies*, New York: Routledge: 242–263.

Cook, P. and Bernink, M. (eds) (1999) *The Cinema Book*, 2nd Edition, London: BFI.

De Lisle, T. (2005, 14 January) "Home Box Office," *The Guardian*, Online. Available HTTP: http://www.guardian.co.uk/print/0,3858,5102376–110760,00.html (accessed 15 June 2007).

DeCoteau, D. (2007) "Re: questions." e-mail (11 June 2007).

Derrida, J. (2004) *Positions*, London and New York: Continuum.

"Ericswrongturn" (2004) "leeches so pathedic that its good [*sic*]," Amazon.com customer reviews of *Leeches*. Online. Available HTTP: http://www.amazon.com/gp/product/customer-reviews/B00011XU6W/sr=1–1/qid=1189590653/ref=cm_rev_next/102–8660110–2308957?ie=UTF8&customer-reviews.sort%5Fby=-SubmissionDate&n=130&s=dvd&customer-reviews.start=11&qid=1189590653&sr=1–1 (accessed 12 September 2007).

Foucault, M. (2002[1970]) *The Order of Things: an archaeology of the human sciences*, London: Routledge.

Friedberg, A. (2002) "CD and DVD," in D. Harries (ed.) *The New Media Book*, London: BFI: 30–39.

Gledhill, C. (1999) "Histories of Genre Criticism," in P. Cook and M. Bernink (eds) *The Cinema Book*, 2nd edition, London: BFI: 137–146.

Goodridge, M. (2004, July 2–8) "Coming out soon . . . ," *Screen International*, 1459: 12–15.

Hawkins, J. (2003) "Midnight Sex-Horror Movies and the Downtown Avant-Garde," in M. Jancovich et al. (eds) *Defining Cult Movies: the cultural politics of oppositional taste*, Manchester and New York: Manchester University Press.

James, N. (2005) "Security blankets," *Sight and Sound*, 15(8): 3.

Klinger, B. (2001) "The Contemporary Cinephile: Film Collecting in the Post-Video Era," in R. Maltby and M. Stokes (eds) *Hollywood Spectatorship*, London: BFI: 133–151.

Klinger, B. (2006) *Beyond the Multiplex: cinema, new technologies, and the home*, Berkeley: University of California Press.

Linna, E. (2007) "Interview with David DeCoteau," *Extraordinary Movie and Video Guide*. Online. Available HTTP: http://www.emvg.net/interviews/decoteau.php (accessed 15 June 2007).

Naremore, J. (1998) *More than Night: film noir in its contexts*, Berkeley: University of California Press.

"Socalraverboy" (2005) "Campy hunky boyz in speedos!," Amazon.com customer reviews of *Leeches*. Online. Available HTTP: http://www.amazon.com/gp/product/customer-reviews/B0001IXU6W/sr=1–1/qid=1189590653/ref=cm_rev_next/102–8660110–2308957?ie=UTF8&customer-reviews.sort%5Fby=-SubmissionDate&n=130&s=dvd&customer-reviews.start=11&qid=1189590653&sr=1–1 (accessed 12 September 2007).

Shone, T. (2005, 19 August) "Busted," *The Guardian*, Online. Available HTTP: http://arts.guardian.co.uk/fridayreview/story/0,,1551526,00.html (accessed 12 September 2007).

Williams, L. (1991) "Film Bodies: Gender, Genre and Excess," *Film Quarterly*, 44: 701–15.

Williams, L. R. (2005) *The Erotic Thriller in Contemporary Cinema*, Edinburgh: Edinburgh University Press.

3 Repeat Viewings
Television Analysis in the DVD Age

James Walters

> Digital and satellite technologies have not only changed the ways in which we watch television, but also improved the quality of sound and image to an extent where aesthetics can be appreciated and analysed as never before
>
> (Akass et al. 2006: 1).

In an episode entitled "I Love Lisa" from season four of *The Simpsons* (20th Century Fox Television, 1989–ongoing), Bart Simpson has characteristically devised an inventive and effective method of sadistic torture for his sister, Lisa. Earlier in the episode, Lisa had expressed her sympathy for a fellow classmate, Ralph Wiggum, by presenting him with a hastily-written valentine's card, having discovered that he had in fact received none from any of his female peers (the class had been making valentine's cards and distributing them to one another). Ralph misreads her platonic gesture, taking the punchline of her card "I Choo-Choo Choose You!" literally, and subsequently pursues Lisa as an object of his affection.[1] Against her better judgment, Lisa accepts Ralph's invitation to attend the prestigious 29th Anniversary Special of the Krusty the Clown show, sitting with Ralph and his father, Chief Wiggum, as guest audience members (the widely-coveted tickets having been procured due to Wiggum elder's dubious influence as the town's presiding chief of police).

The live special edition of the Krusty show consists of a number of archive clips from past episodes and so Lisa sits in relative safety until, ominously, Krusty reads from the dummy cards that it is time for his favorite part of the show: talking with the audience, which he himself greets cynically with an exasperated "Oh God, this is always death." Sitting in her chair, Lisa is equally unenthusiastic about this prospect and, hands clutched tightly to her neck, mutters to herself "Oh no, please don't show me with Ralph"—referring, of course, to the rolling cameras that are recording every second of the broadcast live and beaming them into the homes of potentially all who know her. With tragi-comic inevitability, Krusty makes his way over to Lisa and Ralph who, on being asked by Krusty whether Lisa is his girlfriend, proclaims emphatically: "Yes! I love Lisa Simpson and when I grow up I'm going to marry her!" At this Lisa reaches her limit and, throwing her head back, exclaims with equal vigor: "Noooo! Now you listen to me: I don't like you. I never liked you. And the only reason I gave you that stupid Valentine is because nobody else would!"

As Lisa nears the conclusion of this speech, the image on our screen cuts to a new shot incorporating the frame of a television set. A hand clutching a remote control reaches across the set and pauses the television screen with a click, freezing the image of Lisa and Ralph. Thus, this is not in fact the live broadcast of the Krusty 29th Anniversary special, but a recording of it. We draw back to reveal Bart's identity as the operator of the remote control; he looks back across his shoulder, away from the television set, instructing his sister enthusiastically: "Watch this Lis . . ." His words continue in a new reverse shot that frames both Bart and his sister's silent, mournful reaction as she sits on the sofa: " . . . You can actually pinpoint the second when his heart rips in half!" We return to the recorded image of Lisa and Ralph on the screen as Bart uses the remote control to shuffle through the scene, frame by frame, until finding the aforementioned moment of heartbreak where Ralph can be seen to deflate painfully in the wake of Lisa's words: "And . . . now!" As Bart animates the freeze-frame images, Ralph's murmurs of internal anguish can also be heard, elongated in the extended play format. These sounds are then replicated and replaced by Lisa's own groans as, returning to the reverse shot of her and Bart, we observe her clutching her head in shame.

Such events are not untypical in the town of Springfield, the Simpsons' fictional home, and it is certainly not unusual for Bart to find countless new ways to torment his younger sister from time to time. Moreover, it is characteristic of *The Simpsons'* fictional world that a member of the family should by chance appear on a primetime television show, thus providing an opportunity of this kind for Bart: such is the array of extraordinary events that beset the Simpsons' lives. Crucially, however, Bart's act also represents a relatively inventive use of modern technology—the freeze-frame function on his VHS remote—for his particular sadistic purposes. Indeed, we might well conclude that he is engaged in a specific brand of television analysis whereby his ability to define the precise moment of Ralph's heartbreak rests upon his capacity to scrutinize and evaluate the shifting tone and quality of the moving image. The technology of the VHS remote facilitates this method of close appreciation and allows Bart to divide the flow of the television image into a series of interrelated moments, each one significantly different to the next. From there, he is able to evaluate each second of Ralph's changing postures, gestures and expressions in order to pinpoint the exact moment when his physical and mental anguish reaches its pinnacle. In this short sequence, Bart reveals himself to be a somewhat accomplished and insightful student of television.

In this chapter I want to examine the ways in which technology, and particularly DVD technology, helps to facilitate exactly the kind of close analysis of television that Bart engages in during this sequence. The opening quotation from the editors of the journal *Critical Studies in Television* indicates in clear terms not only that a growing appetite exists among scholars for a renewed focus upon television aesthetics but also that advancements in viewing technology have helped to create an arena in which such debates can readily take place. In the course of my discussion I will explore to a greater extent that relationship between technology and television criticism, evaluating the place of DVD within a series of shifts in emphasis recently occurring within the field of Television Studies. Furthermore, I hope to illustrate in more practical terms how DVD technology can enrich our critical awareness of the aesthetic composition of television programs by referring in detail to moments and sequences within their DVD viewing contexts.

Returning to *The Simpsons*, one minor but significant detail in the scene I described concerns the everydayness of Bart's act, the extent to which such manipulations of VHS technology had, by 1993 when the episode was first aired, become so commonplace that the inclusion of their use in a popular cartoon required absolutely no signposting whatsoever. As educated users of such technology, it would be absurd to suggest that we did not immediately understand Bart's actions during the sequence, and thus appreciate the nature of his intentions. However, it may be worth remembering that the advent of home VHS technology did indeed have lasting ramifications for students of film and television engaged in precisely the same analytical process as Bart Simpson (although, clearly, for very different purposes than his own). On a broad scale, it meant that a swathe of titles which had previously been scarce and hard to find were available for analysis at all. As Laura Mulvey observes in relation to film:

> The early 1980s were a period of transition for cinema studies as the widening availability of VHS made the close study of film more accessible. Although there may be no substitute for textual analysis derived from the celluloid original, VHS has brought with it the advantage of repetition and return that was not so easy to secure in the pre-video days. Then, it might have been possible for a film studies department to own one or two, at most a few, prints. Now, individuals as well as institutions are able to build up collections of films that can be seen and re-seen and reinterpreted along lines that might change with changes in interest and knowledge but also are open to the chance insights and unexpected encounters that come with endless repetition
> (Mulvey 2006: 230).

The advent of VHS, of course, profoundly influenced the study of television in similar ways by providing a means by which individual programs and series could be captured and archived with relative ease—although television programs rarely enjoyed the kind of commercial release afforded to film titles at the time. As Mulvey makes clear, this new kind of availability promotes, or at least facilitates, an intimate relationship with the object of study, meaning that insights and hypotheses can be tested and retested against the television program or film itself. The desirable outcome of this development would be that a greater degree of precision and rigor should be accomplished in accounts of both film and television, resulting from a heightened critical sensitivity regarding the style and form of moments, sequences and scenes. Consequently, following the line of Mulvey's assertions, we can trace a firm synthesis between technological advancement and critical endeavor, whereby the former effectively provides an enhanced environment for the latter to take place.

Whether or not this development in playback technology has, in practice, resulted in a recognizably stronger emphasis upon the close appreciation of style and form in film criticism is a matter to be debated elsewhere. Indeed, if "electronic and digital technologies should bring about a 'reinvention' of textual analysis" (Mulvey 2006: 242), there will still remain the fundamental requirement for critics both within and outside of the academy to possess the skills necessary to adequately articulate the nature and achievement of a particular film, however sophisticated the mode of presentation. Within Television Studies, however, the emergence of VHS technology by and large did not result in an enriched focus upon the methodology of textual analysis, a fact that has been debated and elaborated upon by a variety of different scholars within the discipline (cf. Brunsdon 1997; Jacobs 2001; Cardwell 2006). Thus, whilst in Film Studies the debate might well concern the *extent* to which modern technology impacted upon methods of close analysis, in Television Studies conjecture might well centre upon whether a sustained attention to questions of aesthetics was evident *at all*, either before or after such developments. In short, there is almost no discernable tradition of textual analysis within Television Studies against which such trends can reliably be measured. In a landmark essay addressing issues of this nature, Christine Geraghty has explained that:

> There are a number of reasons why making judgments about aesthetics has proved to be a difficult task in television studies and in the broader areas of media or cultural studies. They would include the impact of semiotics on the genesis of media studies with its pseudo-scientific claims about objectivity; the impact of postmodernism with its emphasis on diversity, decentring and play; the need to establish popular culture and television, in particular, as worthy of study that involved refusing the traditional modes of judgment; the impact of feminist work, with its demand that certain kinds of denigrated fiction should be treated seriously; the notion, coming rather differently from Foucault and Bourdieu, that to make aesthetic judgments was to impose the cultural norms of the powerful. We might also include . . . a lack of confidence about television studies as a defining and working discipline
>
> (Geraghty 2003: 27–8).

Geraghty's assertions provide a rich account of the varying factors that impacted upon the progression of Television Studies and, in particular, stunted the growth of aesthetics as a legitimate area of concern within the field. Furthermore, her highlighting of a perceived need for scholarly "objectivity" and the debated worthiness of studying television at all draws attention to the lack of a *critical* tradition within Television Studies. This is distinct from Film Studies, I would suggest, where the practice of elucidating personal interpretations of films is well established over many years and where critics argue for the value and achievement of individual films, directors, actors, even entire genres, without necessarily attending to the merits of thinking about film as a medium capable of art and sophistication.[2]

Whilst a lack of attention to matters of style, meaning and critical judgement in Television Studies has certainly been observed previously (Brunsdon 1997: 117), in recent years a number of critics have sought to actively redress the balance by vigorously engaging in the close analysis of television. For example, a special issue of *Journal of British Cinema and Television* (vol. 3, no. 1, 2006) entitled "Good Television?" deals specifically with the challenges inherent in articulating notions of value and achievement within specific television programs. The guest editors, Sarah Cardwell and Steven Peacock, lay out their aims clearly in an introduction to the journal issue, posing a series of critical questions:

> What is good television? Why are appreciation and evaluation so rarely tackled within television studies? How might notions of critical judgement and value enhance television studies? What new approaches and perspectives might aid the critical assessment of television? What might television criticism within television studies look like? What role might interpretation or analysis play? How useful are criteria borrowed from film studies? Where does the idea of "quality" television fit in?
>
> (Cardwell and Peacock 2006: 1).

Reading this list in the context of Geraghty's earlier characterization of Television Studies and its resistance to aesthetics we come to appreciate, firstly, that an ideological break is being made with the traditions of Television Studies by the journal's guest editors, and secondly that this break is made with a renewed confidence both in television as a worthy object of critical study and in the merits of subjective critical judgement. Thus, the preceding self-consciousness regarding the status of the medium and the validity of the biased critical voice, to which Geraghty draws attention, is discarded at a stroke. The result in the journal issue is the generation of a number of articles that present detailed interpretative accounts of moments from particular television programs, with authors only briefly feeling the need to preface their method of study and, indeed, in some cases avoiding such an asserted justification completely. What emerges here is the event of television scholars abandoning the need to explain why they are placing an emphasis upon television aesthetics and instead assuming interpretative criticism as a wholly appropriate means for approaching the medium.

A further and perhaps more acute example of this tendency occurs in Deborah Thomas's fluent reading of *Buffy the Vampire Slayer* (Mutant Enemy Inc./20ᵗʰ Century Fox Television, 1997–2003) as part of John Gibbs and Douglas Pye's *Close-Up* series for Wallflower (Thomas 2006: 167–244). Here, Thomas presents a monograph-length consideration of the series in terms of its stylistic richness, weight and depth whilst at no point debating the legitimacy of devoting such close attention to television *per se*, despite the appearance of her work alongside two other monographs on film within the collection. The one possible concession to this might occur within Thomas's assertion that Buffy may be "television aspiring to the condition of film" (Thomas 2006: 173), but this is given more as a way of explaining the series' filmic references, drawing attention to its creator Joss Whedon's background as a student of film, and as an access point to debating some of the complexities of the series' mise-en-scène, rather than an explicit comment regarding the worthiness of studying *Buffy* in itself. Indeed, such considerations are fleeting in Thomas's approach to the series and she instead devotes herself to a measured, highly detailed interpretative account of *Buffy*'s narrative intricacies, its visual coherence and the resonances it creates both within and across episodes and seasons. Implicitly, then, we might draw the notion from Thomas's approach that this television series is potentially as worthy of study as any film, to the extent that any reasons for choosing it as a subject for critical scrutiny are taken to be implicit within the quality of the reading.

In the context of the relationship between technology and television criticism, it is noteworthy that Thomas's reading of *Buffy* features a number of references to Whedon's commentary on the DVD releases of the series, either to provide background detail to episodes or to emphasize aspects of Whedon's authorial intentions, such as his desire to invert the stereotype of the victimized blonde female in contemporary horror cinema by having his central character "fight back" (Thomas 2006: 170). In this way, Thomas explicitly engages with television as DVD, highlighting the ways in which extra features such as director commentaries can potentially enrich an understanding of the series' aims and ambitions in this instance. Unmentioned in Thomas's monograph, but equally important, are the ways in which DVD technology, as with VHS, can potentially enhance opportunities for the kind of close analysis that she performs, and which was strongly promoted in the special issue of *Journal of British Cinema and Television*. Indeed, when I came to prepare my own contribution for that issue of the journal, I instinctively turned to a DVD release of the program *Shameless* (Company Pictures/Channel 4 2004–ongoing [2005]) in order to detail "the tensions between individuals' interior emotions and their exterior appearances" as they are expressed within fleeting moments from a particular episode of the series (Walters 2006: 97). In my attempts to articulate the nature of the program's achievements, the DVD format proved wholly apposite for freezing, slowing down and replaying the nuanced gestures, looks and movements of the characters in order to describe the meanings created in the synthesis between performance style, visual composition and thematic progression.

Reading Thomas's rich evaluation of mise-en-scène in scenes from *Buffy*, it seems uncontroversial to suggest that her work might also have benefited from the DVD releases of the series in ways extending beyond the acknowledged addition of Whedon's commentaries. In fact, it would be remarkable if this were not the case: the DVD format certainly provides clear opportunities for extended and heightened engagement with television, supporting the growing appetite among scholars to scrutinize moments from programs in close analytic detail. Matt Hills, in a key article detailing the relationship between television and DVD, makes this connection in astute terms:

> . . . it is tempting to suggest that the rediscovery of "aesthetics" in TV studies . . . is strongly connected to, though not determined by, the rise of DVD culture. The reproducibility of TV (and the near-perfect freezing of its frames) which makes its texts more akin to those of written rather than oral culture certainly supports a level of aesthetic interrogation which would have been less readily possible in the past, even with the lower image quality and degraded freeze-frame facilities of videotape
>
> (Hills 2007: 48).

The notion that technological advancement, from VHS to DVD and beyond, has coincided with a renewed critical emphasis upon television aesthetics is a potent and, I would suggest, tangible concept. Moreover, I would follow Hills's presumption that this connection extends across a number of the expressive accounts of television that I have drawn attention to thus far, where DVD technology has facilitated precisely the kinds of close analyses that television scholars have become increasingly interested in undertaking.

DVD releases in particular also succeed in transforming a television program into an *object* of study: no longer part of an incessant flow of scheduling but an artifact that can be held, purchased, collected, displayed, replayed and revisited. Such processes of consumption equate television with themes of connoisseurship, whereby particular works are selected from a sea of (commercially produced) alternatives and regarded for their individual quality and merit: "symbolically bounded objects more akin to artworks or novels" (Hills 2007: 45). Of course, this repackaging of television as a DVD commodity necessarily removes it from the original broadcast context and, as a result, changes the nature of the relationship between viewer and medium. We might consider that, with the proliferation of DVRs such as TiVo and Sky+, this relationship is becoming ever more complicated anyway as viewers are invited to pause live television, commit programs to hard disk or, indeed, allow a system to record favorite programs apparently on their behalf. Crucially, however, television purchased on DVD is divergent to these modes of viewing as it constitutes a specialized item which is obtained away from the flow of broadcast television entirely: an artifact in its own right.

This kind of transformation in the form and format of television can lead, understandably, to a certain anxiety or insecurity over what exactly is meant by the term "television." This might present an acute dilemma for those intending to engage in textual analysis, given that the "text" in question is seemingly indeterminate and mutable. As Glen Creeber points out:

> Knowing where a "text" starts and ends seems increasingly difficult to ascertain, a problem clearly heightened in the multi-media age. Extratextual material, such as product merchandising, DVD extras, fanzines and Internet sites, made textual analysis frustratingly unsure of its object of study
>
> (Creeber 2006: 82–3).

Such concerns appear increasingly pertinent given that technology continues to shape television into ever more diverse forms. However, I would hesitate to suggest that the boundaries of the television "text" have expanded to the extent that it is no longer discernible what the object of study should be. Rather, I suspect that these parameters might profitably be set according to our own critical priorities, based upon the questions we wish to pursue when we think about television. Indeed, an interpretative or "text"-led approach to television might provide precisely the kind of focus that is less concerned with matters "outside" of the program itself such as merchandising, websites, fanzines and, of course, DVD extras. Interpretative criticism, we might say, is founded upon a personal desire to return to and scrutinize works of art—be that television or something else—that affect us emotionally and that arouse our intellectual curiosity. DVD technology facilitates that process of critical engagement, aiding the inclination to revisit and review any aspect of a television program's aesthetic composition, and in turn revisit and review our own understanding of it. As a sequential medium, television is composed of moment by moment phases of progression, and so it is the case that certain moments can be singled out as they come to encapsulate or exemplify a whole episode's—even a whole series or run of series'—aims and ambitions. I would contend that such a moment can be found in the final poignant meeting of Rose Tyler (Billie Piper) and the Doctor (David Tennant) at the conclusion of the last episode in series two[3] of *Doctor Who* (BBC Television 1963–ongoing [2006]).

The series finale of the popular UK science-fiction drama, revived by Russel T. Davies in 2005 to widespread acclaim, features an epic battle between the Doctor's most famous and formidable enemies, the Daleks and

Cybermen, and concludes with the Doctor and Rose ridding the world of this twin threat by sending both into a "void" between worlds. However, in the effort to accomplish this feat, Rose herself is pulled towards the vortex and her father (Shaun Dingwall) acts to rescue her by transporting her to a parallel earth, separating her permanently from the Doctor who is left in his alternate dimension. Yet, in her parallel world, Rose "hears" the Doctor calling her and, following his instructions, she travels with her family to a beach in Norway where she is confronted by his image, projected across dimensions. As the Doctor puts it, "I'm burning up a sun just to say goodbye." In the course of their conversation, it becomes clear that this will be their last ever meeting as the projection takes place due to one gap remaining between worlds which will soon close forever, a fact that eventually overwhelms them both.

The episode up to this point has been characterized by an array of large-scale action set pieces: hordes of marching Cybermen, swarms of flying Daleks, frantic escapes, the mass destruction of London and so on. Stylistically, the representation of these events has been defined by a diverse assortment of shot types, incorporating a blend of close-ups, medium shots, long shots and extreme long shots to capture the scale and pace of the action. However, the farewell between the Doctor and Rose on the beach is distinct from this previous visual texturing as, during the lead up to their encounter, the vocabulary of shots narrows from long shot to medium shot, from medium close up to close up before finally, when the two characters reach each other, settling into a steady rhyming pattern of extreme close-up reverse shots that frames Rose and the Doctor alternately. (The minor exception being two inserted long shots of Rose's family in the distance as they are referred to during the exchange.) In narrative terms, this shift in visual style succeeds primarily in creating a particular human intensity within the scene as our proximity to the characters through the placement of the camera replicates the emotional proximity that exists between the Doctor and Rose in this moment. Furthermore, the narrowing down of the visual field produces the effect of closing the characters off from the world that surrounds them, providing a space that is certainly intense but also *intimate*: it belongs to them alone.

The closing down of the world around Rose and the Doctor is particularly apt given that their time together was dictated to a great extent by an emphasis upon worlds: traveling between different worlds and invariably saving them from destruction. Indeed, it was through the pursuit of this very goal that the Doctor and Rose find themselves separated by worlds now, trapped in parallel versions of the same existence that can never converge. It is appropriate, then, that in their final meeting the world should be temporarily suspended in visual terms; that their last goodbye should take place against no backdrop considering that, throughout the moments they shared in the past, we were always aware of the changing backdrop of worlds that shaped their behavior and dictated their duties. The confining feature of the mise-en-scène places a limit on the usual dramatic flow of events we might anticipate in an episode of *Doctor Who* (and certainly pace and scale are chief attributes and strengths of the series under Russel T. Davies's recent guidance) allowing time and space for the characters to work through the emotions that threaten to engulf them, and inviting us to appreciate in close detail the relationship that exists between these two people.

Our proximity to the characters, achieved through their style of representation, encourages us to appreciate a series of striking attributes of the writing, direction and the actors' performances. Piper, for example, exhibits a detailed understanding of the conflict between strength and vulnerability that weighs upon her character in this sequence. In the course of conveying this, she balances the delivery of two jokes—Rose's brief suggestion that she's pregnant and pretending to be back working in a shop—with a vocal frailty as she strains to force the words from her throat, a mournful gaze that knots the skin between her eyebrows and renders her eyes glassy with tears that threaten to spill over at any moment, and a brief, hollow laugh that betrays any attempt at genuinely-felt humor. Here, Piper succeeds in weighing twin aspects of Rose's character: her extraordinary bravery which has endured and developed throughout the series, compared with an everyday realness that preserves the founding notion of her being an ordinary girl of nineteen thrown into unusual circumstances. The jokes represent Rose's attempt at a brave face, but this endeavor is undermined by a manner of delivery that references her interior pain. Thus, in the same instant, Rose retains her heroism and her humanity.

Piper further exhibits an accomplished understanding of the scene's direction and her character's place within its drama as she judges and times the moment when Rose should finally succumb to the profound sorrow she has so far been suppressing. When the Doctor informs her "You're dead, officially, back home. So many people died that day and you've gone missing. You're on a list of the dead" she responds with a sharp gulp of breath, biting her lip slightly and looking down, as if battling to keep her emotions in check. But the attempt is futile and, when she looks back up, bringing a hand across her face to mask the onslaught of grief, the gesture serves only to highlight the truth that she is now crying: tears sparkling in the corners of her eyes, dark wet mascara clogging her eyelashes (Figure 3.1). That Piper times her breakdown for this moment may lead us to speculate, reasonably, what element finally brings about Rose's surrender to her emotions. In one sense, it may be that the effort of maintaining her robust act would, over the course of the conversation, have proved too much and in that case she could have become consumed by her feelings at any stage, ·with any word from the Doctor a potential trigger. However, her crying after the Doctor tells her of her "death" in the parallel world seems significant, relating not to the fact of her being dead to another world—their believing her to be dead is a convenient fallacy and patently, as she stands

Figure 3.1 Rose breaks down and cries in *Doctor Who*.

before the Doctor, immaterial—but to the way in which the word "death" forcefully reminds her of the relationship between herself and the Doctor now: they will be dead to one another soon, unable to ever know the other's movements, thoughts and emotions.

This notion had already been suggested to Rose at the beginning of the scene when the projection of the Doctor was weakened and he appeared to her "like a ghost." This motif becomes a thematic pre-echo as, in a matter of seconds, they will indeed be ghosts to each other, made only of memories, and the Doctor's news of Rose's death appears to reinforce this truth painfully for her. From the nature of her performance, we can suggest that Piper is alive to this notion, and this suspicion is reinforced as, in the next moment, Rose asks "am I ever going to see you again?" and Piper flattens the question mark out of the sentence, transforming it into a hopeless statement to which Rose already knows the answer. This fact is made plain as Piper follows the words with a sharp expulsion of breath and sobs silently, burying her forehead into her open palm. For Rose, the possibility of their meeting again is already untenable and the manner of her asking merely reinforces a truth she has already accepted.

These are just some attributes of the scene that, I would suggest, combine to create the force and intensity it possessed in its original broadcast format. There are other aspects of its composition that merit further scrutiny (Tennant's equally strong performance, for example, or the qualities of the music that underscores the drama), both in terms of its specificity and also regarding its relationship to the culture of *Doctor Who* as a whole. I have no doubt that scholarly attention will take that direction in due course. My concentration upon a few of its constituent features here, however, relies upon a journey of privilege and selection: choosing to purchase the DVD after the terrestrial broadcast, choosing to look again at the episode from the menu screen, choosing the final scene from a list of selections offered within the episode menu, and then choosing to focus upon Piper's interaction with the dramatic texture of the sequence. This process perhaps exemplifies the "active engagement of the viewer" which Rob Cover describes in relation to DVD technology, further suggesting that:

> ... DVD media that distribute an entire television series require selectivity, and invite the participation of the user to choose episodes, to segment and re-sequence the television series, view a particular order of episodes, and engage with the narrative by exercising certain choices—even if within various author-given constraints
>
> (Cover 2005: 139).

Implicit in Cover's description of DVD is the extent to which viewers have the potential to embark upon the large-scale narrative restructuring of television series based upon the levels of choice offered by the media through "authorized" menus such as episode, chapter and scene selections. In my analysis, I have resisted engaging in the kind of broader narrative restructuring which Cover identifies as a potential facet of DVD user "interactivity" (Ibid) and, indeed, I would suggest that it is crucial to appreciate the moment I describe as coming at the climax of a series, drawing together broader themes that have developed throughout a run of episodes. However, it is certainly true that the DVD format has not only allowed my case for this scene from *Doctor Who* to be made, it has positively encouraged the kind of repeated engagement I wish to make with elements of the sequence's aesthetic construction. Beyond the singling out of the moment, through controlling the image with the DVD remote the viewer has the opportunity to match Piper's precision in her performance by ascertaining exactly when particular actions are taken and, in close detail, the manner in which they are undertaken. Thus, in this instance, my critical intentions are rewarded by the technology of choice.

There are, of course, other elements of the technology that exist but which I have elected not to rely on in the same way. It may be, for example, that attention to extras such as production documentaries or director commentaries would reveal that some of my observations correlate with or are divergent to the program-makers' decisions, intentions and actions. Pursuing this line of enquiry would, I think, amount to a different kind of criticism than that which I propose to undertake, and in turn might divert from my original aim of wanting to better understand why the sequence in question affected me as it originally did. That process of understanding, in this instance, relies upon my subjective interpretation of the events on screen, rather than an explanation offered by those who produced them. There is merit in analyzing the style and format of DVD extras, but it would be an unusual kind of artist indeed who wished an audience to attend more to an account of their work, rather than the work itself. Furthermore, as Brookey and Westerfelhaus contend in their analysis of "homosexual erasure" (2002: 38) in the various commentaries contained within the DVD release of *Fight Club* (Fincher 1999[2000]):

> The extra text offers consumers access to commentary by those involved with making the film, and it positions this commentary as authoritative. Such extra-text features can direct the viewer toward preferred interpretations of the primary text while undermining unfavorable interpretations, especially those that might hurt the product's commercial success. The DVD format increases the likelihood that viewers will be exposed to these promotional tactics, thereby lending such tactics greater rhetorical force
>
> (Ibid: 24).

In the case of *Fight Club*, Brookey and Westerfelhaus maintain that the result is the suppression of any sustained reference to the film's homoeroticism in the extra features of the film's DVD release. However, it might reasonably be concluded that the commercial imperatives they describe would equally affect television releases on DVD, resulting in a series of "inside" accounts of the work that in fact serve potentially to sponsor preferred, hence favorable, interpretations of the episode or series. Thus, "answers" may be provided to the meanings of certain moments and sequences which rely less on the viewer's subjective interpretative response and more on "authorized" accounts provided in DVD extras.

In the case of the scene from *Doctor Who*, DVD technology provides a means to revisit and reappraise a dramatically heightened and emotionally intense moment from the program's history. However, it is also the case that DVD provides opportunities to re-examine seemingly inconsequential moments from television programs and evaluate them in terms of wider patterns of representation. Here, I want to turn to an opening episode from the fifth season of the US drama *24* (Fox 2001–ongoing[2006]) to emphasize the ways in which DVD technology can help us to understand even the slightest gestures characters make as part of a nuanced pattern of representation. As has already been suggested, watching television as DVD has the potential to disrupt the flow of its broadcast context, and it could be said that this becomes intensified in the case of *24*, where a central conceit of the show is that the events of each episode "occur in real time," interrupted only by the interposition of commercial breaks. Thus, some might argue that the pausing and replaying of moments from the show risks disrupting that temporal flow to the extent that the immediacy and drive of the narrative is lost, "de-24ing" *24*, as it were. However, I would suggest that this position is somewhat disingenuous given that all narrative drama has a temporal flow that is inevitably interrupted in the processes of analysis. It would be nonsensical to suggest that we lose all sense of a narrative's sequential arrangement when engaged in critical enquiry and, although events are shown to occur in real-time in *24*, they are certainly not *recorded* directly in real time but instead shaped and reassembled to convey that impression of immediacy. Indeed, the detailed crafting of episodes may be the very reason we would return to a show like *24*, creating the space to better understand its textured construction. DVD can provide that temporal space. As Steven Peacock suggests in a recent collection examining the show:

> In returning to *24* on repeat broadcast, disc, download, or instant rewind, the viewer can appreciate more fully the attention to detail in the series' visual compositions. Pausing and rewinding points of the series, shuttling to and from different moments, we can discern how (and savor the sense of knowing that) a detail or gesture caught on the periphery of the frame (a glance, a glimpse of information) becomes crucial to the unfolding scenarios of the series; equally, we can appreciate the way *24* builds to pivotal twists and turns, thickening the plot and heightening the tension, taking a scenario to breaking point before performing a volte-face for characters and viewers alike
>
> (Peacock 2007: 33).

Indeed, it is characteristic of the show to offer fragmentary details that can often only be properly appreciated in the final resolution of the narrative, or at some later stage in its progression. Much like the slowly-emerging "24" title that features at the beginning of each episode, events can only be understood fully when the picture is complete. Therefore, *24* can potentially reward repeat viewings as we can better appreciate the role a small, seemingly insignificant, moment played in the development of a scenario or in the construction of a character. The scene that strikes me as particularly appropriate in this regard is the first in the episode involving President Charles Logan (Gregory Itzin) who, in the fourth season, was shown to be disastrously inept in dealing with a national crisis, having to call upon former President David Palmer (Dennis Haysbert) to successfully handle matters. The sequence in question depicts Logan as he prepares to sign a historic treaty on terrorism with the Russian President (season five, episode one). As he meets with various members of his staff, Logan performs a series of hand gestures in which he touches, or attempts to touch, other characters. On first viewing, these gestures struck as somewhat odd and, through rewinding, forwarding, freezing and stop-framing the DVD, they begin to emerge as defining actions that combine within a textured portrait of the character.

Logan performs three different acts of touching in the sequence. Firstly, as he sweeps into the office, he briefly touches the arm of Walt Cummings (John Allen Nelson), his Chief of Staff. There's a buoyant confidence in the gesture, in keeping with the President's exuberance as he stage manages his meeting with his Russian counterpart. This confidence is undermined, however, by the fact that, at the time, he's referring to his desire for a reinforced chair that will increase his stature in the eyes of the viewing public. Indeed, his later advice to his aide, Mike Novick (Jude Ciccollela) to "not underestimate the power of the image" conveys a picture of a man concerned more with outward appearances than substance or, indeed, truth.

The gentle touch on Walt Cumming's arm therefore reads as not simply an instinctive, relaxed gesture, but rather as Logan's visual indication to his Chief of Staff, and perhaps to the rest of the room, of their solidarity. In this context, it is crucial that he doesn't look at Cummings when he performs the gesture, which might have established a more authentic human connection between them. The staginess of Logan's opening line "Walt, my chair?" adds to this apparent concern with surface effect, as Logan raises his arm slightly, as though performing a small show. This notion of a show is continued as Logan describes his remembered images of Churchill and Stalin sitting for Roosevelt: iconic scenes that he clearly seeks to replicate within his own presidency. The show of solidarity with Cummings, the insistence on the raised chair and the allusions to Roosevelt combine to form a picture of insecurity, of a man needing to manage his image to create an illusion of himself as a respected statesman.

Whereas the hand brushing against the Chief of Staff's arm can be seen as a fleeting, somewhat disingenuous act, later in the scene President Logan makes a much more tangible connection with Cummings. As Novick takes a phone call, Logan chooses the moment for a discrete discussion with his Chief of Staff. The purpose of this is to ascertain the condition of the First Lady, although the tone of the President's inquiries is set by his abrupt opening line "have you checked on my wife?" and his firm contention that "she cannot have one of her meltdowns today." These words are hardly imbued with careful concern, so further defining the President again as a man distracted with how things might look at the expense of underlying truths or sensitivities.

The coldness of the President's tone undermines the potential warmth or intimacy that might have been conveyed in his placing a hand on the Chief of Staff's shoulder when he asks him to personally check on the First Lady. The gesture could, in another circumstance, indicate one man's trust in the other and the strength of their bond both professionally and personally. Here, however, in the context of Logan's behavior, it reads as a controlling gesture, creating a forced bond of dependence that the Chief of Staff is unable to politely break. In this sense, it ensures that Logan's demand has to be met so that Cummings is effectively given a definite order, rather than a compassionate request. This degree of manipulation is emphasized in Cummings' letting his gaze drop momentarily before reengaging the President, as though acknowledging he has been left with little choice in the matter (Figure 3.2). The hand on the shoulder, rather than suggesting an amicable connection, becomes a symbol of the President's calculating but nervy control; a control that extends through the Chief of Staff to the First Lady as he attempts to regulate her behavior by proxy.

The President's final gesture of touch occurs as he reaches out to his advisor, Mike Novick, but unlike his previous gestures, Logan does not actually complete the potential moment of contact with his associate. Novick had previously worked closely with President Palmer, Logan's predecessor, but betrayed him in an earlier series. After delivering the shocking news that Palmer has been assassinated, Novick stands by the window, visibly shaken. President Logan leaves Novick and as he passes him raises his arm as if to lay a supportive hand on his obviously grieving colleague's shoulder. However, he doesn't follow the action through, and instead his fingers barely touch Novick as he passes. Indeed, Novick doesn't respond even marginally to the President's touch, suggesting that he in fact made no contact at all. This lack of sincere connection represents a failure on the President's part to adequately respond to Novick's loss, as his gesture lacks both compassion and meaningful impact. In this sense, he reveals himself to be somewhat incapable of displaying genuine human understanding.

President Logan's touching of other characters in this scene becomes a metaphor for his underlying traits and characteristics. Each inflection of the gesture serves to index a series of attitudes inherent in his character. His personal shortcomings are exemplified in his physical interactions with others, and these shortcomings spiral out as the series progresses, becomes ever more sinister and dangerous. The show succeeds in taking a small action—one character briefly touching another—and teasing out the ambiguities of that gesture, demonstrating how it can translate differently in a series of contexts. The tenor of Logan's small physical acts then comes to

Figure 3.2 The use of gesture in *24*—President Logan gives Chief of Staff Cummings a direct order.

function as part of a wider pattern of character representation, building a picture of a man who, it turns out, is eventually unfit for the position he holds. The ways in which he touches each of the characters in the sequence thus become guiding constituent parts in the construction of his character, shaping an impression of the President that endures throughout the series. In this way, the character's movements, actions and gestures, connect with the series' wider fictional world and consequently its wider dramatic aims as elements taking their place within a coherent whole. Isolating these gestures for extended consideration can help to advance our appreciation of the complexities inherent in *24*'s moment-by-moment narrative development, allowing us to evaluate even slight moments as part of an overall representational strategy.

It has been my contention in this chapter that DVD technology presents a series of benefits to the attentive television viewer, promoting sustained engagement with moments and sequences through a process of repetition and return. One product of this might be a brand of television criticism centred upon the close appreciation of program texture, tone and composition, which I have attempted as part of my discussion and is performed elsewhere as part of a growing scholarly interest in questions of television aesthetics. Thus DVD technology, although removing television from an original broadcast context as we stop, slow down and replay the image (Cover 2005: 141–3), might succeed in supporting greater precision in accounts of the medium, making us ever more alert to its particular qualities and achievements. Of course, the term "DVD" may itself be rapidly passing into the confines of history (taking its place alongside VHS) due to the advancement of digital technology represented in the competition between Blu-ray and HD-DVD, for example (Bulkley 2007). While this kind of development may understandably be equated to an expansion of the television "text," I hope to have suggested ways in which new formats can also complement critical practices founded upon detail, focus and precision, narrowing down the area of consideration in order to better understand the whole.

NOTES

1. This misunderstanding is characteristic of Ralph's "slowness" which the show frequently references, often for comic effect. However, while the representation of this aspect of Ralph's character might implicitly suggest acute learning difficulties of some variety, the portrayal is not consistent across episodes and seasons. Indeed, in this very episode Ralph's basic inability to understand the nature of Lisa's gesture combined with his tendency to eat wax crayons and paste his head to his shoulder, for example, seems to exemplify his possessing a mental age well below his physical age. Yet, in the episode's conclusion, he gives a powerfully melodramatic performance as George Washington in the school President's Day pageant that reduces the audience to tears and prompts a group of notorious school dropouts to

make their way to the library in order to "learn more about our founding fathers."

2. The status of interpretative criticism as a practice within Films Studies has not been entirely secure and without question however, a fact that George Wilson attends to in his essential article, "On Film Narrative and Narrative Meaning" (Wilson 1997).

3. The second series since the show was re-launched in 2005.

BIBLIOGRAPHY

Akass, K. et al. (2006) "Editorial," *Critical Studies in Television: scholarly studies in small screen fictions,* 1(1): 1–2.

Brookey, R. A. and Westerfelhaus, R. (2002) "Hiding Homoeroticism in Plain View: The *Fight Club* DVD as Digital Closet," *Critical Studies in Media Communication,* 19(1): 21–43.

Brunsdon, C. (1997) *Screen Tastes: soap opera to satellite dishes,* London: Routledge.

Bulkley, K. (2007, May 3) "No Punches Pulled in High Definition War," *The Guardian,* Online. Available HTTP: <http://www.guardian.co.uk/technology/2007/may/03/newmedia.media> (accessed 2 August 2007).

Cardwell, S. (2006) "'Television Aesthetics' and Close Analysis: Style Mood and Engagement in *Perfect Strangers*" in J. Gibbs and D. Pye (eds) *Style and Meaning: studies in the detailed analysis of film,* Manchester: Manchester University Press: 179–194.

Cardwell, S. and Peacock, S. (2006) 'Introduction,' *Journal of British Cinema and Television,* 3(1): 1–4.

Cover, R. (2005) "DVD Time: Temporality, Audience Engagement and the New TV Culture of Digital Video," *Media International Australia Incorporating Culture and Policy,* 117: 137–147.

Creeber, G. (2006) "The Joy of Text? Television and Textual Analysis," *Critical Studies in Television: Scholarly Studies in Small Screen Fictions,* 1(1): 81–8.

Geraghty, C. (2003) "Aesthetics and Quality in Popular Drama," *International Journal of Cultural Studies,* 6(1): 25–45.

Hills, M. (2007) "From the Box in the Corner to the Box Set on the Shelf: "TVIII" and the Cultural/Textual Valorisations of DVD," *New Review of Film and Television Studies,* 5(1): 41–60.

Jacobs, J. (2001) "Issues of Judgement and Value in Television Studies," *International Journal of Cultural Studies,* 4(4): 427–47.

Mulvey, L. (2006) "Repetition and return: textual analysis and Douglas Sirk in the twenty-first century," in J. Gibbs and D. Pye (eds) *Style and Meaning: studies in the detailed analysis of film,* Manchester: Manchester University Press: 228–243.

Peacock, S. (2007) *Reading 24: TV against the clock,* London: I.B. Tauris.

Thomas, D. (2006) 'Reading *Buffy*,' in J. Gibbs and D. Pye (eds) *Close Up,* London: Wallflower.

Walters, J. (2006) "Saving Face: Inflections of Character Role-play in *Shameless*," *Journal of British Cinema and Television,* 3(1): 95–106

Wilson, G.M. (1997) "On Film Narrative and Narrative Meaning," in R. Allen and M. Smith (eds) *Film Theory and Philosophy,* Oxford: Oxford University Press: 221–238.

4 "The DVD of Attractions?"

The Lion King and the Digital Theme Park

Tom Brown

Understanding "new media" in the light of the "old" provides something of an antidote to the hyperbole of modern multi-media institutions, which seek to frame innovations such as the DVD in terms of unprecedented access to the previously mystified workings of media production. In the case of this entry, I draw upon the paradigm of Tom Gunning's "cinema of attractions" (1990[1986]). The question mark in the title indicates the evident tension between the use of a concept originating in the study of early cinema and my subsequent analysis of conventions (relatively) specific to the new media object DVD.

This chapter does not seek to reduce the newness of DVD, but rather use the "aesthetic of attractions" as a heuristic through which to investigate key aspects of the DVD's audience address. Attractions provide a useful springboard for the close textual analysis of DVD menuing, a defining characteristic of the platform that is receiving increased attention.[1] The choice to focus on Disney's special edition DVD of *The Lion King* (Allers and Minkoff 1994[2003]) engenders tensions, not only that between the general discussion (the relationship of DVD to the cinema of attractions) and more specific factors (Disney as a company renowned for its particularly controlling attitude to its own texts), but also that between the DVD as a novel kind of "intra-text" (Brookey and Westerfelhaus 2002) and its relationship to previous notions of filmic textuality. As a DVD, *The Lion King* is an extras-laden package, which includes various documentaries and interactive games; *as a film,* notwithstanding its status as animation, it can be related to the history of attractions in musical/comic traditions.[2] The cinema of attractions provides a useful starting point for understanding this and other DVDs' direct address of their audience, their combination of the spectacular with the intimate, and their technological anthropomorphism. Furthermore, the aesthetic of attractions sheds light on the historic connections between film and the fairground, amusement and theme park, physical spaces that provide the organizational logic to the digital spaces of *The Lion King* DVD.

THE CINEMA OF ATTRACTIONS
AND THE DVD INTRATEXT

The cinema of attractions is a familiar concept for both critics of film and new media. According to Tom Gunning, it is the dominant cinematic mode until about 1906–1907, at which point the so-called "cinema of narrative integration," which will come to be associated with D.W. Griffith, takes over (1990: 57). The cinema of attractions is more concerned with showing off the technological possibilities of the cinematic apparatus than the subsequent, more narrative-driven cinema: "contrasted to the voyeuristic aspect of narrative cinema analyzed by Christian Metz, this is an exhibitionist cinema" (Gunning 1990: 57). This exhibitionism is technological (the apparatus and its illusory tricks are on show), but it is also performative. This performative exhibitionism is manifest in the predominance of direct address in the cinema of attractions—"the recurring look at the camera by actors" (1990: 57). Direct address is not only intrinsic to the cinema of attractions through the on-screen actor, conjurer or illusionist, but is also, importantly, a feature of the film's exhibition by an exterior showman (Gunning 2004: 45–46). Indeed, in the cinema of attractions, the exhibition of the film and the film itself were not easy to distinguish; the notion of the film text as discreet entity did not exist. It is perhaps for this reason above all that the concept has attracted theorists of new media. In the case of abundantly packaged DVD intratexts cited here, it is just as difficult, indeed, inappropriate, to extricate the film from the context in which it is presented.

Gunning's innovation was chiefly to question previously dominant models for early cinema which worked upon a clear teleology, the dominant force being the inexorable move towards greater realism. So, whereas some histories have seen the development of the close-up as a move towards continuity editing, in the cinema of attractions the close-up is considered primarily as unabashed technological exhibitionism (Gunning 1990: 58). Partly because of Gunning's brief allusion to the continuation of the cinema of attractions as an undercurrent emergent in later genres (he cites the musical; Gunning 1990: 57), the concept has been called upon in a variety of critical contexts. For example, it has been evoked in "national cinema" approaches that seek to resist the dominant paradigm of classical (Hollywood) cinema (Vincendeau 2004: 138) and in other work historicizing recent special-effects spectaculars (King 2000: 29–30). The cinema of attractions is also used to link the cinema to other forms of sensation. For example, both Andrew Darley (2000: 31–57) and Geoff King (2000: 178) link the visual and experiential spectacle represented by "special venue attractions" such as "Back to the Future: The Ride" to the attractions of early cinema. (Later, we shall note the re-inscription of such ride experiences into many DVD extra activities aimed at children).

Particularly relevant here is Bolter and Grusin's comparison of the cinema of attractions with recent Hollywood blockbusters within the context of "transparent immediacy" ("the denial of the presence of the medium") and "hypermediacy" ("a fascination with the medium itself"):

> The set-piece attacks of the dinosaurs in *Jurassic Park* [Spielberg 1993] and *The Lost World* [Spielberg 1997] seek to invoke a sense of wonder in the contemporary audience similar to what Gunning describes for the French audience in the Grand Café [the site for the first exhibition of the Lumières brothers' films]. The audience for Steven Spielberg's films knows that the dinosaurs are animatronic or wholly computer generated, and the wonder is that these devices look so lifelike and interact so realistically with the human figures . . . We go to such films in large part to experience the oscillations between immediacy and hypermediacy produced by such special effects. Unlike the early cinema of attractions, the effects in today's films are, as most of the audience understands, computer-controlled or computer-generated remediations of traditional film
>
> (1999: 157).

If, as Bolter and Grusin point out, modern viewers are aware of the special effects *as* special effects, this awareness is now promoted most explicitly by the DVD. Many of the "extras" included on DVDs, from audio commentaries to behind-the-scenes documentaries, provide details of the technical procedures used to create the film's spectacular set pieces. Though the first supposedly credulous spectators of the films at the Grand Café may not have possessed this degree of extra-textual knowledge, one should acknowledge the promotion of such awareness by various means during classical, studio-era Hollywood (roughly 1927–1960).[3] The genre Gunning alludes to as a continuing source of "attractions"—the musical—would regularly offer the "oscillation between immediacy and hypermediacy produced by [its] special effects." Writing of the spectacle of Fred Astaire's dance routines, Steven Cohan compares two numbers in *Royal Wedding* (Donen 1951), "Sunday Jumps," a dance solo in which Astaire's seemingly boundless energy entangles him in gym apparatus, and "You're All the World to Me," in which the dancer seems to defy gravity by dancing on the floor, walls then ceiling of his room: "If the first solo [in 'Sunday Jumps'] makes an audience think, 'wow, look what he can do!' the second [in 'You're All the World to Me'] makes them wonder, 'wow, how did they do that?'" (2002: 91–92). As Cohan suggests, the Hollywood studios devoted considerable resources and energies to the promotion of such moments as technical *tours de force* "not to be missed." As with *Royal Wedding*, magazine and newspaper advertisements/articles, press books, and, later, television shows, would reveal the secrets behind the cinematic tricks of a man dancing on a ceiling. However, until the DVD, these extra texts remained spatially and temporally separate from the film text itself. As Brookey and Westerfelhaus have discussed, the DVD thus participates in a transition from a particular kind of industry-sanctioned intertextuality to *intratextuality*, which connotes a different kind of synergistic control:

> The DVD format collapses exposure to promotional material into the experience of viewing the film by bringing the film and its makers' commentary about it into close proximity, temporally and spatially; hence, DVD-extra text's *intratextual* advantage over traditional forms of secondary texts
>
> (2002: 24).

Across this transition from the intertext of film with ancillary promotional material to the DVD as an *intratext*, combining film with promotional material, Disney displays its mastery. Through television shows such as NBC's *The Wonderful World of Disney*,[4] hosted by "Uncle Walt" until his death in 1966, Disney personified his company's "family values." These TV shows promoted the films, the technical innovations used to create them, and of course the theme park based around them. This can now be achieved on the DVD, which, in its interactive novelties, can also promote other media products and experiences such as computer-game spin-offs.

The gap between Disney's initial cinematic release of *The Lion King* and its special edition DVD illustrates the evolution of these promotional strategies. One of the film's most spectacular scenes sees the stampede of thousands of wildebeest and this scene was repeatedly singled-out in the promotion of the theatrical release. News spots and television programs stressed the state-of-the-art technology used to animate this scene—it was said to have been innovative in combining two-dimensional, conventional, hand-drawn animation with three-dimensional computer rendering. On the DVD, both the audio commentary on disc one (which describes the scene as "probably the center-piece of the movie;" seven minutes that apparently took three years to complete) and a documentary on disc two entitled "Computer Animation" unveil the technical processes employed. The wildebeest scene represents a fairly typical moment of spectacle familiar to viewers of contemporary cinema; its prominence on the DVD illustrates the importance of the connecting promotional discourses.[5] Its scale, its abundant visual and aural qualities encourage us to ask: "Wow, how did they do that?"[6] Within the DVD intratext, this question is no longer merely symbolic of the awe experienced by the spectator, but is answered explicitly by the extra materials.

I would argue that the oscillation between "immediacy" and "hypermediacy" discussed by Bolter and Grusin is further reconfigured by the temporality of the "DVD of attractions." The particular temporality of the DVD is evident in the way it allows the user to access moments of the film (typically through "chapters"), and in the way that some DVDs enable the user to access extras from within the film, sometimes by clicking an icon or by the abrupt insertion of extra materials into the normal passage of the film—the latter is illustrated by the *Moulin Rouge!* (Luhrmann 2001[2003]) example cited below. In relation to chaptering, one can draw clear parallels with the promotion of early cinema. Gunning emphasizes the raw, quantifiable relationship between spectacle and narrative in the cinema of attractions. As evidence, he cites a Boston theatre's advertisement for the 1924 [sic] version of *Ben Hur*, which included a timetable of its key moments of spectacle. This menu might remind one of the chapters present on almost all DVD discs:[7]

8.35 *The Star of Bethlehem*
8.40 *Jerusalem Restored*
8.59 *Fall of the House of Hur*
10.29 *The Last Supper*
10.50 *Reunion*

(Gunning 1990: 61).

It is debatable what contemporary patrons of *Ben Hur* did with such information, aside from perhaps recognizing it as a gimmicky way of advertising an abundance of spectacle—it is hard to imagine many spectators wandering in at 10.29 to catch The Last Supper. However, DVDs organize their chapters in a similar way, often providing a brief title to describe the main events contained in each. In many DVDs, this appears simply to be a means of convenient access to key points of the narrative—fast-forwarding in a way not dissimilar to VHS. However, those genres offering more prominent non-narrative pleasures arrange their chapters around their main moments of spectacle. This is especially evident in the case of musical films. For example, classic MGM musicals, such as *Singin' in the Rain* (Donen and Kelly 1952[2006]) and *The Band Wagon* (Minnelli 1953[2005]), the "postmodern musical" *Moulin Rouge!*, and, indeed, the animated musical *The Lion King* all organize their chapters around their musical numbers. This is scarcely surprising since musical filmmaking is particularly well suited to the viewing of spectacular moments out of narrative sequence—the MGM compilation films of the 1970s (starting with Jack Haley's *That's Entertainment* of 1974) demonstrate the genre's suitability for this sort of viewer appreciation.

To understand more fully the potential impact of chaptering conventions on the DVD's intratext and film, one might look to Gunning's reflection on "the temporality of the cinema of attractions," an essay usefully entitled, "Now you see it, now you don't:"

The temporality of the attraction . . . is greatly limited in comparison to narrative, albeit possessing its own intensity. Rather than a development that links the past with the present in such a way as to define a specific anticipation (as an unfolding narrative does), the attraction seems limited to a sudden burst of presence

(2004: 45).

The cinema of attractions is thus defined by "a jagged rhythm [which] catches the irruption of a different, nonconfigured temporality" (Gunning 2004: 45). Such temporality finds echoes in more modern cinema, as in the transition to a number in a musical or, perhaps somewhat smoother, the way the obligatory awe-struck crowd prepares us for a moment of Steven Spielberg spectacle. Of course, in these two examples, the spectacular moments are molded and contained by narrative. However, such a temporality is much closer to the "not-so-linear" functionality of DVD.

The disc for the animated film *Shark Tale* (Bergeron et al. 2004[2005]) provides a more unusual instance of chaptering than the musical DVDs cited above. *Shark Tale* contains a standard chapters function available from the main menu of the disc, but, within a menu named "Dreamworks Kids" (Dreamworks is the studio behind the film), there is an alternative means of accessing scenes of the film. Named "Fin-filled scenes" (the menus reproduce the fishy puns of the film text), this function differs from standard menuing in a couple of crucial ways. Firstly, moments of the film are grouped into categories rather than into chronological order. These categories are "Laugh Out Loud," "Gross Out!!," "Dance Scenes," "Lenny & Oscar" and "Ernie and Bernie." The categories offer the user a variety of moments, or attractions, arranged, respectively, into general comedy, more scatological humor, musical numbers and two different comic character double-acts. Another crucial difference from normal DVD chapters is that these are not simply access points to the film, but are moments made discrete by the DVD's encoding. One chooses a category, then a particular moment within that category, and is then given a brief burst of action, which can last from around ten seconds to a couple of minutes. The disc then returns to the root menu. These are moments of pure spectacle made separate from narrative in a way reminiscent of the sudden burst of presence of early cinematic attractions. Of course, on a DVD, this is interactive and user-led, but the effect is the same: it distils linear filmmaking down to its base spectacular elements and stresses the "jagged rhythm" of the attraction. While this function is particularly fitting for numbers in a musical, it is also suited to comedy, that most "alienated" of genres (Naremore 1988: 114). It can also be seen to enrich the repeated home viewing of a film text such as *Shark Tale* for its young viewers. One can imagine the thrill of re-watching the film and anticipating a favorite moment—anticipation built in the DVD viewer with a temporality announced by "Now you see it, now you don't." Indeed, added to the exclamations Cohan imagines ("Wow, look what he can do!" and "Wow, how did they do that!"), this phrase may help us define the temporality of the DVD of attractions. Crucially, it addresses the audience directly and, in the later analysis of disc one of *The Lion King*, direct address is central to the linking of DVD to the aesthetic of attractions.

This jagged, non-configured temporality is even more prominent in special features that combine extra materials with the primary film text. For example, the *Singin' in the Rain* special edition [2006] includes a feature entitled "Singin' Inspirations." When activated, icons appear during the film, generally during the musical numbers, allowing the viewer to click enter on their remote control and view the original rendition of, for example, "Singin' in the Rain" from *The Hollywood Revue of 1929* (Reisner). This function is almost identical to the "Follow the White Rabbit" feature on the DVD for *The Matrix* (Andy and Larry Wachowski 1999), which shows brief documentary films on the special effects work behind a particular scene.[8] A more intrusive version of this function appears on the *Moulin Rouge!* DVD, with its "Behind the Red Velvet Curtain" special feature. The back of the DVD box proclaims how this special feature "lets you glimpse a historical, technical, and artistic view of *Moulin Rouge!*" In practice, when activated, the function interrupts the normal narration of the film with a short documentary on the history of the Parisian night club or, more frequently, with material detailing the "extraordinary artistic endeavor" that is Luhrmann's film. All these functions are indicative of the limited interactivity of the DVD intratext. Indeed, the term "reactive" seems more appropriate to the "Behind the Red Velvet Curtain" feature—but even this implies that the audience has much more control than they have in reality. As Brookey and Westerfelhaus note, "the rhetorical advantage of DVD intertextuality" is evident, as it "invests the viewer with a greater *perceived* sense of agency" (2002: 24).

Before we turn to one particular case study, it is worth noting some other correspondences between the aesthetic of attractions and certain kinds of DVD intratexts. So far, we have emphasized attractions as embodied in moments of filmic spectacle—for example, a musical number or the stampede of thousands of animated wildebeest—and how these moments are differently emphasized by various DVD intratexts. In DVDs aimed at children or a family audience, the attractions of theme parks and roller coasters are also recreated in a variety of extra activities, particularly in "set-top games." This helps to reformulate previous links between cinematic spectacle and the thrills of the theme park. Indeed, this link was a tenet of the initial formulation of "the cinema of attractions," a term borrowed from Soviet film director Sergei Eisenstein's "montage of attractions:"

> ... It is important to realize the context from which Eisenstein selected the term. Then, as now, the "attraction" was primarily a term of the fairground, and for Eisenstein and his friend Yutkevich it primarily represented their favourite fairground attraction, the roller coaster, or as it was known then in Russia, the American Mountains
>
> (Gunning 1990: 59).

Not only do many modern children and family DVDs seek to recreate the thrills of theme parks and fairgrounds, some such films are themselves based on rides.

Unsurprisingly, Disney offers the most famous examples of film-theme park ride synergy. DVDs of *The Pirates of the Caribbean: The Curse of the Black Pearl* (Verbinski 2003[2004]) and Disney's *The Haunted Mansion* (Minkoff 2003[2004]) contain documentaries about the rides that inspired them and special features that, to a greater or lesser extent, recreate the experience of the rides (with the added appeal of "interactivity"). For example, the DVD of *The Haunted Mansion* (a film seeking to make up for poor theatrical release figures with an abundance of DVD extras) contains a feature entitled "Disney's Virtual DVD Ride." The viewer takes the position of one of the theme park's "doom buggies" and moves through the spooky spaces of the DVD by following on-screen arrows. *Pirates of the Caribbean*'s "Below Deck" feature is not so much a recreation of the thrills of a ride, but a way of navigating historical information about real pirates through a feature that recreates something of the experience of the original audio animatronics of "The Pirates of the Caribbean." The viewer "travels" below deck through various rooms and clicks on particular parts of the ship to uncover its history, which also underlines the research that went into the film's production. Cross-platform and cross-media convergence takes many directions and many forms in these two films.

The kind of gimmickry cited above is not limited to the more playful genres aimed at children. For example, the DVD of Scorsese's *Gangs of New York* (2002[2003]) allows a 360 degree view of the "Five Points" set, a function that enables the DVD user (however superficially) to penetrate space in a way denied to the film spectator. (In this same collection, Jo T. Smith notes the "clunky" interactivity of this feature.) Many other DVDs base their menus around the spaces of their films and echo the "enclosed environmental artworks" of the Disney oeuvre—a metaphor for DVD intratextuality that I shall return to below. It is worth noting, however, the prevalence of set-top games on children's DVDs, games that one might better term virtual roller coasters. The DVD release of *Harry Potter and the Chamber of Secrets* (Columbus 2002[2003]) contains one such game called, "Escape from the Forbidden Forest." The DVD user is required to steer this ride with touches of the DVD remote control, the on-screen image speeding and swooping through a dark, digital forest. Reactivity is however rather limited; the aim instead seems to be to dazzle or distract the user with the aesthetics of a high-speed ride. Clearly one is seeing the combination of older forms of sensation, such as the roller coaster, and the experience of the computer game. Indeed, *Spy Kids 3-D: Game Over* (Rodriguez 2003[2004]) is perhaps the ultimate convergence text in this regard. Taking video games as the premise for its narrative, this risible piece of filmmaking becomes a slick DVD package. The DVD contains a relatively sophisticated game, which reproduces a high-speed, roller coaster-like scene from the film—a spectacular set piece surely designed partly with the DVD or a computer-game tie-in in mind.[9] As early cinema often sought to emulate the thrills of the fairground, these kids' DVDs simulate theme park simulation rides.

THE LION KING'S DIGITAL DOMINION

The Lion King Special Edition won a British Academy of Film and Television (BAFTA) Interactive award for best DVD in 2003. It is exemplary as a quality DVD object, due to the wealth of material on its two discs, the sophisticated animated menus, the relative status of the film (seen as a high point of the last golden age of Disney feature animation), and the package's apparent aspirations towards some educative value—the "natural history" dimension must have attracted the BAFTA voters.

The elements of exhibitionism, direct address of the audience and the importance of a showman figure intrinsic to the cinema of attractions are clearly illustrated by *The Lion King* as with other DVDs. First, following convention, the technology and illusory techniques behind the original theatrical release are prominently exhibited through a variety of extra features. Direct address is the structuring mode of address of DVD presentations generally, in ways that parallel the televisual but often go beyond it. DVD direct address ranges from behind-the-scenes documentaries to optional aural direct address by, mainly, the filmmakers on commentary tracks. (Furthermore, that menus are the basis for the DVD underlines the *direct, reactive* relationship the text requires of the viewer.) Finally, we have remarked on the dissolution of traditional boundaries between primary film text and secondary promotional material in the constitution of DVD as intratext. In the case of *The Lion King* disc one, this is exemplified by the creation of a virtual showman figure (an animated bird) who addresses the audience directly in order to act as a guide through the entertaining extra spaces of the DVD.

The Lion King is divided into two discs, the first containing the film and extras clearly aimed at the younger members of the family, disc two containing more weighty material (a "virtual safari" aside), such as behind-the-scenes documentaries. This division between discs one and two is itself revealing, but first, one must examine the introductions to each disc separately, and pay close attention to the flow of their menus, warnings, advertisements and various brand markers.

After the obligatory FBI warnings and the Disney Home Entertainment ident, disc one opens with a series of advertisements. (Disney DVDs and videos are well known for heavily advertising other Disney products, particularly films.) The first is for Disneyholidays.co.uk, featuring a child chasing a Mickey Mouse balloon through Disneyworld. There are then trailers for the theatrical releases of *Brother Bear* (Blaise and Walker 2003) and *Finding Nemo* (Stanton and Unkrich 2003), and for the direct-to-video/DVD release of *The Lion King 1½* (Raymond 2004).[10] All three animated films are made by or affiliated with Disney. The significance of the placement of the Disney resorts advertisement will become more apparent later, but it is first worth remarking on a couple of interesting characteristics of the *Brother Bear* and *The Lion King 1½* trailers. While *Brother Bear* is announced as "only in theatres," the trailer curiously resembles that for a DVD. Scenes from the finished film are interspersed with the original line drawings for the animation (Figure 4.1) along with behind-the-scenes footage of the voice artists, the recording of the soundtrack and the real bears used to model the film characters. Recognizable conventions of DVD deconstruction are thus projected onto a film even before it was released in the cinema.

The entirely animated advertisement for *The Lion King* prequel is also highly reflexive. The characters of Timon (voiced by Nathan Lane) and Pumbaa (voiced by Ernie Sabella) sit in front of a television screen showing the original *Lion King*. Timon than holds up a remote control and fast-forwards "to the part where we come in." Pumbaa counters, "You can't go out of order . . . [otherwise] everyone is going to get confused." After battling over the remote, they agree to rewind before the beginning of *The Lion King*'s story to tell their part in it: "Let's take them on a backstage tour, behind-the-scenes for a revealing and intimate look at the story within the story." The language is notable for its arch-knowingness and its clear use of a discourse now very familiar in DVD extras. While clearly aimed at children, they joke with concepts of multiple entry points and viewer control familiar from theories of home media consumption. It shows a level of self-referentiality intrinsic to our understanding of DVD and attractions.

When the advertisements and trailers are finished, we move into the disc's main menu. A sophisticated piece of animated filmmaking in its own right, the menu is remarkable first of all for its duration—over two minutes by the time the animation and main part of the accompanying voiceover has completed. The menu begins with an extreme close-up of a chalk image of the lion-cub hero Simba. This image is recognizable to viewers who have already seen the film as one from a prophetic chalk drawing by soothsaying baboon, Rafiki, in his home, "the tree of life." His voice whispers, "It is time," and Rafiki's thumb wipes across the forehead of the chalk drawing.

Figure 4.1 Trailer for theatrical release of *Brother Bear* intersperses final animation with original line drawings.

The image then dissolves into a continuous shot following the king's chief aide from within the film, a bird named Zazu, as he flies across the kingdom ("the Pridelands") of the film. African-esque music, like that featured within the film, accompanies Zazu's flight as he soars and swoops across the digital landscape—it is clearly a computer rendition, prepared specially for the DVD, of the traditionally animated landscape of the film. The qualities of Zazu's flight and the camera's movement around him (it sometimes appears to strain to keep up, falls behind, then catches up) parallel those in the virtual roller coasters cited earlier.[11] There are moments (for example, when Zazu flies through a skull in the elephant's graveyard) when it appears as if we might crash into some object, only for the camera/Zazu to effect some spectacular maneuver to avert disaster.

The dialectic between spectacle and intimacy could be said largely to define the aesthetic of attractions. In the cinema of attractions, this would be achieved in the combination of moments of cinematic shock, rupture, or artifice (as in a Georges Méliès special effect) with the central place of direct address by a filmic or extra-filmic agent (actor or showman respectively). More fundamentally, a moment of spectacle in the cinema of attractions marks itself out as artifice and thus affects a kind of intimacy/collusion with the audience. The menu of *The Lion King* disc one moves from the spectacular to the intimate as Zazu lands on "Pride Rock," a central setting for the film and the seat of the lion king's throne. He turns to the camera and, apparently startled by our presence, exclaims, "Visitors!" in a double-take. It is thus doubly a moment of intimacy via this character's direct address and the use of a key space within the film to anchor it.

Steadying himself after this shock, Zazu gathers his dignity (his character's pomposity and rigid adherence to courtly etiquette is a joke within the film) and says he will have to "improvise." He moves in closer to the camera, then sweeps his wing across the screen (Figure 4.2), telling us, "Behold! The wondrous realms of the Pridelands." With the movement of his wing, the rock on which he is standing recedes to show a landscape, the bottom half of which is taken up by DVD menu options, which include "Scene Selection," "Play," "Tree of Life," "Grasslands," "Set Up," "Jungle," "Elephant Graveyard," "Index" and "Disc Two Preview." Aside from the self-explanatory standard DVD functions, these denote different spaces from within the film, which, in the DVD menu, represent different kinds of extras. (This disc being aimed at younger children, most of these spaces contain games, while the "Elephant Graveyard" holds deleted scenes.) His voiceover tells us that each area is hosted by its associated character(s) from the film, and in a bit of comic business, he favors certain hosts (principally himself) over others. In the context of the attractions schema, what is interesting about his gesture over the landscape is how much it resembles the theatrical gestures of early cinema showmen. However, his "Behold!" does not announce the arrival of a moment of spectacle. The landscape that follows is relatively flat and uninteresting in comparison to that which was spectacularly traversed in the opening of the menu. Instead, it is a gesture of digital dominion, as the wealth of extra material is what is on display. Aside from being in the middle, the film ("Play") is no more favored than any other, and the voiceover does not mention it at all. Seen from this viewing platform, the film is just one small element amongst others.

TOTAL ENVIRONMENTAL CONTROL

As with many special editions, disc two does not contain the film but rather the majority of extra features. After a choice of language, we go straight into an animated menu, which has a more adult address than that on disc one. While of a similar length, the animation is much simpler than that analyzed above. The menu is designed with a savannah landscape at the bottom silhouetted against a huge globe (Figure 4.3). The globe begins its movement focused on Africa and then continues to rotate, the color changing as if day turns into night and back again. In front of the globe there are six options designated by the continents Asia, Africa, Australia, Europe, North America and South America. A different set of options are marked over the dark landscape at the bottom: "Story," "Film," "Stage," "Virtual Safari," "Music" and "Animals." The animation is simple compared with the flight of Zazu, but has a grander feel. This is underscored by the bombastic orchestral music, and also by the explanatory voiceover which accompanies it. Whereas disc one offers an animated bird as a guide, on disc two the disembodied, well-spoken, British voice of Jeremy Irons (also a voice actor in the film) intones:

Figure 4.2 Disc one "host," *Zazu*, presents *The Lion King*'s digital dominion.

Welcome to the world of *The Lion King*. Within this chronicle, there is more to be seen than has ever been seen. The history, stories, people, places, art and artifacts of this majestic world fable have been collected here for your enjoyment. For the adventurous, take a self-guided tour and select individual items within each continent. This way, your exploration of *The Lion King* is different each time you visit. For the curious, embark on one of the special journeys based on filmmaking, music, theatre, mythology or animals. These chartered tours are always waiting for departure. For the daring, Timon and Pumbaa are waiting to guide you on a virtual safari. It's a thrilling ride where you'll meet some of the more wild residents of the Pridelands. For no matter which method you choose, the magnificent worldwide phenomenon of *The Lion King* awaits your exploration. Pleasant journeys

The length of this voiceover is itself noteworthy, but the touristic language is of particular interest here. DVD producers often experiment with how to make large amounts of material easily navigable. While other DVDs offer filmed introductions (like that for Disney/Pixar's 2001 *Monsters Inc.* [2002]) or pull-out maps (such as those for Peter Jackson's 2001–2003 *The Lord of the Rings* films [2002–2004]), here a high-toned voiceover is employed to explain the purpose of the different sets of categories. These categories in fact represent two different means of accessing the same material (which of

Figure 4.3 "The majestic world fable of *The Lion King*."

course creates the illusion that there is more material than there actually is). Aside from *The Lion King* being referred to as a "world-wide phenomenon" and a "world fable," the logic in arranging the menu in terms of continents seems at first elusive, since the film itself is as tied to an image of *one* particular continent as one could imagine. Indeed, when one travels (and imagery of travel and tourism abound in the voiceover) into most of the individual continents, there is only a very loose relationship to those places, with no relationship at all to Australia or Asia, though obviously a more identifiable relation to the Africa section. However, in familiarizing oneself with the various sub-menus, the promotional-documentary materials therein, and particularly when one enters the North America section, one gets a sense of an organizational logic circulating around various aspects of the Disney brand.

The North America section is arranged around key seats of the Disney corporation: Burbank (home of the corporation's headquarters); Orlando (Disneyworld); Glendale (traditional home of Disney animation). The exception is New York; however, this section focuses on the Broadway musical adaptation of the film. The different sub-sections relate to different aspects of the corporation: "Burbank" includes general material on "Disney and animals;" "Glendale" contains technical documentaries on animation; and of particular interest when considering the question of attractions, the Orlando section provides information about Disneyworld's loosely *Lion King*-themed "Animal Kingdom Park." The rhetoric of Iron's voiceover can thus be understood according to the logic of the Disney theme park. Indeed, as the disc is organized into different continents, so too the Disney theme park seeks to offer "a whole world in one place." This world includes "Mainstreet USA," the nostalgic heart of both parks, the vaguely European fairytale space (with castle) of the "Magic Kingdom" and the newer "Animal Kingdom Park" centering on a safe and sanitized version of an African safari. Margaret King writes:

> In keeping with the "total environmental control" plan of the parks, Disneyland and Disney World are designed as enclosed environmental artworks; in Disney's words, "I don't want the public to see the real world they live in while they're in the park . . . I want them to feel they are in another world." Power and utility lines are buried and the world outside the parks is invisible from inside them (and each theme land invisible from the others), enforcing an automatic selective perception for those in any single area; only the medieval castle in the center serves as a focal point of reference from all points of the park, much like the central clock in a medieval town
>
> (1981: 121).

The "total environmental control" of the Disney theme parks and their status as "enclosed environmental artworks" provide compelling metaphors for the organization of the DVD intratext, and may bring us back to the notion of a "DVD of attractions." Gunning, along with other theorists and historians, has cited the World Fairs of the nineteenth and early twentieth centuries as sites for early cinema exhibition and important precursors to cinematic modes of viewing (see also Friedberg 1993: 68–90). The World Fairs were also the prototypical theme parks, often arranging sights and spectacles into different countries or continents (this was particularly the case with the colonial powers). By creating an immersive landscape, the Disney *theme park* emulates this model, but also tames the more heterogeneous arrangement of attractions found in an *amusement park*.

The invisible infrastructure of the theme park Margaret King cites could equate with the digital encoding that makes one's "journey" through *The Lion King* more carefully managed than the menu's language suggests— this is more the tourism of a coach tour than a real adventure. Indeed, it becomes clear when accessing the extra materials of disc two either through a "self-guided" or a "chartered tour," one ends up seeing all the same material. To follow a path though disc one to disc two is not simply to view a series of activities and materials "extra" to *The Lion King* film; it is to circulate through "an enclosed environmental artwork" akin to the Disney theme park itself.

As noted earlier, disc one opens with an advertisement for Disney Holidays, which features a child chasing a balloon through the "magical" landscape of Disney World. The "guide" for the disc one menu similarly demands childlike wonder, his "Behold!" (see figure 2) indicating a series of spaces devoted largely to play. To follow the path further, disc one's "Disc Two Preview" trumpets in particular the "virtual safari," the name for a set-top game, but also a term one could use to describe Disneyworld's "Animal Kingdom Park," which will also be promoted on disc two. Both the "virtual safari" game and the documentary about Disney's "Animal Kingdom Park" promote the park in differently synergistic ways. The first simulates the spectacle and experience of a roller coaster, to the extent that, at the end, the animated guides jokingly reassure the viewer that "it was only a ride," and offer photos much as one may purchase at the end of a ride in a real theme park. The documentary featurette about the "Animal Kingdom Park" echoes the quasi-educational discourses that have long underpinned the family appeal of the corporation, its parks and its products. The immersive world of a Disney holiday is promoted to young and old alike (the latter importantly holding the purse strings) as a space in which "there is more to be seen than has ever been seen," a line from *The Lion King* repeated in Jeremy Iron's promotion of the "added value" of materials on disc two of the DVD. That large multimedia corporations such as Disney like to promote themselves and their products across various platforms is not in itself much of a revelation. However, the DVD provides an invaluable modern media object in which to remark the complex circulations of media and corporate convergence. Furthermore, the jagged temporality of the aesthetic of attractions, its forms of display and spectacle, and its historic links to the early cinematic exhibition contexts of fairs and amusement parks, are largely tamed by the "total environmental control" of a family DVD like *The Lion King*.

CONCLUSION

The term "DVD of attractions" is followed by a question mark in the title of this chapter and, by way of conclusion, we can now reflect on the benefits and limitations of this concept. The model of the cinema of attractions may firstly be useful in searching for the equivalent aesthetic consequences, the artistic and commercial logic of a booming technology in its first ten years of mass exposure. The attractions paradigm enables close attention to precedents for the technological exhibitionism of DVD technology and its more direct address of the audience. DVD in the late-twentieth and early-twenty-first century, like the cinema of attractions a hundred years earlier, attempts to familiarize a new form of visual spectacle and display through the intimacy of direct audience address and even anthropomorphic/virtual interlocutors. "DVD of attractions" also puts into relief (and some historical context) the convergence of home cinema with the sights, sounds and experiences of the fairground, amusement arcade and theme park. Where the concept of a "DVD of attractions" may appear less useful is in relation to the more pessimistic portrayal of a particular DVD like *The Lion King* as a carefully managed intra-textual whole. Rather than an emergent medium at play with its own conventions, the DVD seems to have come fully formed as a tool for the (multi)media conglomerate. However, the account pursued here is not dependent on technological determinism, nor a fixed notion of DVD's "political economy." I hope my attention to the constitution of particular DVDs underlines the importance of close attention to the object itself, and one hopes that future close analysis of individual DVD intratexts will uncover some of the format's alternative, more open potentialities. It is apparent, however, that such work must give due consideration to the extra material that increasingly surrounds and structures our interactions with/reactions to the primary text. How one conceives this textuality is of course partly determined by questions of disciplinarity.

This chapter has sought to promote the benefits of a broadly Film Studies approach to the DVD, but it also admits the limitations of that approach. New Media Studies may be better placed to conceptualize the particular interface of the digital versatile disc—for example, as a "database" into which a film or television text is inserted—and to assess the extent (and limits) of the format's reactivity. Neither has there been sufficient space here to consider the televisual qualities of DVD textuality. For example, Nick Browne's concept of the "super-text" (1984), with its emphasis on television network control, could be related to the kinds of corporate self-promotion I examine in *The Lion King* DVD. Similarly, the combination of segments, clips, and extras, on a DVD perhaps relates more closely to theories of televisual "flow" than to concepts of cinematic narration (see Raymond Williams 1974).[12] Furthermore, in this collection, John Caldwell asserts the importance of television industry marketing techniques as precedents for the organization of DVD "extra" features. Ultimately, however, the crucial lesson was suggested by Charlotte Brunsdon at the conference that inspired this collection, when she observed that contemporary media studies must "converge its disciplines" if it is to understand a convergent object like the DVD. The interdisciplinarity of *Film and Television after DVD* provides the ideal forum for such a project. Moreover, the variety of complementary, sometimes conflicting paradigms for understanding DVD textuality offered within this collection attest to the richness of the object of study.

ACKNOWLEDGMENTS

This essay is reproduced (with minor amendments) by permission of Sage Publications Ltd: Tom Brown: "The DVD of Attractions'? *The Lion King* and the Digital Theme Park," *Convergence: The International Journal of Research into New Media Technologies* 2007 13(2): 169–183 (© Sage Publications, 2007). Earlier versions of this work were presented at the Cinema and Technology International Conference, Institute for Cultural Research, Lancaster University (7 April 2005) and the Society for Cinema and Media Studies (SCMS) Conference, London (31 March 2005). I am also greatly indebted to the observations and advice of Pat Brereton (Dublin City University), Janice Brown and, especially, James Bennett.

NOTES

1. See for example, Jo T. Smith and John Caldwell's entries in this collection—though my consideration of, for example, the "physical" gestures of a virtual interlocutor engages with DVD menus through a different methodology. Craig Hight (2005) also attends, to some extent, to the organisational logic of DVD menus.
2. For the sake of this discussion, I make no distinction between musicals (which, in the Hollywood tradition, are almost always also comedies) and Disney's musical animated films. See Rick Altman (1987: 103–106) for a discussion of this issue. Subsequent observations about the "attractions" of musical films are equally relevant to films like *The Lion King*. It should also be noted that I am not considering audience uses of these technologies, only the DVD's address of its audience, which may say something of the uses these texts presuppose. See Kerr et al. (2006) for some exploratory research into audience use of DVD amongst other new media technologies.

3. This periodisation is generally agreed upon, thanks in particular to Bordwell et al. (1985). See Gunning (1999) for a discussion of the mythic credulity of the first film spectators.

4. Between 1954 and 1990, the corporation's main flagship television show went under a number of titles and was subsequently broadcast also on ABC and CBS. It is often known as *Disneyland*.

5. The film's status as animation complicates the implicit comparison with the Fred Astaire numbers—clearly there is no human performer about whom one might remark, "Wow, look what he can do!" However, the issue is no less complicated in other genres of modern filmmaking which are most often associated with attractions, and in which computer- generated imagery is particularly prominent—for example action-adventure/fantasy films (*The Lord of the Rings* trilogy, for example [2001–2003]) or superhero narratives (see the often computer generated heroics displayed in Raimi's *Spiderman* films [2002/2004/2007]).

6. The aural qualities of the scene are the focus of a short documentary extra entitled "DVD sound design." Technicians from the film stress the richer, more "aggressive" sound available on the home cinema system mix. Director Roger Allers comments, "The wildebeest stampede now is incredible!" And the re-recording mixer Terry Porter, says with glee, "It will test your home system!" Porter's comments underline the machismo of the technophilia so prominent on many DVDs; part of a much broader "masculine" technophilic culture that Barbara Klinger examines elsewhere in this collection.

7. The most famous resistance to the pervasive convention of DVD chaptering has come from filmmaker David Lynch. Lynch refuses to allow the use of chapters in the DVD releases of his films, presumably seeing it as an affront to the unity of his cinematic vision.

8. This function bears perhaps greatest resemblance to the hyperlink, and could profitably be considered through concepts such as the database, which Manovich has written, "is the natural enemy of cinema" (2001: 225). See also Craig Hight (2005: 9–12), who combines Manovich's arguments about "database" with Brookey and Westerfelhaus's (2002) "intra-textual" model for DVD. Though in many ways, Hight shows a preference for the model provided by Manovich, he makes the important point that "there is nothing on special edition discs . . . analogous to a 'random' [e.g. database] feature for accessing content" (2005: 11).

9. These kinds of set-top games can also be seen to hark back to what Gunning sees in the cinema of attractions, that is " . . . a peculiarly modern obsession with violent and aggressive sensations (such as speed or the threat of injury)" (2004: 44).

10. The British title for the latter (and that presented on the DVD I have worked from) was *The Lion King 3: Hakuna Matata!*

11. Obviously there is no "camera movement" in an animated film like *The Lion King*, and effectively no camera in a computer generated menu like the one here. However for the sake of descriptive clarity, it is worth describing the effect rather than the technical procedure. It is often remarked how CGI, including that in computer games, seeks to reproduce the effects of a camera—for example, light "bleeding" into the lens.

12. The suitability of this paradigm for television has been widely debated. John Ellis's concept of "segment" (1982) constitutes the most prominent addition to Williams's account and James Bennett's recent addition of "fragment" (2006) aims to create a model more appropriate for contemporary "interactive" television. (Bennett's analysis of the limited and often clunky interface of UK digital television's "red button" interactivity does

have resonance for understanding the DVD—see, also, in this collection, Jo T. Smith's description of the "clunk effect" of DVD interactivity.) Ultimately, one does not feel one can entirely resolve these questions of terminology. However, my preference for "intratext" as a descriptive term for DVD emerges from the discovery of a case study that is remarkably un-"fragmentary," though of course that does not mean to say one may not view/interact with *The Lion King* Special Edition DVD in a number of different ways.

BIBLIOGRAPHY

Altman, R. (1987) *The American Film Musical*. Bloomington: Indiana University Press.

Bennett, James (2006) "The Public Service Value of Interactive Television," in *New Review of Film and Television Studies*, 4(3): 263–285.

Bolter, J.D. and Grusin, R. (1999) *Remediation: understanding new media*, London: The MIT Press.

Bordwell, D, Staiger, J.D., and Thompson, K. (1985) *Classical Hollywood Cinema: film style and mode of production to 1960*, London: Routledge.

Brookey, R. A. and Westerfelhaus, R. (2002) "Hiding Homoeroticism in Plain View: The *Fight Club* DVD as Digital Closet," *Critical Studies in Mass Communication*, 19(1): 21–43.

——— (2005) "The Digital Auteur: Branding Identity on the Monsters, Inc. DVD," *Western Journal of Communication*, 69: 109–128

Browne, N. (1984) "The Political Economy Of The Television (Super) Text," *Quarterly Review of Film Studies*, 9(3): 174–182.

Caldwell, J. (2003) "Second Shift Aesthetics: Programming, Interactivity and User Flows," in A. Everett and J.T. Caldwell (eds) *New media: theories and practices of digitextuality*, New York: Routledge: 127–144.

Cohan, S. (ed.) (2002) *Hollywood Musicals: the film reader*, London: Routledge.

Darley, A. (2000) *Visual Digital Culture: surface play and spectacle in new media genres*, London: Routledge.

Ellis, J. (1982) *Visible Fictions: cinema, television, video*, London: Routledge & Kegan Paul.

Friedberg, A. (1993) *Window Shopping: cinema and the postmodern*, London: University of California Press.

Gunning, T. (1990) "The Cinema of Attractions: Early Film, its Spectator and the Avant-garde," in T. Elsaesser (ed.) *Early Cinema: space, frame, narrative*, London: British Film Institute: 56–62.

——— (1999) "An Aesthetic of Astonishment: Early film and the (In)credulous Spectator," in L. Braudy and L. Cohen (eds) *Film Theory and Criticism: introductory readings—fifth edition*, Oxford: Oxford University Press: 819–832.

——— (2004) "'Now You See It, Now You Don't.' The Temporality of the Cinema of Attractions," in L. Grieveson and P. Kramer (eds) *The Silent Cinema Reader*, London: Routledge: 41–50.

Hight, C. (2005) "Making-of documentaries on DVD: *The Lord of the Rings* trilogy and special editions," *The Velvet Light Trap,* 56: 4–17.

Kerr, A., Kücklich, J. and Brereton, P. (2006) "New Media—New Pleasures?," *International Journal of Cultural Studies*, 9(1): 63–82.

King, G. (2000) *Spectacular Narratives: Hollywood in the age of the blockbuster.* London: I. B. Tauris.

King, M. J. (1981) "Disneyland and Walt Disney World: Traditional Values in Futuristic Form," *Journal of Popular Culture*, 15(1): 116–140.

Manovich, L. (2001) *The Language of New Media*, London: MIT Press.

Naremore, J. (1988) *Acting in the Cinema*, London: University of California Press.

Vincendeau, G. (2004) "The Art of Spectacle: The Aesthetics of Classical French Cinema," in M. Temple and M. Witt (eds) *The French Cinema Book*, London: British Film Institute: 137–152.

Williams, R. (1974) *Television: Technology and Cultural Form*, London: Fontana.

5 Auteur Machines?
Auteurism and the DVD

Catherine Grant

... [We have] to recognize also the fascination of the figure of the auteur, and the way he [or she] is used in the cinephile's pleasure

(Caughie 1981: 15).

AUTEURIST AWARENESS

Auteurism, like many other features of cinema, is a matter of supply and demand. It is a way of both making and experiencing films, and increasingly of selling them, in which the largest part of the control of the intellectual and creative work involved in the filmmaking process, or of the responsibility and credit for this, is actively taken up by or ascribed to the film's director. Contemporary auteurism comprises a complex series of interrelated film production, marketing, and reception practices and discourses which are all underpinned by a shared belief in the specific capability of an individual agent—the director—to marshal and synthesize the multiple, and usually collective, elements of filmmaking for the purposes of individual expression, or to convey in some way a personal or, at least, "personalized" vision.[1]

This mutual belief is evidently akin to other, longer-established, "authorial" convictions at work in the cultural field. As Donald Larsson has put it in an essay on authorial agency:

> our experience of any form of art, in any medium, entails to at least some degree a dual awareness: an experiential awareness that seeks to engage the work on its own formal level (whether as a narrative or as another form), and a contextual awareness that understands the work as an artifact, a made object produced by human beings within a particular time and place
>
> (Larsson 2000: 1).

The practices and discourses of auteurism help to promote and inform, if not solely to generate, our authorial-contextual awareness of cinema. For example, such an awareness may be especially encouraged by our experience of the seemingly deliberate placement of auteurist cues in a film (say, our recognition of a particular director's filmic "signature"), as well as by the ancillary texts and discourses which emerge from, or in response to, the film's promotion (which may also flag up for us the existence of such a signature). Indeed, in an important essay on questions of agency and the commercial and critical practices surrounding contemporary film director interviews, Timothy Corrigan (1991) argued that auteurism had paradoxically come to constitute a quite autonomous form of intertextual film consumption, which did not always have to involve the viewing of a particular film. We can quite satisfactorily, indeed lovingly and pleasurably, "consume" the director-auteur, or to indulge our authorial-contextual awareness of particular forms of cinema, simply by reading or viewing directorial interviews or press commentaries on their work, along with other related ancillary discourse and media forms.

In her groundbreaking work in the late 1980s, Barbara Klinger understood the intertextual encouragement of particular "awarenesses" about films, like these auteurist ones, as part of a range of "digressive" practices at work in commercial cinematic reception. Digressive readings draw upon ancillary discourse as a kind of intertextual *"life-support system* for a film,"* existing as part of "a socially meaningful network of relations that enter into the arena of reception around it" (Klinger 1989: 5; my emphasis). Klinger also wrote of the crucial role that intertextual factors, such as what she called "a commodified version of auteurism" (Klinger 1989: 12), play in the "semantic actualization of a text" (Klinger 1989: 6). But for Klinger, importantly, such intertextual factors do not only have a semantic function:

> the industry that creates these commercial epiphenomena [textual "side-effects," accompanying phenomena, or "by-products"] is not primarily concerned with producing coherent interpretations of a film. Rather, the goal of promotion is to produce multiple avenues of access to the text that will make the film resonate as extensively as possible in the social sphere in order to maximize its audience
>
> (Klinger 1989: 10).

In their respective seminal works on cinematic promotion and intertextuality, both Klinger and Corrigan were describing modes of film consumption, including auteurism, the best part of a decade before the introduction of the DVD to the home-video marketplace. These early accounts end, therefore, before the widespread public circulation on DVDs of directors' audio commentaries, and directorial appearances and discourse in "making-of" documentaries.[2] Unlike the separable, or ephemeral, digressive forms of auteurism that Corrigan and Klinger were writing about, ones materially available away from, or consumed at a different time from, the viewing of the film, these newer digital-auteurist "paratexts" ("liminal devices . . . that mediate the relations between the text and reader" [Genette 1997: xi][3]) are permanently conveyed by the hypermedia technology of DVD *alongside*, *over*, or even *during* the film (should the spectator-user choose an audio commentary option, for example). That is to say, the new forms are potentially delivered to the spectator-user in ways that may serve to "re-direct" not only some of our metaphorizations of the spaces of cinematic intertextuality but also to alter our practical experience of this intertextuality as a whole, in ways which may emphasize its immediacy or "directness."

In the rest of this chapter, I will examine some of what is at stake in these new modes of delivery of auteurism in relation to the interactive medium of DVD.[4] It is worth noting at the outset, though, that, in content at least, much of the auteurist material that we can now access through "extra features" on DVDs is not altogether "new." A large part of it resembles certain pre-existing forms of directorial and promotional film culture, as other contributions to this collection also argue.[5] Yet I believe that the new medium does make a difference to the ways in which the current forms of auteurism "work." To use a phrase that Klinger employs a couple of times to signify the generative nature of auteurism in her 1994 study of the reception history of Douglas Sirk's melodramas, for me, DVDs often, if by no means always, function as *"Auteur Machines"* (Klinger 1994: 10, 17), potentially engendering different, more comprehensive forms of auteurism than were previously possible.[6] These include, on occasion, the actual "production" of auteurs, that is, the bringing into discursive existence commercially- and critically-defined "significant directors," where before not all would have been construed as discursively or commercially necessary.

I will go on to survey some of the key aspects of the auteurist "machinations" of contemporary DVD culture, focusing above all on directors' commentaries, as the most "pure" of all of the new paratextual forms of DVD auteurism, in order to examine the role that "live and direct" auteurist address to the viewer-user plays in the production of multiple and resonant avenues of access to the text (to paraphrase Klinger 1989: 10).

IN ITS MASTER'S VOICE

As Corrigan argued in "The Commerce of Auteurism," directorial interviews, in which filmmakers are prompted to tell stories about their film and to explain their creative choices, are "one of the few documentable, extratextual spaces where the auteur, in addressing groups of fans and critical viewers, can engage and disperse his or her own organising agency as auteur" (Corrigan 1991: 118). Justifying the attention he pays in his essay to the paraphernalia or ancillary discourses of film culture ("extratexts," such as interviews) rather than to films themselves, he writes:

[I]n linguistic terms, the mechanisms for identifying with a speaking subject, usually a director, have become as important to communication in film culture today as the so-called textual statement of a movie itself or the different ways it is received by different audiences: the commercial drama of a movie's source can say as much today as the drama of a movie and the dispositions of its viewers

(Corrigan 1991: 118).

DVD directors' commentaries, in particular, have much in common with the promotional strategies Corrigan describes, sometimes even taking the form of an interview, or dialogue. Yet, as I have already noted, unlike other kinds of auteurist explanation, these commentaries are not placed "before," "after" and "outside" the film, but *over* it: the director's enunciation providing a simultaneous and aural "re-writing" of the film, an optional, *documentary* voice-over, which cannot be accessed autonomously from the film, at least not in isolation from its visual track. So, what happens to the ways in which we might engage and identify with the "drama of a movie's source," given these new aspects?

Some substantial work has already been carried out on audio commentaries and other extra features. As Robert Alan Brookey and Robert Westerfelhaus wrote in a early article on the DVD format:

Like traditional secondary texts [criticism, interviews, promotional articles and other materials], the additional material included on DVDs also can be used to increase a film's profitability. We suggest, however, that they do so in a way that blurs the distinction between primary and secondary texts as they have been conceived and made use of in the past. . . . By including such distinct but interrelated texts in a self-contained package, the DVD turns this intertextual relationship [between primary and secondary texts] into an intratextual relationship. Thus, the DVD is perhaps the ultimate example of media-industry synergy, in which the promotion of a media product is collapsed into the product itself

(Brookey and Westerfelhaus 2002: 22).

In relation to the auteurist bent of many of the extra features on DVDs (making-of documentaries as well as audio commentaries, for instance), Brookey and Westerfelhaus argue that these "can evoke the ideological residue of the 'auteur,' and do so in a way that [rhetorically] directs the viewers' experiences of the film" (Brookey and Westerfelhaus 2002: 25).

Their article then analyses the ways in which the audio commentaries on the DVD of *Fight Club* (1999[2000]) use the power of "intratextuality" and auteurism (or privileged readings) to direct the viewer's attention away from what they argue are the homoerotic or queer readings suggested by aspects of David Fincher's film, thus protecting "the film's [mainstream] commercial appeal through dual forms of homosexual erasure." They write:

[*Fight Club's*] narrative, while depicting a relationship that can be easily interpreted as homosexual, incorporates violence and a heteronormative ending to render the homoeroticism merely homosocial. The running commentaries provide a second line of defence, with the film's auteurs providing an interpretation that either denies that the homoeroticism represents homosexuality, or distracts the viewer from the issue. In this way, the *Fight Club* DVD constructs a digital closet that provides pleasures associated with such eroticism while at the same time assuaging any guilt that might potentially accompany such pleasure on the part of homophobic and/or heterosexist consumers

(Brookey and Westerfelhaus 2002: 38).

While their arguments about *Fight Club* as a narrative are quite compelling, the usefulness of their approach to theorizing DVD culture is limited. Brookey and Westerfelhaus do not examine the question of the documentary quality of the commentaries, nor, to any great degree, that of viewer-user interactivity. Their overwhelming focus precisely on *narrative* interpretation or preferred readings of the film, as these may or may not be facilitated or encouraged by audio commentaries, bespeaks the degree to which even those of us who write critically of auteurist ideology are often caught up in its terms. As David Bordwell writes of auteurist culture, in his book *Narration and the Fiction Film*:

Directors' statements of intent guide comprehension of the film . . . More broadly, the author becomes the real world parallel to the narrational presence "who" communicates (what is the filmmaker saying?) and "who" expresses (what is the filmmaker's personal vision?)

(Bordwell 1985: 211).

For Bordwell in this quotation, and also for Brookey and Westerfelhaus, this kind of auteurist "communication" or "expression" is always (or almost always) subordinated to *filmic narration*, the telling of a particular story-meaning *in* a particular film. But when one looks closely at a broad cross-section of directors' commentaries (and indeed at DVD audio commentaries in general), the telling of a particular story-meaning *in* a particular film in order to communicate a privileged reading of the film is only one of a number of concerns, and often one of the least important, of those participating in the production of these intratexts. A director's vision of a film, as expressed in DVD discourse, is often focused much more on the other things a film might be selling, beyond the particular nuances of its narrative meaning.

Before I go on to explore an example of the directors' commentary format, I wanted, first, to briefly illustrate at least one of the means by which DVD culture can function, in contemporary cinema, to generate a thoroughly "commercial auteurism" in ways which were not really predicted

by Corrigan back in 1990. Upcoming young "director-for-hire" Antoine
Fuqua was contracted by established "star-producer" Jerry Bruckheimer
to direct the epic adventure film *King Arthur* (2004[2004]). While Bruckheimer had nurtured Fuqua's early career in music video directing, the
latter was, nonetheless, a somewhat unlikely choice for a costume epic,
although he was well versed in directing effective action-crime thrillers
(such as *Tears of the Sun* [2003], *Training Day* [2001], and *The Replace-
ment Killers* [1998]). While Fuqua believed he had been hired to shape *King
Arthur* as an R-rated film, like all his previous films, at some point in the
production it was decided to tailor the project to a much more commercial
PG-13 rating for its theatrical release.[7] Despite this, with a production budget estimated between $90–$120 million, the film failed critically and also
performed very disappointingly at the US box office. To improve the film's
ancillary revenue performance, it was decided to release it, rapidly and
almost simultaneously, in two different DVD formats: a less widely advertised "Theatrical Release" version (126 minutes long) and a highly promoted, so-called "Director's Cut" version/AKA in the USA "King Arthur:
Extended Unrated Edition (140 minutes long), the latter containing a somewhat more "adult" or violent version of the film, though with the same
"Hollywood" ending. Interestingly, neither DVD made any mention of the
director's name on the front cover. Both DVDs carried the same 18 minute
long making-of film (*Forging King Arthur: The Behind-the-Scenes Making of*). This was principally focused on Fuqua. Each section of the film
contains reference to his overall contribution and there are repeated men-
tions of his "dark, gritty" vision for the film by each significant actor and
technician, as well as by the producer. The US extended edition also carried
a director's commentary. Despite the fact that Fuqua has not been critically
recognized or received as an auteur (he doesn't write his own scripts, he
now makes exclusively studio films, and he is not particularly obviously
employed on the basis of a signature style), and the film is not exactly clas-
sically auteurist material, the *King Arthur* DVDs nonetheless "produce"
Fuqua as an auteur. This seems to have been done, at least in part, in order
to be able to *re-narrativize* (Klinger 1989: 14), or, in retrospect, to justify
creatively, the highly *commercial* decision to release two DVD versions to
maximize financial returns. As Klinger has written:

> The process of commodification is socially meaningful, in that the
> mini-narratives that it produces in order to background the production
> of a film encourage the spectator to internalize the phenomena of the
> film, by becoming an expert in its behind-the-scenes history.
>
> (Klinger 1989: 17)

In order to further explore the ways in which these commodifying
"mini-narratives" work in contemporary film culture, I turn now to the
instance of a director's commentary that I would like to explore in some

detail. It is an inventive example of format on the DVD of Mike Figgis's *Timecode* (2000[2001]). Like the film of *Timecode* itself, and like many audio commentary tracks in general, the two commentaries featured on the DVD constitute the record of live events, improvised around predetermined structures.[8] In them, as in the multiple versions of the split-screen film, key, contradictory aspects of authorship—chance and control—are at once thematically foregrounded and synchronously played out.

The *Timecode* DVD was clearly one spin off product from the theatrical version of the film that *added value*. As one reviewer of the DVD release had it:

> [T]he supplemental material found here, like no other release, is almost crucial to completely understanding and enjoying a film that seems to be rather shallow and gimmicky at first glance. This is a film that supports repeated viewing, even if your first reaction to it isn't favourable, and this disc supports that in spades.
>
> (Burger 2001: 1)

From the rest of the review it becomes clear that what this reviewer means by "understanding the film" is not reducible simply to understanding the story *told by* the film, but instead to understanding the story *of* the film, "the drama of the movie's source," as Corrigan would put it.

Timecode was ideal material for an auteurist film audience, marketed as it was from the outset as the singular result of the experimental vision and skills of its writer, director and co-producer, the British filmmaker Mike Figgis, who operated on this low-budget film with a very high degree of control. But it was also an ideal project from the point of view of the particular interactive potential of DVDs, given that the form of the film's own experiment with digital technology and filmmaking practice was highly "interactive" and, to a certain extent, "dialogic." Using a quartered screen format for the display of four separate but interconnected narrative sequences, recorded by four digital cameras in real time across 93 minutes without cuts, the theatrical release of *Timecode* presented the most accomplished (and final) version of a script-less ensemble film-story improvised and shot fifteen times over two weeks in 1999. The DVD release contained two versions of the film, the first and the last of the fifteen takes, with a large number of interactive features, providing the viewer with the ability to zoom in and follow action on any or several of the four screens, or to follow their individual audio tracks, as well as to access other extras (for example an interactive making-of documentary presented in the form of Mike Figgis's video diary through pre- to post-production).

There are different directorial audio commentaries provided for each of the two versions of the film on the DVD. Both focus principally on the process of making the film (rather than, say, gossip about its cast), although this is not surprising given its unusual nature. It is worth examining one segment at length. Some 52 minutes 35 seconds into the commentary on "version 15," an unnamed interviewer asks Figgis: "What would you say you have discovered in doing the process, in doing this kind of filmmaking with four screens?"

Figgis's reply is voiced over four minutes of screen-time, and I have transcribed it as follows:

> I think I've discovered that I don't know anything—and that's the good news . . . If you think you know what's going on you're in deep trouble, because it's only when you understand that you don't understand, that you understand. You know . . . your life is not really about understanding and controlling. It's about the ability to let go, and . . . observing, and making, as it were, small observations about certain connective ideas. But . . . one of the problems . . . one of the vulgarities of filmmaking is that most contemporary films come with the idea that they understand what's going on. I mean, this is absurd, and storytelling techniques are obsessed with the idea of wrapping up ideas, of saying: here's an idea, here's an expansion of that idea, and here's the resolution of that idea. It's a nonsense. And so, what I love about this possibility of this film technique is that it's a way of observing certain things which you can structure loosely and then it's almost like the accidents of coincidence.

> *[Figgis suddenly interrupts his flow, at 54 minutes two seconds into the commentary].*

> Ah! My favourite moment, bottom right *[as an extradiegetic music track begins, Stellan Skarsgård backs through a door into the light in the bottom right of the four screens]*, and bottom left *[as, in the bottom left screen, filmed by a camera on the other side of the door, we see the same actor entering the room, synchronously with the other screen image]* of the door closing. Now one could argue that, as a plot point, this has a kind of zero value. But as a kind of profound visual moment, in conjunction with the music that's now playing *[Figgis tells us briefly about the music]*. . . . And now a purely visual piece of filmmaking where the plot, you could argue, is standing still, but Stellan Skarsgård is having a cigarette next to Jeanne Tripplehorn *[she is singled out in a medium close up in the top left screen segment, but also shown, at the same time, in a differently angled medium shot in the bottom left screen, walking forwards and backwards past Skarsgård]*, who's just heard him making love to her girlfriend and they don't know who they are. And where Saffron's crying in the toilet *[Saffron Burroughs, Skarsgård's character's wife—in the top right screen]* and Salma's crying in the toilet *[Salma Hayek, Tripplehorn's character's girlfriend—in the bottom right screen]*.

It's almost like this is what everything I've done has led up to, the ability to make this kind of a statement. Now if I tried to integrate this into a conventional, singular film, it undoubtedly would have to answer the question: is the plot moving forward? If I didn't ask it, several junior executives would, and I would lose the fight because there's no way I could say the plot was moving. The plot stands still for five minutes, but it's riveting, in my opinion. It's an absolutely compelling piece of storytelling because it's about life. It's about . . . those things that we never normally see, because we can only see ourselves, and the idea that these things all parallel.

So, in answer to your question: it's almost like I've only just scratched the surface of what it is you could possibly do with this kind of technique, and I don't know what it is. But I do know that it has infinite possibilities that other forms of filmmaking don't have because unfortunately they will always be story-based, and they will always be "plot-points." Julian Sands appears to be standing on someone's head there *[in the bottom right screen]*. I quite like the fact that we never go back and visit that again. And . . . *[Figgis laughs]* . . . it's just a Julian Sands moment.

We can see from my transcript that there is some brief, authorial, "narrative anchoring," as Figgis uses the particularly felicitous moment of visual synchronicity across the screens—the kind for which he had strived in a number of places throughout the fifteen takes of the film—to articulate his story-themes of for what appears to be the only time in either commentary. But, even in this instance, this kind of "semantic actualization" is noticeably only put to the service of distinguishing Figgis's experimental storytelling techniques from those of conventional cinema. These filmmaking *techniques* are the major selling point of *Timecode*, perfected, as far as they could be in commercial cinema, across the fifteen versions.

Although *Timecode* is obviously unusual in the degree to which it is designed and articulated around chance, synchronicity, synchronous-ness and the control it takes to achieve the latter, Figgis's teleological story of the mastery-of-chance ("It's almost like this is what everything I've done has led up to, the ability to make this kind of a statement"), told on the DVD in the voice of the directorial "master" himself, is a common feature of much of the discourse of audio commentaries. Even as the director-as-collaborator pays direct homage to his actors for their work in the service of his vision, as he does here, the director-*as-auteur* cannot help but remind us that it is *his* vision.

Nonetheless, directors' commentaries would not "work" to promote the film, and certainly not to encourage the interactive choices necessary to access and experience them, if they were simply (or always) monomaniacal monologues of self-promotion. Frequently, as is the case in both commentaries on the *Timecode* disc, they are framed as interviews or dialogues, either between a journalist and the filmmaker or between two members of a filmmaking team, usually including the director. But even when they are monologues, audio commentaries are never "monological." The directors on all the commentaries I have accessed address themselves to a particular kind of perceived audience: always one of sympathetic and interested viewers-users, usually "fellow connoisseurs" (or budding fellow connoisseurs) who are most likely to tune into commentaries, and often to an audience of "aspiring filmmakers," as is the case here. The very next question that the unnamed interviewer asks Figgis, after the answer transcribed above, is: "If you were to say something to aspiring filmmakers what would it be?"

In his work on earlier forms of commercial auteurism, Timothy Corrigan writes of personal appearances by directors at cinemas showing special screenings of their films as a repositioning of the authorial source as a "critical interlocutor defined by the diversity of his audience;" "[t]he auteur becomes literally realized as an agency constructed across the diverse response of a genuinely public sphere" (Corrigan 1991: 119). With DVD commentaries, we have the expression of an agency directed only to *potential* viewers, constructed in a virtual, but seemingly *private* sphere. It is, nonetheless, equally dialogic in nature. As is the case with the *Timecode* commentaries, there is often a focus on semi-intimate or familiar forms of address, occasional or frequent use of the first and second-person pronoun, and there is almost always a whispered or confessional quality to the recordings, encouraged perhaps by the silencing or lowering of volume of the film's actual soundtrack.

Making-of documentaries do not usually interpellate their viewers in quite such obviously "intimate" ways, although, in the "featurette" on the *Timecode* DVD, Figgis does look and speak directly into the camera at the beginning of each chapter or segment to set out his inspiration for different aspects of his film. One might also add that the encouragement to interactivity offered by the increasingly common division even of these frequently short documentaries into chapters is also part of inciting a different, and even more dialogic, approach to their viewing than that provoked by substantially the same documentary material when broadcast on television, in longer blocks, as part of a film's pre-release publicity.[9]

And yet, despite this construction of intimacy (which, through the connection with confession and quasi-religious reverence, seems paradoxically fused with the *auratic* qualities of aspects of directors' commentaries),[10] the actual exchange that takes place between producers and consumers is a highly codified one, indeed. As Barbara Klinger writes, in particular of making-of culture, in her recent work on new cinema technologies:

> Let in on industry "secrets" and capable of mastering further enigmas if need be, the viewer enters the world of filmmaking to reside in the

privileged position of the director and other production personnel. . . . Far from demystifying the production process, these revelations produce a sense of the film industry's magisterial control of appearances. . . . As viewers are invited to assume the position of an expert, they are further drawn into an identification with the industry and its wonders. But this identification, like any identification viewers may have with the apparently seamless diegetic universe of the film itself, is based on an illusion. Viewers do not get the unvarnished truth about the production; *they are instead presented with the "promotable" facts*, behind-the-scenes information that supports and enhances a sense of the "movie magic" associated with Hollywood

(Klinger 2006: 73; my emphasis).

THE MAKING OF (AND THE SELLING OF) AUTEURISM

The authoring presence of the filmmaker is represented by the commentary and sometimes the (usually unseen) voice of authority will be that of the filmmaker him or herself

(Nichols 1991: 37).

Barbara Klinger is right to argue, in her recent work, that media industries offer film consumers a "rhetoric of intimacy (i.e., 'secrets' of the cinema) and mastery (i.e., technological expertise and media knowledge);" in this way they enhance the "sense of owning a personalized product" (Klinger 2006: 89). But what has not yet been sufficiently emphasized in academic work on these matters, in my view, is the documentary status of much of this rhetoric. Indeed, in the case of what I have tried to establish as the "intimate" address of DVD audio commentaries, the preceding quotation (from Bill Nichols's work on representing reality), should help to remind us that we usually experience filmmakers voicing a narration over their films precisely when we are watching documentaries. The act of selecting the director's commentary turns the "original" (theatrical) experience of watching the film *as fiction* into one of watching it "re-directed," or literally re-performed, *as a documentary*, one in which the film's existing visual track is employed as graphic illustration of a teleological story of its own production.[11]

Earlier in my chapter I referred to Donald Larsson's understanding of "dual awareness"—the "two minds" in which we engage with or experience cultural texts, as both forms "in themselves" (a narrative, say, or a comedy) *and* as created products issuing from a particular authorial context. Much DVD documentary content potentially results in the balance of our awareness being tipped in an "artifactual" direction, that is, in favor of a more comprehensive attentiveness or responsiveness to the film's authorial context. Directors' audio commentaries on DVDs, in particular, cue this awareness on a moment by moment basis, reminding a viewer-user throughout their duration, that the work *really* is "an artifact, a made object produced by human beings within a particular time and place" (Larsson 2000: 1).

Klinger writes of cinematic promotion that the success of commodification "relies on a personalization or privatization of what are originally public discourses." She continues that "the further a text can be extended into the social and individual realm by promotional discourses, the better its commercial destiny" (Klinger 1989: 17–18). These coterminous processes—the across-the-board (re)-experiencing of an existing film text as at once authorial product and auteurist making-of documentary—potentially, at least, encourage the "internalization of the phenomena of the film" (Klinger 1989: 17) to a much deeper level than other forms of "digressive" cultural practice in which the intertextual cues are less directly experienced or are less "present."

As for the supply side, once again, the kinds of enunciatory performances taking place in DVD commentaries, and also in director's contributions to and appearances in making-of documentaries, are not reducible to monological narrational expression, or simply to auteurist disquisitions on, or "actualizations" of, the "meaning of the story," or the "moment." Rather, the commentaries and documentaries can be seen to provide broader forms of identificatory and dialogic "infotainment," ones predicated on authorial and auteurist discourses of vision, control of chance, achievement, and occasionally on the failure or inability to achieve. They often attempt to interpellate a connoisseur community or a community that may construct itself as connoisseur, as is the case with the *Timecode* disc. But they are always "commercial;" indeed they are usually primarily commercial in the case of contemporary films gaining a rapid release on DVD. They focus above all on the particular selling points of the individual film: thus an experimental film commentary or documentary focuses on the difficulty and success of the experiment; an "event" film making-of documentary concentrates on the magnitude of the managed event.[12] Unlike practically the same stories of the "drama of the movie's source" as told in press interviews, which are always only auxiliary discourses, connected to but separate from the films, DVD director's commentaries and, to a lesser extent, making-of documentaries, directly turn their authorized, documented, and intimate stories of the filmmaking process itself into a product. At the same time, they turn their directors into a product, too, using whatever means necessary. It is hard indeed to imagine a more perfectly conceived, commercial-auteurist artifact than those DVDs which choose to combine the movie with, or to "re-direct" the movie as, a documentary performance of the "drama of the movie's source."

NOTES

1. Early versions of this work were first delivered as conference papers, as follows: "In Its Master's Voice: *Timecode* and the Director's Commentary," at "Screen Studies Conference," University of Glasgow, 2–4 July 2004; and

"Re-directing Cinema: Authorship and the DVD," at "'Some people Are disappointed to only get the film' . . . What is a DVD? Conference," University of Warwick, 23 April 2005. Thanks to the audiences at these conferences for their feedback, as well as to the editors of this collection for their support and patience.

2. As I will go on to discuss, Barbara Klinger has brilliantly incorporated some discussion of these forms in her recent book *Beyond the Multiplex: cinema, new technologies and the home* (2006).

3. In Gérard Genette's discussion of forms of biblio-cultural intertextuality in his book *Paratexts*, the "peritext" of a book includes "extra-textual" elements "inside" the confines of a bound volume—everything between and on the covers. The "epitext" denotes elements "outside" the bound volume—public or private elements such as interviews, reviews, correspondence, diaries etc. Thus, for Genette: "Paratext = peritext + epitext" (Genette 1997: 5). Although the French theorist does comment that "in principle, every context serves as a paratext" (8). Jonathan Gray (2006) uses Genettian concepts such as paratexts in his discussion of the DVD extra features of *The Lord of the Rings* trilogy. Perhaps DVD "bonus features" should perhaps be more properly considered to be "peritexts," as they are "extratextual" material that falls inside the confines of the DVD object.

4. This chapter draws upon more extensive work on film directing and auteurism in my book: *Directing Cinema: the new auteurism* (forthcoming Manchester University Press). This book attempts an in-depth investigation of the ways in which contemporary film directors, their discourse, and discourse about them act in the contemporary global practices of film production, distribution and exhibition, and in contemporary film cultures more widely. Commercial developments in film production and marketing, especially since the 1970s (Neale 1981; Caughie 1981; Corrigan 1991), and geocultural, technological and structural developments since the 1990s have meant that a much larger number and a wider variety of directors than ever before acquire a public prominence that was once the preserve of established "auteurs" (Grant 2000). I consider directors as agents, or subjects, who have direct, intentional and reflexive, if obviously not completely all determining, relationships to the cultural products they help to produce, as well as to their reception (Grant 2001). Following Judith Butler I see agency as a "reiterative or re-articulatory practice, immanent to power and not as a relation of external opposition to power" (Butler 1993: 15). This means that, for me, while directors (as agents) make or direct films, by choosing, doing and saying (sometimes) original things, as individuals what they cannot make or "direct" is the discursive or conceptual framework of "directing" itself. In order to be seen as directors (and as particular kinds of directors), they can therefore only "re-make" or "re-direct," or, cite or repeatedly perform, the kind of work that is socially constructed as being that of a "director," the kind of work that we, the audience, want from directors (see also Grant 2002, for further theorizations of contemporary auteurism)·

5. Making-of documentaries, directors' cuts, and even the idea of directors commenting over their work all circulated as realized forms or ideas in film culture, or in television's treatment of film culture, before DVDs came onto the market—for example in such forms as Electronic Press Kits and live directorial "master classes." (See John T. Caldwell's entry in this collection for a discussion of the Electronic Press Kit's relationship to DVD.)

6. DVD directorial extra features of the kind I have described are not yet equally commonplace in all film territories. Even if they were, it is clear that the DVD viewer is precisely not compelled to access these features. One can

take a horse to water but one cannot make it drink. In addition, in the case of media reception, we cannot always be sure if the water has been drunk or not.

7. See Fuqua (2005).
8. Totally "live" audio commentaries are often recorded in one sitting, and usually run the length of the feature film unedited. But commentaries may of course be recorded in stages, and also further edited. Some DVD audio commentaries are only partial ones, covering only selected parts of the film; others may be entirely composed of pre-recorded (archive) interview segments. Academic commentaries tend to be prepared as written texts, then read and recorded—see Ginette Vincendeau's entry in this collection for an insider's account of this process.
9. See the very interesting work by Hight (2005) on the structure and address of making-of documentaries.
10. Two researchers write very compellingly of the Benjaminian notion of "aura" in contemporary auteurism in relation to the new technologies of cinema: Notaro 2006: 96; and Gray 2006.
11. In an as yet unpublished conference paper, Dana Benelli, a specialist on the films of Werner Herzog, argued that attention be paid to the ways in which: a documentary content which is otherwise limited, ambiguously present, or not apparent at all in a fiction text becomes actualized and enhanced, and author-ized, by the addition of directorial reminiscence, anecdote and commentary. [. . .] [D]irectorial commentaries explicitly point out and testify to the authenticity of the realities embedded in the fiction text. [. . .] [T]he contemporary practice of providing director commentaries creates a post-theatrical presentation of these Herzog films that offers viewers the option of a fictional or travelogue viewing experience, both of which use the same image track (Benelli 2005).
12. As well as on the absolute "necessity," the commercial "generosity," of releasing a DVD version to more perfectly render the director's R-rated vision of "his" or "her" film, as was the case with King Arthur.

BIBLIOGRAPHY

Benelli, D. (2005) "Werner Herzog and Frank Buck," unpublished paper at the Conference on "Werner Herzog's Cinema: Between the Visionary and the Documentary," University of Kent/Goethe Institut, London, 16–18 September.
Bordwell, D. (1985) *Narration and the Fiction Film*, Madison: University of Wisconsin Press.
Brookey, R.A. and Westerfelhaus, R. (2002) "Hiding Homoeroticism in Plain View: The *Fight Club* DVD as Digital Closet," *Critical Studies in Media Communication*, 19(1): 21–43.
Burger, D. (2001) "Review of *Timecode* DVD Special Edition," DVD Tangle Reviews. Online. Available HTTP: http://www.dvdangle.com/reviews/review.php?Id=1314 (accessed 1 June 2001).
Butler, J. (1993) *Bodies That Matter*, London: Routledge.
Caughie, J. (ed.) (1981) *Theories of Authorship*, London: British Film Institute.
Corrigan, T. (1991) *A Cinema Without Walls: movies and culture after Vietnam*, New Brunswick: Rutgers University Press.
Fuqua, A. (2005). "Interview: Antoine Fuqua—*King Arthur*," DVD Interviews at DVDtalk. Online. Available HTTP: http://www.dvdtalk.com/interviews/003567.html (accessed 6 March 2005

Genette, G. (1997) *Paratexts: thresholds of interpretation.* Translated by Jane E. Lewin and foreword by Richard Macksey. Cambridge: Cambridge University Press.

Grant, C. (2000) "www.auteur.com?," *Screen*, 41(1): 101–108

––––––– (2001) "Secret Agents: Feminist Theories of Women's Film Authorship," *Feminist Theory*, 2:1: 113–130.

––––––– (2002) "Recognizing *Billy Budd* in *Beau Travail*: Epistemology and Hermeneutics of an Auteurist 'Free' Adaptation," *Screen* 43(1): 57–73.

––––––– (forthcoming) *Directing Cinema: the new auteurism*, Manchester: Manchester University Press

Gray, J. (2006) "Bonus Materials: The DVD Layering of *The Lord of the Rings*," in E. Mathijs (ed.) *The Lord of the Rings: popular culture in global context*, London and New York: Wallflower Press: 238–253.

Hight, C. (2005) "Making-of Documentaries on DVD: *The Lord of the Rings* Trilogy and Special Editions," *The Velvet Light Trap*, 56: 4–17.

Klinger, K. (1989) "Digressions at the Cinema: Reception and Mass Culture," *Cinema Journal*, 28:4: 3–19

––––––– (1994) *Melodrama and Meaning: history, culture and the films of Douglas Sirk*, Bloomington and Indianapolis: Indiana University Press.

––––––– (2006) *Beyond the Multiplex: cinema, new technologies and the home*, Berkeley: University of California Press.

Larsson, D.F. (2000) "Every Picture Tells A Story: Agency and Narration In Film," paper delivered at "MLA Conference," Dec. 28, 2000. Online. Available HTTP: (long version) http://english2.mnsu.edu/larsson/agency1.html) (accessed 9 February 2007).

Neale, S. (1981) "Art Cinema as Institution," *Screen*, 22(1): 11–39.

Nichols, B. (1991) *Representing Reality: issues and concepts of documentary*, Bloomington and Indianapolis: Indiana University Press

Notaro, A. (2006) 'Technology in Search of an artist: Questions of Auteurism/ Authorship and the Contemporary Cinematic Experience,' *The Velvet Light Trap*, 57: 86–97.

6 The Place, Purpose, and Practice of the BFI's DVD Collection and the Academic Film Commentary
An Interview with Caroline Millar and Ginette Vincendeau

James Bennett and Tom Brown

[The BFI shall] encourage the development of the arts of film, television and the moving image throughout Our United Kingdom, to promote their use as a record of contemporary life and manners, to promote education about film, television and the moving image generally, and their impact on society, to promote access to and appreciation of the widest possible range of British and world cinema and to establish, care for and develop collections reflecting the moving image history and heritage of Our United Kingdom.

(*BFI Royal Charter* 1933[2000]: 2)

As attested to by Caroline Millar, DVD producer for the British Film Institute (BFI), DVD publishing goes to the heart of the institute's promotion of film culture in Britain. Since the first BFI DVD in 1999, *The Seven Samurai* (Kurosawa 1954), the institute has released 172 films and (to a far lesser degree) television programmes on DVD.[1] Something of a British, publicly-funded equivalent to Criterion (a US DVD producer with whom Millar's department has exchanged numerous films and extra materials), the BFI's focus is the dissemination of classic films from throughout the history of world cinema. However, DVD "extra" features have also proved crucial to the way in which the institute frames its output and Millar provides a valuable insight into the pragmatic as well as ideological factors that determine the kinds of "extras" attached to film texts.

The interview that follows focuses particularly on the audio commentary; more specifically still, the academic audio commentary and the "in-between space" ("between cinephile engagement and the cinema as a social product") into which it fits. The example of the BFI is particularly revealing in this regard, as the institute has found itself caught in a similar "in-between space," that is, between its profit-making imperative (DVD is one of the BFI's most lucrative revenue streams) and the obligations encapsulated in its Royal Charter. The British government's inconstant commitment to arts funding, together with incremental shifts in the institute's direction since the 1980s, have led to recent controversy in the academic community. The announcement in 2007 of the BFI's plans to effectively abandon book publishing was the cause of consternation amongst many British and American media academics. The current climate, in which Film and Television Studies' expansion is accompanied by increasing uncertainty about the future of many academic publishing houses, makes it even more imperative that we interrogate the scholarly labor performed by many DVD extras.

Ginette Vincendeau, one of the UK's leading film scholars, and a regular contributor of "extras" to various BFI DVDs and the DVDs of other major producers (Criterion, Optimum, Masters of Cinema) provides another insider's perspective on this kind of labor. At the time of writing, Vincendeau has provided audio commentaries for four films, filmed introductions to ten as well as numerous sleeve notes. Vincendeau offers the perspective of both audio commentator and teacher, noting the DVD's fetishization of long-standing "film buff" discourses familiar to film educators in students' work. Vincendeau's comments explore her own position across the "in-between spaces" opened up by many DVDs. For example, Vincendeau's publications (particularly *Jean-Pierre Melville: an American in Paris* [2003]) along with her DVD work (for example, on Melville's 1970 *Le Cercle rouge* [2004] and his 1969 *L'Armée des ombres* [2006]) have contributed to the rediscovery of a previously forgotten auteur. However, Vincendeau is also conscious that the academic commentary should achieve some distance from discourses familiar from other kinds of commentary (particularly director commentaries), which can function, in the words of another contributor to this volume, to make the DVD into a kind of "auteur machine" (see Catherine Grant's entry).

Amidst these discourses, it is clear that the BFI's DVD catalogue plays an important role in both the teaching of film as well as the formation of a critical canon. As work by Nathan Carroll (2005) and a similar interview to the one here by Bradley Schauer with Criterion's DVD Producer Susan Arosteguy (Schauer 2005) attest, particular DVD publishing houses—most notably Criterion—have become associated with a high-cultural position that sees film as art. In turn, the decision by such companies to produce a DVD of a film—or, indeed, an alternative version of the same DVD, such as the many releases of *La Haine* (Kassovitz 1995[various]) that Millar cites below—implicitly lends that film such artistic status.

Drawing on James Kendrick's research on the Criterion Collection (2001), Nathan Caroll provides an interesting examination of the process of canonization, and the way in which the representation of DVD restoration by a number of publishing houses is implicated in this process, to suggest that the publication of a film on DVD by Criterion not only "confers cultural legitimacy to a film," but goes towards creating the "digital canon" (Caroll 2005: 25). Similarly, Schauer notes, again drawing on Kendrick, that "the Criterion Collection has come to symbolize quality in home video" (Schauer 2005: 32), which, despite its apparent variety, is a selection quite clearly defined and delimited in terms of era, genre and national origin. There are two interrelated points worth picking up on here in relation to this interview's focus on the BFI's DVD collection and the place and purpose of academic commentary: namely, the role of BFI as archivist (and its difference from Criterion as a public institution), and the "aura of quality" that Paul McDonald (2007) attaches to DVDs.

As the Royal Charter quoted at the start of this chapter sets out, the BFI aims to promote education in film and television as well as promote access to and appreciation of the widest possible range of cinema. Nevertheless as Caroll notes, archives—such as that formed by the BFI's decisions on DVD publishing—act as "more than repositories for truth, knowledge, and art;" they also speak to "cultural impulses, fears and desires through exclusionary acts" (2005: 28), whereby the politics of taste affect canonization. One might expect, therefore, the following interview—which is focused on the provision of academic commentaries on the films of, particularly, Jean-Pierre Melville, decisions implicitly related to his recovery as an auteur—to reveal an elitist project in the BFI's archiving through DVD. However, whilst it is beyond the scope of the following discussion to fully interrogate the institution's wider archiving processes, the interview reveals much finer and complex points about the BFI's role and the place of academic audio commentaries therein. We might link this to the issue pointed out in this volume's introduction regarding DVD's "aura of quality," which noted that whilst such understandings of DVDs might go towards a reification of the cannon, DVD's "aura of quality" is not conferred solely on those films deemed "art." An accompanying "aura of quantity" also sees the massive circulation of all kinds of film and television on DVD, suggesting that the medium plays into what Gay Hawkins notes is a general movement away from claims that "aesthetic knowledge and judgment are restricted to an elite minority of audiences and forms" (2005: 342)—Glyn Davis's entry in this volume offers a similarly optimistic reading. In this context, whilst one may not wish to go as far as John Frow's (1995) claims that the contemporary era sees a profound restructuring of taste and valuing regimes, whereby any opposition between high and low taste has dissipated, it is worth noting that the BFI have produced DVDs such as *Ghost-watch* (1992[2002]). This programme, a forerunner to the current trend of "paranormal" programming—such as *Most Haunted* (2002–) and *The 6th Sense with Colin Fry* (2002–)—is implicitly positioned as "low" culture, demonstrating a more populist concern in the BFI's archiving of film and television on DVD than one sees in, for example, the Criterion Collection. Furthermore, and more importantly, the elucidation by Vincendeau and Millar of the place and purpose of academic commentaries in the DVD's archiving process suggests a concern to move away from canonization as an elitist project of restriction, towards facilitating a "knowledge transfer" between the academy, the canon and the general public, thereby promoting access to and education in film and television.

We hope that the interview and ensuing conversation between Millar and Vincendeau will point to some of these issues and help generate a self-reflexive debate within the academy. As Vincendeau's comments below attest, the DVD commentary both opens up critical debates to a wider audience, but also constitutes a new, and performative, kind of scholarly work. The audio commentary's direct and intimate relationship to the film should make us more aware of the kinds of questions we ask of the film. For as Vincendeau wryly notes, the filmmaker has "rather thoughtlessly" not made the film with such academic work in mind.

> *Tom Brown: Caroline, what is the BFI's approach to DVD produc-*
> *tion and how do you decide about what extras will be included?*
> Caroline Millar: Essentially, we include extra features because they
> are at the core of the BFI's work and are inherent in the BFI's mis-
> sion statement. DVD extras come in many forms: voice-over com-
> mentaries, interviews, documentaries, deleted scenes and, at their
> best, these extra features can work to shed new light on the film-
> making process as well as deepen our experience of the film, add-
> ing layers and perspectives that the average viewer may never have
> considered—this makes the film less sacrosanct and the domain
> of a privileged and knowing few. The BFI releases films that have
> usually established themselves as classics in domestic and world
> cinema, silent cinema, animation, documentary and experimental
> cinema. As such, these titles demand extras that respect the value
> of the film and remain consistent with the overall program.
> *James Bennett: How does this ethos inform the way the BFI designs*
> *its DVDs' menus?*
> CM: The best ones can be works of art in themselves. The BFI prides
> itself on creating menus that complement the film, that work
> in harmony with the style of the film, not imposing a design or
> graphic upon the film which is anachronistic or overtly modern
> or flashy. We try to create moving menus which suggest or touch
> upon themes of the film but without giving too much away. Some-
> times our menus are quite minimal, but this is a conscious deci-
> sion. Artfully designed menus can suggest the mood of the film,
> hopefully allude to its themes and most importantly complement
> the directorial style and also the art direction of the film itself.
> After all we're lucky enough to be working on films made by such
> directors as Jean-Pierre Melville, Jean Renoir, Michael Powell,
> Dziga Vertov, and Akira Kurosawa—some of the best filmmakers
> in the world.
> *JB: When you buy the rights to release a film on DVD, does that*
> *give you rights over the extra materials and/or access to produc-*
> *tion personnel or any of those sorts of things?*
> CM: No, nothing. You're just buying the rights to the feature film
> and anything else you license in or create yourself. Some rights-
> holders are better than others, but generally the only materials

that might be "thrown in" are, at most, production stills. The use of material such as existing documentaries is often very expensive. So on the one hand, there are DVD extras that we produce ourselves, where we go out and shoot and edit and produce the whole package or there are programmes that have already been made. For example, there is a documentary on *La Règle du jeu* (Renoir 1939[2004]), which we bought and put out on the DVD but often these bonus films can cost as much to license as the main feature. There are great interviews with filmmakers languishing in archives because the rights holders are demanding fees like £900 per minute to use the material.

JB: *Is it cheaper, then, to go out and film your own documentary?*

CM: It is, yes. We've got a crew and we've got decent rates so we tend to do that more. But obviously a lot of people are dead and if you're releasing an older film you don't necessarily have a lot of access to living people. You have to talk to somebody like Ginette!

JB: *Has the BFI released films that other producers have already released and how does the BFI differentiate what it does?*

CM: Yes, many times, is the answer to the first question and I should say it's getting more and more difficult to differentiate ourselves. As Ginette and I were discussing earlier, multiple DVD releases are not the preserve of, say, *The Lord of the Rings* films (2001–2003[2002–2004]), or other blockbuster fare. For example, there have been four or five versions of *La Haine* (Kassovitz 1995[various]). And in terms of competing in the marketplace, Criterion can release a film before we do and they have huge budgets. Also, particularly if Criterion are releasing an American film, they've got good access to people who were in the film (the cinematographer or people like that) who we would find difficult to get access to. So there is competition because we look at the DVD they bring out and think, "What more can we do now?" Often, for example as with *L'Armée des ombres* (Melville 1969[2006]) where they looked at our commentary and realized (perhaps) they couldn't improve upon it, they ask, "can we use the commentary?" So we do a direct swap with them. They've given us commentaries in return.

TB: *Does that mean there's no fee involved? It's just a straight swap?*

CM: Yes.

TB: *So, do you negotiate rights on a film-by-film basis?*

CM: Yes, although there are blanket deals that get done. Recently in order to buy the rights for *The Innocents* (Clayton 1961[2006]), we had to buy a bunch of other titles: some early Otto Preminger, a John Ford film called, *What Price Glory* (1952[2005]). These are minor films, really, that have not performed well on DVD. They've disappeared in terms of sales but we had to buy them and we had to put them out as a part of the contract that included *The Innocents*. So you can't just cherry-pick from a rights holder's best films.

JB: *And then how is the decision reached as to which films will receive an academic commentary?*

CM: Well, it was interesting that at the "What is a DVD?" conference, many of the delegates were preoccupied with the issue of DVDs and the presence of an academic commentary creating or reinforcing the film canon. In reality, for us, the decisions about what films will feature commentaries are more arbitrary really. There's not a decision at the point of licensing the film. For the BFI, anyway, it comes just from looking at the bottom line. You look at your figures and then you, as a producer, make your own decision as to which films are worth going the extra mile on. With the Melville films, they hadn't been on DVD before so we knew that they would sell, and Ginette's book had come out and, as Melville wasn't well known to the average punter, it seemed like a really good opportunity to do a commentary and a few extras. People needed to know about Melville. What would you do if you brought out a Hitchcock? The stories have been told so many times, I think you'd be scrabbling around to find something fresh to say.

TB: *How do you go about choosing who will do your commentaries?*

CM: We spend time researching to find a critic or academic who has both written well on the director and/or genre and is considered an expert in that field, but who can also deliver on the day. In the past, we have made the mistake of reading an article by a well respected academic, commissioning a script, and then being faced with the nightmare of precision—of timing the voiceover to match the picture. With several retakes needed, a voiceover for a 40-minute film can sometimes literally take all day.

We make these choices very seriously because we consider commentaries as one of the most important extras. We look for someone who can offer material that is a piece of original research. Working with the text of the film that closely can force a new reading of certain scenes, even though sometimes contributors find it difficult to find something original to say over every single scene of the film. However, if it is not relevant to comment on scenic analysis, they can then give background information on the director, the actor, the cinematography, genre etc. Normally, we request that a contributor writes the commentary to include both the general and the specific, and achieve a balance. Where necessary, we then edit the general comments over the sections which have no specific commentary. I should say that we are always aware that the accessibility of commentaries is one of our key concerns, as the average consumer, as opposed to a film student, probably wouldn't choose to read or might feel excluded from a publication on Melville, Michael Powell and Visconti. But by simply pressing a button on their remote control, they can access a director or academic commentary whilst at the same time still being entertained by the film itself. Perhaps commentaries can work better than books in analyzing a scene as we can watch it at the same time as the voiceover is telling us what to look out for.

JB: Ginette, as an academic, when you're doing the commentaries, do you differentiate it from other sorts of academic work, for example, writing a book?

Ginette Vincendeau: I think it's an interesting question because one must consider the status and identity of the academic commentary. This certainly impacts upon where one puts it on the CV! Certainly one of the headings it comes under as an academic is "knowledge transfer," which is something we're very much encouraged to do—that is put out academic work into the wider community and outside the "ivory towers." One of the main criteria is that you popularize your work and you address another audience. The commentary is a product of one's academic work—one gets asked because one is an expert—but it's part of a slightly different sphere. I think a comment I found by Jean Michel-Frodon is useful in this regard: "The DVD renews and problematises in a very fruitful and democratic way the tension between cinephile engagement and the cinema as a social product" (2003). The DVD commentary is halfway between academic research proper and cinephilia. I think it's an intervention into that in-between space.

CM: That's where we try and pitch our work at BFI DVD. However, it's difficult to predict who's going to buy the DVDs. One of the challenges in this regard is that we don't have any market research. We don't actually know who's buying and who's listening. Obviously, university libraries would normally acquire them and keep them on their shelves. We do try and pitch it in a way that the man on the street can get into the film. For academics, there are so many other resources available but, for the average person who wants a night in with a good film, they can turn on the commentary and listen to someone like you, Ginette, someone who achieves the right balance. Someone who still uses film language but makes it understood, not obscuring what they're saying in any way. If academics use and consume commentaries, that's great. But it's not really for them, it's for the average consumer.

GV: I completely agree and of course that's the ideal if you're an academic: this idea of knowledge transfer and that the work is going to reach a wider audience. Of course, one also hopes it reaches students and if a commentary has some sort of weight, if it is done by an authoritative person who knows their subject, one may recommend it to the students. I remember at the conference, "What is a DVD?," Charlotte Brunsdon made the point that this created another layer of material you had to look at when you were preparing your teaching. And it's true that when I'm preparing to teach classic films, for example a course on the New Wave, films which are now all available on DVD, I check which films have commentaries and I try to listen to them. I do this partly so I know what's in the public domain, what students might have access to. Unfortunately, one also needs to do this so one can check that they have not plagiarized these resources.

CM: It can be a good starting point, a way in for average consumers, because if you watch that commentary, as you say, it gives you an insight and then you can investigate further. Of course, there's only so much a commentary can do but hopefully it can stimulate people to look a bit deeper. I think it should really be standard practice to include a critical bibliography on each DVD.

TB: *Ginette, what particular challenges does producing a DVD commentary present?*

GV: I'll start with someone else's example which unfortunately, or perhaps luckily, Caroline sent me only after I had done my first commentary. Scott Eyman, in his "Confessions of a DVD extra" (2003) tells of his problems writing the audio commentary for *Trouble in Paradise* (Lubitsch 1932[2003]), based on his having written a book on Lubitsch. He says: "the section of *Trouble in Paradise* takes up five pages. Read out loud—slooowwwll-lyyy—and it might last 10 minutes. That left me 75 minutes to fill." I approached the problem in a slightly different way. Having been told that 180 words a minute was the standard BBC delivery, I was horrified to find that my commentary for *Le Cercle Rouge* (Melville 1970[2003]), a film which is 140 minutes long, would have to be over 25,000 words. Scaled down to 150 words a minute, a more relaxed delivery, this still meant 21,000 words. (I had noted that many audio commentaries suffer from being rather breathless). With a few brief pauses, for instance, to point out Melville's use of silence or music, this means that my commentary in the end was 17,000 words long—almost the length of a BFI film classic book. Of course, part of the problem was that there is no clear template for the format. Listening to previous commentaries was useful but still did not really give me an insight into the practice of writing and delivering my own commentary. What I did decide, however, was that I wanted to provide the right amount and balance of information and to avoid what I saw as the pitfalls in what I had listened to: principally breathlessness, rambling, redundancy and irrelevance.

CM: I've witnessed those pitfalls first-hand a number of times, for example with breathlessness, you'll have some commentators who, when they see a moment coming, they rush to get to it or they slow down so they don't hit that point too soon.

GV: Yes, I heard that in a number of examples. Also, with redundancy (telling the spectator what they can perfectly well see) you might have someone stating, for instance, "Octave is now walking out of the Marquis' bedroom." Ironically having the film running with the audio commentary heightens the risk of redundancy (in a written essay one moves from description to analysis but here description is unnecessary, yet difficult to do without entirely).

TB: *So from this experience, Ginette, would you consider that audio commentary represents a particular form of film analysis?*

GV: Well the issue of redundancy, or rather avoiding it, goes to the heart of this. When you *write* film analysis for a book or article, one of the main problems, you feel, is not having the film. One has to write something about another medium, and so you have to somehow evoke, describe. Perhaps you will have some images, though you're always conscious of what's missing: the movement. Though when you have the movement, and you have the flow of the image, that creates another problem! All that description has to go, because otherwise the listener is going to ask, "Why am I listening to this when I can see and hear perfectly well myself?" So that is a great pitfall, as you must add something to the images and the sounds and not just describe them.

CM: Also, what often crops up when people have run out of things to say, is that they start going into real biographical detail about the actor, what they were in, their whole history, and it's not relevant to this film and it takes you out of the moment of that film; it takes you into the actor's life.

GV: Well, yes, irrelevant details may often creep into commentaries and there might be a mismatch, bad timing or general material that can go anywhere. This is very difficult because the filmmaker, rather thoughtlessly, has not made the film with your commentary in mind! For example, one very brief moment in a film might spark off a lot of commentary while you also encounter long scenes where not much happens. There is a six minute scene in *Le Cercle rouge*, which needs to be "filled" with 900 words, when "nothing happens"—characters silently walk from the street to the scene of the burglary—I solved this one by linking Melville's minimalism with his hostile reception by *Cahiers du cinéma* at the time. For, while speaking too fast and breathlessly is a problem, at the same time, when I was doing some research into the reception of DVD commentaries, the worst sin consumers pointed out was too many silences! As on the radio, a few seconds of silence feels very long on a commentary and the best thing is to motivate and signpost those silences—for example, "let us just remark on Melville's use of silence for a few moments. . . ." For me, the ideal in academic commentaries is where you have the textual and the contextual analysis and the information is all woven into what will hopefully appear as a seamless narrative; it sticks to the image but brings in contextual information.

JB: *How do you approach the task from a purely practical point of view?*

GV: Well, when I researched the practical dimension before doing my first commentary, I noted that Scott Eyman said he spent about six weeks on his 55-page manuscript and then had to write some more. My experience is also that the process is amazingly time-consuming. I remember vividly the first day I sat down to it and spent an entire afternoon on the first *four* minutes of the film, and came very near giving up, although I did speed up as I went along. So, for what it's worth, here is the "Vincendeau method:" I started by watching the film and making rough comments on what was going on and what I wanted to say over each scene, speaking it into a tape recorder. Then I transcribed this and checked for repetitions but also for gaps against my chapter on this film in the book—my first commentary was on *Le Cercle rouge*, a film I wrote about in *Jean-Pierre Melville: An American in Paris* (2003). Then I started working on the detail. It immediately became obvious that I needed to time things incredibly minutely. I used a computer, a video player and a tape recorder and in the end the minute plotting paid off, and I did not have Scott Eyman's nightmare recording session, although it still took more than four hours.

TB: Caroline, have you produced many filmmaker commentaries at the BFI and are there different issues involved in that?

CM: Yes, there are. They're completely different really because with an academic commentary, we agree on a fee for one thing and it's a piece of original work that will go on a DVD. But with a director commentary, they're really doing it out of goodwill. They don't require money or it's not really a money thing. It's their film and they're happy to talk about it. You can't prepare, really. You can prepare some questions and hope that they'll be amenable to being asked questions but often you've just got to book a studio and hope for the best really. Then you may have a massive editing job!

JB: *It's interesting listening to Ginette talk about all the work that goes into commentaries, particularly when you read about big stars like Schwarzenegger refusing to do commentaries unless they're paid separately for them. These commentaries tend to entail stars or directors being paid to just chat about the film in order to say how, "It was really hard when we did this thing," or "It was really fun when we did this." An academic commentary seems very different, much more like a form of labor.*

GV: That's funny because in my research I saw that often it was actors' commentaries that would sell a DVD but they were almost universally reviewed as being the worst ones. I listened to the one for *The Magnificent Seven* (Sturges 1960[2001]), with Eli Wallach and the other actors who were still alive at that time. They were obviously completely drunk and it was all "Do you remember this?," "Do you remember that . . . ?"

CM: It's like a meeting of the old boy's club.

GV: Also, from what Caroline was saying, you can see how so much of it is reliant on the actor/director being in the right mood. For example, on one of the many versions of *La Haine*, Mathieu Kassovitz was clearly hung-over and for the first 30 minutes or so, he offers a really stumbling commentary. Aside from that, his commentary is pretty good, but there are quite a few directors' commentaries that are not very insightful. I imagine someone like Martin Scorsese, a more cinephile director, might be more interesting and might have that critical stance. But to me, the value of a director's commentary, when it's there, is factual. Often it's bringing out facts about the background behind the scenes, the making of the film. Sometimes it's very anecdotal in the "do you remember?" mode but occasionally there are little nuggets of information. From a pedagogical point of view, one may tend to recommend the academic ones.

JB: Do you find that students use the commentaries, regardless of recommendation?

GV: You definitely see references to DVD commentaries creeping into students' work. It's quite common in essays now and it's raised an issue about how you cite commentaries and we've all incorporated that into our guidelines for the presentation of student essays. It's a small matter but it's revealing.

TB: If you remember at the "What is a DVD?" conference, Helen Wheatley commented that she found this quite unhelpful in seminars, that it could shut down critical debate because a student would say, "the director says this, so this is the way it is." As a film lecturer, have you had experiences of this?

GV: I don't think that's necessarily an issue of DVDs alone. It goes with a certain kind of film student who occupies the position of film buff rather than student or academic. So they would tend to go to all the interviews and would have read all the interviews with Martin Scorsese, Mathieu Kassovitz etc. They would always go for this kind of knowledge, this film buff knowledge, rather than more critical material. What you could argue is that DVDs make this more prominent because the student's favored way of seeing film is on the DVD. However, I don't think it shuts down discussion any more than a student picking up this information from an interview. The DVD is an elaborately packaged object, an object that can be fetishized, so the sort of student that would be very much into a film buff approach to Film Studies will own the DVDs and will have seen all the extras and listened to all the commentaries. However, I don't think it's a problem that is generated by the DVD. It pre-exists DVD.

CM: I think it can cause problems, because when a director remembers something, they may not remember it the same way someone else does. I have come across the problem where a director has claimed that something was his idea, while the production designer claimed it was hers. So one has to be very diplomatic about such contentious issues. For various reasons, the record of events that goes went on the disc became the director's, solely his vision, and so, in instances like this, the contribution of other crew members becomes downplayed in favor of the director. So, whoever happens to be available or amenable to contributing to the disc, it is their story or their version of events that goes down in history, or at least as long as the DVD is available.

GV: So, the director's voice does go down in history as the authoritative one.

JB: *In such cases, the DVD seems to be working, as Catherine Grant suggests in this collection, as a kind of "auteur machine." It generates a discourse about the director as the owner of the film. Ginette, how would you relate your work on commentaries to the idea that DVDs inscribe a preferred/authorial reading of the text?*

GV: I would say that, again, ideally, the academic commentary should be able to situate the author's positions and situate one's own voice in relation to other critical material. Certainly, in the Melville material, with the very elongated sequences, I was able to bring information, for example, the reception of *L'Armée des ombres*, when Melville was accused of being Gaullist. In my commentary, I'm trying to situate a number of readings, but if the commentator is the director, obviously a whole different agenda is at work.

NOTES

1. Figures correct as of November 2007.

BIBLIOGRAPHY

British Film Institute. (2000) "Royal Charter." Online. Available HTTP: http://www.bfi.org.uk/about/charter.html (accessed 15 December 2007).

Caroll, N. (2005) "Unwrapping Archives: DVD Restoration Demonstrations and the Marketing of Authenticity," *The Velvet Light Trap*, 56: 18–31.

Eyman, S. (2003, 23 February) "Confessions of a DVD Extra," *The Palm Beach Post*. Online. Available HTTP: www.criterionforum.org/forum/viewtopic.php?p=140374(accessed 15 December 2007).

Frodon, J. (2003, December) "Le travail critique à l'épreuve du DVD," [round table discussion], *Cahiers du cinéma*, 66.

Frow, J. (1995) *Cultural Studies and Cultural Value*, Oxford: Oxford University Press.

Hawkins, G. (2005) "Taste," in T. Bennett, L. Grossberg and M. Morris (eds), *New Keywords: a revised vocabulary of culture and society*, London: Blackwell Publishing: 340–342.

Kendrick, J. (2001) "What Is the Criterion? The Criterion Collection as an Archive of Film as Culture," *Journal of Film and Video*, 53(2–3): 124–39.

McDonald, P. (2007) *Video and DVD Industries*, London: BFI Publishing.

Schauer, B. (2005, Fall) "The Criterion Collection in the New Home Video Market: An Interview with Susan Arosteguy," *The Velvet Light Trap*, 56: 32–35.

Vincendeau, G. (2003) *Jean-Pierre Melville: an American in Paris*, London: BFI Publishing.

7 DVD Technologies and the Art of Control

Jo T. Smith

The technological make-up of the DVD invites us think across the gap between Film, Television and New Media Studies. The DVD is not strictly cinema, nor is it a computer, television or computer game. It is a complex combination of older media forms and new digital technologies that produce cinema as data that can be reconstituted in a multiplicity of social settings. This hybrid status contests traditional approaches to film as a discrete object and encourages us to think about this multimedia phenomenon in more transversal and interconnected ways. Indeed, the material and discursive dimensions of the DVD point to its own conditions of production and consumption and reveal something about the dynamics of contemporary media cultures. The DVD references earlier industrial cinematic practices (visual spectacle and immersion) as well as new media practices (the DVD as a digital database). The DVD is an outcome of the practices of repurposing common to capitalist creative industries and, as such, demonstrates the endlessly extendable technological apparatus of contemporary media industries. Accordingly, contemporary media scholarship needs to chart the movements and shifts of new media forms in ways that address the speed with which contemporary audiovisual culture changes. We need methods of analysis that can adequately map the complex interactions between social, aesthetic, economic, and technological forces that the DVD embodies and produces.

The constantly changing nature of audiovisual culture draws attention to the logic of continuous variation that characterizes capitalist creative industries. These industrial practices involve the production of new desiring subjects and the invention of new techniques of capturing consumer attention. Outlining a nascent political economy of attention, this chapter assesses the contribution made by DVD culture to the industrialization and virtualization of contemporary audiovisual culture. As well as discussing the impact of DVD on contemporary culture, this chapter also demonstrates the continuing relevance of the philosophical work of Gilles Deleuze, who predicted that we are in the midst of emerging societies of control that are intimately connected to new forms of communication. Situating DVD technologies in relation to these emerging societies of control, I suggest that we must investigate the promise of greater control apparent in discourses of contemporary audiovisual culture. We must examine how the promise of greater control invites the media consumer to contribute their time, attention and labor to emerging media products that subsequently expose the consumer to new modes of social regulation and normalizing regimes. At the same time, we must examine how new forms of audiovisual culture also provide the conditions from which we can begin to think in different directions. By privileging the pedagogical function of DVD culture, we are not only able to identify emerging systems of control but also those new possible modes of agency given in contemporary audiovisual culture.

DELEUZE AND CONTEMPORARY AUDIOVISUAL CULTURE

Deleuze's most explicit discussion of contemporary audiovisual culture and emerging control societies occurs in his engagement with the writings of Serge Daney, a film and television critic notable for his emphasis on the changing conditions of film culture in light of the advent of television (Deleuze 1990). In his commentary "Letter to Serge Daney: Optimism, Pessimism, and Travel," Deleuze gestures towards the demands of contemporary culture where images are increasingly interchangeable, instantly reproducible, and caught up in the frenzied activity of endless and perpetual production. He notes that Daney invites us to consider how contemporary forms of cinema seek new audiovisual combinations that give rise to new kinds of social and aesthetic powers. As the title of Deleuze's commentary suggests, these new audio-visual relations generate both pessimistic and optimistic responses. Pessimism arises due to the fact that cinema now circulates within an episteme based upon surveillance and control, with television (particularly game shows and news) functioning as the most virulent machine of direct social engineering. However, there is also cause for optimism due to the aesthetic dimensions of cinema that have a supplementary function from which a new form of resistance to surveillance and control might emerge (1990: 76). For Deleuze, cinema is not a representational medium; it is a machine that produces affects, intensities and a logic of relations that subsequently generates new modes of thought. While Deleuze devotes two books to the study of these cinematic concepts (*Cinema 1* and *Cinema 2*), in his letter to Daney he includes other forms of media such as pop videos, special effects, and footage from space as being capable of generating "new associations" and "new domains" of possibility. Deleuze also notes how quickly these possibilities can be turned into domains of control where the potentials of pop video quickly change to "marketing jingles" and space footage becomes just another banal act of a "regular guy" (1990: 77). Here, Deleuze gestures to the realm of informatics where an idea, concept and thought itself, becomes the object of calculation, quantification and reification, a domain that his philosophical work seeks to interrupt. In their final book together, both Deleuze and Felix Guattari note how the realm of informatics is not the solution to contemporary social situations, but the domain where market forces, advertising and the glib rhetoric of communication reign. As they write, "We do not lack communication. On the contrary, we have too much of it. We lack creation. We lack resistance to the present" (Deleuze and Guattari 1996: xx). Accordingly, the supplementary force of audiovisual culture offers up the brief potential to break with the banal habits of the realm of informatics, and to re-engage our thought and our attention in creative ways and directions hitherto unthought of.

Following this logic, one could examine the supplementary forces generated by DVD versions of cinema as well as consider how the DVD's connection to the domestic realm of the home brings this medium close to the social function of television. That is to say, the DVD bridges the fields of both cinema and television as it is a technology that involves the domestic context of exhibition more familiar to Television Studies at the same time as it announces itself as an authentic reproduction of cinematic conditions.[1] The DVD thus offers a unique insight into the new forms of social engineering that are linked to television's social function as well as the possible new forms of creativity linked to the aesthetic and supplementary dimensions of cinema.

Jack Z. Bratich confirms Deleuze's critique of the social function of television when he suggests that reality television (RTV) programming is a cultural form of control societies, which does not attempt to *represent* changes in the world as much as function to *produce* these changes (2006: 65). Bratich reminds us that the reality of RTV is the result of strategic interventions and that RTV functions as a training ground for the production of compliant social subjects. Makeover shows such as *Extreme Makeover* (2002–2005), *Queer Eye for the Straight Guy* (2003–2006) and *The Swan* (2004–2005) demonstrate the deployment of certain techniques and expertise that can change the life and circumstances of their participants. These powers of direct intervention catch up the TV participant (and increasingly the TV *audience*, if we think of the polling systems incorporated into shows such as *Big Brother* [2000–ongoing] and *American Idol* [2002–ongoing]) in a circuit of exchange where television producers reap the benefits of this televisual labor.[2] This is not a one-way mode of exploitation. As Rachel Moseley has argued in relation to the transformation of audience members into "televisual spectacles," RTV makes ordinary people "über-ordinary" and thus celebrities of the small screen (2000: 306). The very promise of this shift from ordinary to extra-ordinary is the key to the genre's success. Accordingly, RTV contestants are not the passive dupes of a domineering broadcast industry in that the benefits of participation flow in diverse directions. It is precisely these feedback loops that capture the dynamics of current audiovisual practices and that require analytical attention from media scholars. Indeed, by investigating the ambivalent powers of this feed-back-hungry, milieu we can glimpse more clearly the new forms of freedom as well as the new modes of social regulation now emerging.

The concept of a feedback loop as a dynamic and responsive circuit of exchange suitably sums up the guiding logic of control systems. Deleuze's most explicit discussion of control societies occurs in *Negotiations* (1990) and *Foucault* (1986), where he addresses the misconception of Foucault as a theorist of "confinement" and instead identifies him as a thinker of the "outside," who develops diagrams and maps of supple and diffuse forms of power (1986: 42). Foucault (in Deleuze's reading) defines the diagram of discipline as that which functions "to allocate, to classify, to compose, to normalize" (Deleuze: 28), whereas a diagram of control operates through a logic of modulation, transformation and continuous variation that is closely aligned to the self-perpetuating and transversal logic of capital. Control societies have more transversal systems of domination that break down the confined spaces of schools, prisons, and factories. The disciplinary pow-ers of education no longer stop at school, but continue in the workplace where performance reviews, promotions and mechanisms of accountability depend on the consistent upgrading of skills. In another context, innova-tions in business management blur the strict division between workers and owners by paying workers company shares as part of their wage agree-ment. Communication technologies contribute to these shifts via email and mobile phones, which make the home a virtual office on the weekends and after 5 p.m. at night. Indeed, Deleuze identifies the diagram of control as having "a varying geometry whose language is *digital*" (1990: 178) and firmly linked to a contemporary form of capital that privileges meta-pro-duction over production, and diffused systems of exchange over the con-centrative form of capital found in disciplinary societies.

Under such conditions the individual becomes distributed across overlap-ping social systems alternately occupying, for example, the role of worker, student, shopper, or creative producer, while confined to a single social space such as the home. The seriality of disciplinary societies, where one moves from the family to the school to the workplace, is replaced by simul-taneity in control regimes, casting the individual as someone who is "spun into a net of and perpetually controlled by immediate communication" (Busk 2001: 105), a situation where one is never finished with anything. This image of a "spinning net" suggests two kinds of effects in control soci-eties: the ability to be caught up, coded and regulated by systems of control (forms of unfreedom) *and* a chaotic and potentially deterritorializing sense of flow and movement which constitutes breaks with these regimes of cap-ture (new possible modes of freedom and creativity).

In the case of RTV, Bratich links the displays of change, responsiveness and renovation (the spectacle of perpetual production) to capitalist tech-niques of labor management where the individual (as worker) is able to per-form a variety of tasks in a flexible, interchangeable and mobile manner.

RTV then becomes understood less as a genre than "as a loose assemblage of techniques and experiments, a mechanism for conducting powers of transformation" (2006: 77). Where Deleuze identifies TV game shows as a "perfect reflection of how businesses are run," Bratich updates this critique by noting that "gamedocs," such as *The Apprentice USA* (2004–ongoing), *Survivor* (2000–ongoing) and *Fear Factor* (2001–2006), now incorporate gaming dynamics into the workings of everyday life (2006: 70). This leads Bratich to conclude that "just as factory techniques have left the factory, so programming has left television, and the whole of reality has become programmable" (77). Yet, rather than ending on a dystopic note, Bratich attends to the affirmative tenor of Deleuze's writings by reminding us that:

> RTV multiplies life's points of contact with networks of power, a wired habitat that delivers instructions and takes feedback. Making reality programmable means mechanisms are widely distributed, and thus the mechanisms are loosened from their own channels. They open up cultural domains vulnerable to the autovalorization of subjects and social cooperation
>
> (Bratich 2006: 78).

Bratich thus agrees with Deleuze who argues that systems of control regulate social relations as much as provide the necessary conditions for producing new forms of social agency. According to this logic, multiplying "life's points of contact with networks of power" produces the conditions for resistance. While Bratich identifies a productive ambivalence at the heart of RTV control mechanisms that could be exploited for affirmative ends, Deleuze continues to consider the aesthetic function of cinema as potentializing a radical critique of this age of instant communication. Contrasting the socially engineered eye of TV with the creative forces of cinema, Deleuze argues for an "art of control" that might give rise to a new form of resistance when he writes:

> To get to the heart of the confrontation [between TV and cinema] you'd almost have to ask whether this control might be reversed, harnessed by the supplementary function opposed to power: whether one could develop an art of control that would be a kind of new form of resistance. Taking the battle to the heart of cinema, making cinema see it as *its* problem instead of coming upon it from the outside
>
> (1990: 75).

By "taking the battle to the heart of cinema," Deleuze recommends a form of resistance that is less an oppositional practice than an intensification of, and experimentation with, the given conditions of control. One must ask then, what might cinema as an "art of control" look like? Do DVD versions of cinema attempt to take us *in* to the image so that we might touch the technology that harnesses our attention? What is the "supplementary function" of DVD versions of cinema? How might the DVD offer a brief break with the banal habits of informatics, in ways that re-engage our attention in new and critically creative directions?

Where Bratich sees the emergence of RTV as an assemblage of techniques and experiments that demonstrates the logic of perpetual production, so too we can see how DVD versions of cinema function as a productive assemblage that intensifies the feedback loop between production and consumption. The DVD's capacity for storing information, for re-purposing the theatrical release and for extending the life of the film's production and consumption (through "making-of" documentaries and special features) suggests that digital forms of cinema contribute to intensified forms of control. Yet what of the creative and resistant potential of DVD cinema? Perhaps the DVD's position as hybrid object (neither cinema nor television but a database linking both) allows us to map the social engineering function of the DVD as well as the potentially creative forces of changing forms of cinema? While DVD culture promises to perpetuate the industrialization of audiovision, it also forms new relations and combinations between images. As I shall argue, the DVD parallels the "wired habitat" of RTV through its intimate connection to home theatre entertainment systems and its promise of interactivity.[3] This connects the DVD with the social function that Deleuze attributes to television. At the same time, the digital promise of pristine reproduction and visual spectacle embodied by the DVD echo the aesthetic appeal of cinema as an intensive and immersive experience where new relations and ideas might emerge. These televisual and cinematic attributes are enabled and harnessed by the database structure of the DVD, an intriguing blend of material and immaterial components that gesture to the changing conditions of production and consumption practices of contemporary media industries. As such, the DVD offers us a unique opportunity to investigate the social, industrial and aesthetic function of recent audiovisual developments. I will suggest that the peculiar status of the DVD (its rather awkward manifestation as TV, as database *and* as cinema) constitutes an art of control that provides a glimpse of the optimistic and pessimistic dimensions of emerging control systems.

THE PROMISE OF GREATER CONTROL

A parallel logic runs between the reality TV genre and new media discourses in that each share the promise of personal and social transformation, and subsequently, disseminate the illusion of greater control and more personal freedom. RTV opens up the possibilities of participants sharing in the pleasures of celebrity, fame and fortune as well as the ability to control one's appearance or social circumstances. The promise of greater control is also a hallmark of commercial discourses surrounding digital technologies and home theatre systems. The consumption of a DVD in your home can shield you from the discomforts of going out to endure a public screening where popcorn munching neighbors or unruly children can spoil the viewing pleasure. The recording function of your VCR or DVD machine can enhance your control over exhibition conditions by allowing you to tailor your television viewing according to your own particular domestic rhythms. In his analysis of the commercial discourses surrounding home theatre systems ("Now You're Living," as one marketing slogan goes), Raiford Guins notes that this promise of greater consumer control and autonomy is most often restricted to selecting from an array of predefined choices rather than convincingly challenging the producer/consumer division. That is to say, one is more likely to replay, freeze-frame and record mass-produced media content than to make media content of one's own (2001: 353–354). By participating in these activities (choosing what to record, when to watch and under what conditions), the media consumer becomes part of a cycle of perpetual innovation and enhancement that has no distinct horizon, other than the promise of continuous variation. Where the RTV participant is caught up in a network of direct social programming and instant transformation, the consumer of home theatre systems is incorporated into a "wired habitat" of perpetual technological upgrade which trades on the promise of greater control over the immersive nature of audiovisual culture. DVD technologies are a vital component of this culture of continuous variation, and, as new media critics, we must attend to the ways in which new desiring subjects are produced by this system of perpetual upgrade, a process that I want to suggest, nonetheless links back to prior institutional norms of cinema.

Technological innovations in home theatre entertainment systems enable the techniques and institutional cues of earlier film industrial practices to penetrate and break down the discrete social space of the domestic sphere and to recondition existing social relations. Raiford Guins ends his discussion of home theatre systems by urging media scholars to produce more nuanced assessments of the way that our private viewing conditions are informed by the "power-knowledge technologies that assert norms for cinema" (2001: 362). Guins is not alone in paying attention to the relationship of home entertainment technologies to the norms surrounding film culture. Barbara Klinger argues that home theatre systems enable the repurposing of a theatrical release across a myriad of media platforms, thus maximizing, expanding and increasing the possible revenue of the initial filmic release (2006: 7). According to Klinger, these repurposing techniques not only facilitate an emerging new media aristocracy, but also consolidate gender norms. The promotional strategies of the home entertainment business make appeals to greater consumer control that reinforce the bond between men and machines, using promotional appeals that urge us to "master time, memory, and circumstance" or "Take Complete Control with Home Theatre Master" (2006: 43). Here the promise of greater consumer control meshes with orthodox discourses of gender and technology to enable the media industries to infiltrate the domestic sphere, a process that perpetuates existing social inequities. Yet (if we are to hold true to an analysis of audio-vision in emerging control societies) how are these conditions of commodi-fication and control also the conditions necessary for the transformation of orthodox social discourses? What new freedoms are enabled by these shifts if indeed the promise of more control is paradoxically a very mechanism of regulation and capture? In particular, in light of Guins's reference to home theatre discourses ("Now You're Living!") and Bratich's earlier observation about the dual effects of control systems (both regulatory and enabling), how do DVD technologies multiply "life's points of contact with networks of power" in any affirmative or transformative way?

It is easy to argue that DVD technologies contribute to the dead heart of informatics, where an increasingly information-based society leads to the degradation in thought and experience. It is a more difficult task to iden-tify and assess the supplementary function of DVD culture and the new modes of thought (and forms of social agency) enabled by the increased penetration of audiovisual technologies within the domestic environment. However, it is precisely to this promise of greater control that we must pay critical attention if we are to assess the social impact of contempo-rary media culture. The contradictory logic of greater control is expressed directly in the promotional discourses surrounding DVD technologies and we can look to these discourses to understand more fully how systems of control depend upon an ambivalent productiveness.

The promise of greater control and freedom that dominates home the-atre discourses is also a feature of DVD promotional materials. Adverts surrounding DVD culture normalize the relationship between audiovisual pleasure, the technological interface and our desire for the new. These kinds of normalizing discourses suggest that what we want from "a life" depends upon our relationship to the technologies that surround us and that the quality of this life is measured by our participation in an endlessly upgradable and ever-improvable techno-ecology. By affirming social life as a techno-ecology, these industry discourses ask us to imagine new modes of subjectivity and new forms of agency that depend upon the purchase of the latest technologies. Prior to the large-scale uptake of domestic DVD players, video retailers included promotional materials for DVD players on their VHS copies of feature films. One such *Touchstone* promotion begins with a voice-over that announces that the ensuing shots you will see are examples of "what happens when you watch DVD." Subsequent shots of exploding airplanes, tankers, houses and cars are interspersed with extreme close-ups of the depicted "home viewer" responding to these scenes. These spectacular action sequences attempt to demonstrate the superior sound and visual quality of the DVD, while paradoxically relying on a VHS for-mat to do so. These affective sequences are interrupted in the middle of the advert where shots of an actual DVD player and chapter menus provide the consumer with more analytic information. Interspersed between action shots and information sequences is the recurring image of a flying DVD disk (accompanied by hi-tech sounds of metal and air). At this point the technology takes on a life of its own with the DVD disk appearing in mid-air and then inserting itself into a player seemingly without need of human intervention. The life-like quality attributed to the disk echoes the promised augmentation and enhancement of the implied consumer's audiovisual pleasures. The advert suggests that if you own this technology you can have greater control over your immersive audiovisual pleasures, an immersive state paradoxically given through our interaction with home entertainment and DVD technologies.

Such promotional materials demonstrate exuberance and enthusiasm for the superior sound and visual quality of the DVD (particularly when hooked up to a plasma screen and home theatre system). Agitated by such hi-fidelity reproductions, the implied consumer would react with shock, surprise and apprehension, which should then shift to delight, pleasure and amazement. Presumably, then, "what happens when you watch DVD" involves participating in a more intensive and immersive sense of "being there" for the viewer, which other forms of display and exhibition do not provide. The variable levels of emotion and affect (surprise, delight, joy and then ecstasy) expressed by these human faces demonstrate the capacity for DVD to simulate perceptual environments that generate embodied intensities to a greater degree than earlier mediums. This is visual culture multiplied to the nth degree: a form of life that depends crucially on the "wired habitat" (or techno-ecology) of the DVD-user assemblage.

This DVD advert privileges an *embodied* concept of perception where the digital reproduction of a film text is augmented by the home theatre system to intensify viewing pleasure. Following the logic of this promotional discourse, the viewing body becomes an agitated body that is hardwired into the extended technological set-up of the DVD-home entertainment system. The illusion of greater control, better sound reproduction, enhanced verisimilitude and immersion, works at the level of embodied interaction in ways that parallel the logic of spectacle, which informs traditional forms of cinema. Home theatre systems and DVD technologies thus contribute to the continued industrialization of the domestic sphere, where the media consumer is caught up in a net of perpetual communication and thus the banal realm of informatics. At this point we can begin to see how the DVD might be the most overt embodiment of cinema as a mechanism of control not only in its augmentation of bodily affects, but in the way that the consumer is invited to get caught up in audiovisual technological techniques and experimentations. But what of Deleuze's notion of "an art of control" as a practice that can reverse the constant drive for information as informatics? While the *Touchstone* promotion works to secure new consumers for its products, this advert also tells another kind of story, one that provides us with a glimpse of how important consumers are to the media industries. While the consumer is increasingly caught up in the "wired habitat" or techno-ecology of contemporary capitalist industries, this environment is not the sole domain of media producers. This is also a domain where consumer labor is of increasing importance and where the feedback loop between production and consumption becomes the object of intense innovation and experimentation. Accordingly, it is in this domain that we might search for the supplementary function of contemporary audiovisual culture.

THE *DIVIDUAL* AND DVDS

According to Deleuze's reading of Daney, the optics of contemporary culture no longer function as a "window or a door . . . nor a frame or a surface . . . but as a computer screen on which images as 'data' slip around" (1990: 76). In this third phase the world resembles a bad film, where habit, opinion and consensus prevail and where "the quest for 'universals of communication' ought to make us shudder" (1990: 175). DVD technologies are an excellent example of this quest for instant communication in their packaging and promotion of excess amounts of information that blur the boundary between primary and secondary texts. Brookey and Westerfulhaus use the term "extra-texts" to describe how the DVD blurs the conventional differences between primary and secondary texts (2002). The DVD enables special features such as the audio commentary (a secondary text) to be played at the same time as the feature film (conventionally understood as the primary text). Where the more traditional notion of primary and secondary texts refer to an intertextual relationship between two distinct texts (an actual film versus criticism or promotional articles concerning the film), Brookey and Westerfelhaus argue that the DVD's technological capabilities now produce an *intratextual* relationship between primary and secondary texts, that blurs the distinctive time and space of each text. Brookey and Westerfelhaus suggest that these technological shifts impact on the ways that an industry can harvest added value from their media products. Referring to this intratextual relationship, they write:

> Thus, the DVD is perhaps the ultimate example of media-industry synergy, in which the promotion of a media product is collapsed into the product itself. Judicious use of the DVD-extra text can exploit this intratextual advantage as a means of promoting the film.
>
> (2002: 23)

Not only does the intratextual nature of a director's commentary help to guide the preferred meaning of the film (and Brooker and Westerfelhaus provide an intriguing reading of *Fight Club* [1999 (2000)] to demonstrate these practices), the intratext also uses "insider knowledge" and excess information to add value to the film itself. Here, DVD producers pursue a packaged form of information that promises a complete and total bundle of knowledge (special edition DVDs in particular). In Deleuze's terms then, the DVD trades on its potential to provide a "universal" form of communication. This "total package" approach is facilitated by the digital technologies that make up the DVD. Menu and chapter selection options remind us of the database nature of this medium.[4] To add value to the original feature film, the industry includes "behind-the-scenes" documentaries, scholarly voice-overs and director commentaries and trailers to the original feature release. The possibilities of "add-ons" are endless, and these extra-texts overlap with a variety of older media forms to repurpose and expand the potential revenue from the primary product.[5]

The endlessly renewable nature of a DVD film is also coupled with the refashioning of the media consumer. From literature to film, art, and computer technologies, the DVD is a hybrid form of media that makes an appeal to a wide variety of taste formations, classes and ages and also calls for a form of interaction from its user that intensifies the relationship between the consumer and the media object. In Deleuze's terms, the individual becomes a *dividual*, amenable to the multitasking nature of contemporary culture where flexibility, interchangeablity and mobility are premium qualities. Indeed, the very structure of the DVD mimics the characteristics of control societies by overlapping with a variety of older media forms in their packaging, navigational features and formal properties. For example, the New Line Platinum Series of *The Lord of the Rings: The Fellowship of the Ring* (2001[2002]) presents itself as a gold-trimmed book, a commodity that would not look out of place on a bookshelf. The artworks that form part of the production design for the feature film are also evident in the cover design of the DVD, as well as in the chapter menus and navigational features within the DVD. These techniques raise the aesthetic level of the packaging far beyond its functional purpose in order to extend the media producer's vision of the filmic world into every stage of the commodity's life. The cover art extends, transforms and repurposes the design of the filmic world in ways that make a diverse appeal to a range of consumer desires. These techniques enhance the collectible nature of the New Line Platinum Series, an appeal that extends itself to film purists as well as to book collectors and fans of special media editions.

The broad-based and yet simultaneously elite appeal of the special edition DVD scrambles the received wisdom of consumer identity and suggests more interchangeable and mobile taste formations. The technological and aesthetic dimensions of DVDs constitute a retooling of consumer desire in their diverse appeal to a consumer who is an assemblage of media categories that include cinema, television, computers and books. Consequently, the multi-mediated nature of the DVD appeals to a vast array of social identities. The technological dimensions of the menu screen (which invokes the similarly embodied logic of computer gaming) make an appeal to the computer user, while the aesthete can admire the artworks on special editions and indulge in their identification with the taste-formation surrounding literary authors and film auteurs. The TV buff can manufacture a hybrid tele-cinematic flow by viewing documentary footage, commentaries and behind-the-scenes footage back-to-back, while the high-definition rendering and surround-sound of the DVD production (coupled with immersive home entertainment systems) can absorb the cinephile. Indeed, as Laura Mulvey notes, new developments in technology (the freeze-frame, the scan feature and slow motion) enable the spectator to "possess" the film image more definitively, thus leading to enhanced forms of cinephilia and star-worship. She writes:

> With electronic or digital viewing, the nature of cinematic repetition compulsion changes. As the film is delayed and thus fragmented from linear narrative into favourite moments or scenes, the spectator is able to hold on to, to possess, the previously elusive image. In this delayed cinema the spectator finds a heightened relation to the human body, particularly that of the star
>
> (2006: 161).

In these appeals to a diverse range of consumers, the media industry produces new orders of consumption through incremental modulations across established consumer categories and taste formations. These appeals include the promise of greater control over the audiovisual event, the most obvious example being the DVD's promise of greater consumer interactivity. These appeals to some form of interaction from the DVD user intensifies the relationship between consumer and media object, and thus emphasizes the "wired" nature of the habitat in which the dividual is caught up.

The material structure of the DVD (their bookish cover design, the complex navigational structure and the excess of information available) accentuates the fact that the user must *do* something with this media package. At the very least, one must navigate the chapter structure of the DVD menu in order to access the content. One must pause or restart viewing in response to changes within the exhibitionary setting. Users load their disc on a player connected to increasingly hi-tech display and sound systems that accessorize the mise-en-scène of the living room, or the traveling subject. These instances of engagement (with the technology itself or the environment in which it is housed) produce a form of interactivity that invites the consumer to touch the technology that provides them with their visual pleasure. Yet it is always a form of interactivity regulated and enabled by the media producer. Commenting on the six-part structure of the New Line *The Lord of the Rings* series, Craig Hight notes:

> Users of the *LOTR* DVDs will gradually work their way through the considerable amount of material on these disc, accessing and engaging with the various aspects of these frames through a variety of pathways.

The key point, however, is that while our specific viewing trajectories may differ, we are still engaging with a static text, one that is clearly constructing a specific and limited set of perspectives on the film trilogy
(Hight 2005: 12).

These invitations to interactivity involve increasingly novel features. In the case of the DVD version of *Gangs of New York* (2002[2003]) the media producers were not content to simply make available to the consumer a study guide of the Five Points, a music video, movie trailers as well as a behind-the-scenes featurette; they also offer the consumer the novelty of a 360-degree tour of the film's "awesome sets" (DVD cover). The playful form of investment involved in revealing this hidden space mimics the techniques of computer gaming (a form of labor that is also a feature of DVD chapter organization in general). The user must activate the arrow icon that appears as the making-of documentary unfolds. Once this option is selected the making-of documentary freezes on a screen shot and the user must select an additional arrow icon that simulates a 360-degree camera movement that encompasses the surrounding set. What is perhaps surprising about this novel feature is that this rotating shot reveals an empty set. There is no information in the frame that throws light on the production process or the actors and technologies involved on this particular set. The outcome of the physical investment of the consumer (who must interrupt Scorsese's commentary to enjoy this panoramic shot) is simply the enjoyment of a novel technological feature that makes the shot of the set appear as if the result of an omniscient camera presence able to penetrate any given space. There can be no doubt that this technological feature is purely a novelty with no inherent value in terms of enriching the consumer's understanding of the film. It is there to contribute to the "additional features" taxonomy of the DVD and to contribute to the illusion of meaningful informatics. It is there to invite consumers to interact with the information it provides, an invitation to interaction that simultaneously asks consumers to immerse themselves within the conditions surrounding the production of the feature film. It is there, in other words, to capture consumer attention, and to invite immersion and interaction without any meaningful outcome. The promise of greater consumer control and interactivity thus contributes to an ever-expanding regime of capture and immersion that paradoxically enables the media producer to assert a firmer control over the audiovisual market.

As the *Gangs of New York* example also suggests, the invitation to interaction is an increasingly prevalent part of additional extras. The viewer as active user is taken to a new degree in Mike Figgis' digital feature film *Timecode* (2000[2000]), which features a screen divided into four quarters with each quadrant showing concurrent action in four different locations. To assist the viewer's comprehension of the overall plot, Figgis manipulates the volume of each quadrant during important scenes. But the purpose of the split screen technique is to allow the spectator to imaginatively edit the film by simply looking from one frame to the next. This novel interactive mode of spectatorship is taken to the next level in the DVD version of *Timecode*, where the DVD user has an option that allows them to select the audio on any quadrant at any time, so that one can produce a multiplicity of narratives within the four-frame structure. The interactive dimensions of *Timecode* differ significantly from that of the tour featured in *Gangs of New York*, and yet *Timecode*'s interactivity remains linked to the pre-defined options set by the media producer. The consumer can choose from a fixed array of choices, but she/he cannot change the audio and visual content. The playful and interactive dimensions of *Timecode* thus gesture to an illusory form of freedom that maintains and extends the overall control held by the media producer. The DVD industry thus actively experiments with the boundary between producer and consumer, inventing new techniques of control and interaction, using the promise of digital technologies to fine-tune this "art of control."

Brookey and Westerfelhaus view interactivity as part of the many ways that consumers become "invested viewers;" however, they link this investment to the newness of the technology rather than understanding visual techniques and technological experiments as an *inherent* aspect of an emergent DVD culture (2002: 40). *Timecode* and *Gangs of New York* demonstrate the persisting need of media producers to attract consumer attention by using new and novel features. The New Line edition of *Se7en* (1995[2000]) includes a multi-angle "exploration" of the opening credit sequence. The 20th Anniversary Edition of *Alien* (1979[1999]) includes hidden extras that require time and patience to discover them. The *Die Hard* Five Star Collection (1998[2001]) features a "Cutting Room" where viewers are invited to re-edit three scenes from the feature film, using alternate shot sizes and angles.

These examples of the increased interactive appeal of DVDs involve a mode of address that invites us to *do* something with our media objects, whilst many may not move beyond the most banal activity of slotting the software into the DVD player, this appeal nevertheless invites us to spend time conducting these novel activities. This appeal is embedded in the aesthetic, informational and navigational attributes of the DVD itself. The excess of information contained in special edition DVDs invites us to store up specialist knowledge of cinema that will make experts of us all. The chapter navigation structure compels us to move our hands and eyes in ways that mimic the PC, gaming console or laptop. This impetus to action is as much abstract as it is embodied. As such it links to what we might call *ludic labor*, which is (rather broadly) a playful form of investment in objects, information, sounds and images. This ludic appeal parallels other digital media products that invite consumers to *do* something in relation to their digital media objects (be it the iPod, the mobile phone, iMovie software or Photoshop), a phenomenon that increasingly blurs the distinction between workplace media (the database, the spreadsheet, the mouse and computer screen set-up) and leisure time activities. I suggest that these synergistic relations are the hallmark of regimes of control, regimes intimately tied to capital. Accordingly, while the promise of interactive media positions the viewer as an active user, one must interrogate the kinds of investment of time, attention and labor that this technology promotes.

AUDIOVISION AS LABOR

The central logic prevailing in control societies is that "you never finish anything" (Deleuze 1990: 179). This is certainly the case with DVD versions of feature films that refashion, extend and upgrade earlier modes of cinematic production, so much so that one is "never finished" with the cinematic text. Arguably DVDs extend the experience of theatrical display into the quasi-public space produced by home entertainment systems. This mode of production involves the promise of greater consumer interaction and control over the conditions of exhibition. Yet paradoxically this greater control results in the quantification and regulation of human time and attention. Home entertainment systems demonstrate the centrality of the domestic sphere in this mode of production while the DVD demonstrates the increasing importance of audiovisual experience as a prime site of commodification. DVD producers invent new and novel forms of interaction that work at the boundary of producer/consumer functions, thus functioning to extend the limits of production into the realm of consumption and circulation. The dividual as consumer is hardwired into this feedback system through the ludic engagement with DVD technologies. At this site of sight and interactivity, audiovision becomes a form of labor.

In *The Cinema Effect*, Sean Cubitt argues that since the late 1920s, the time of media consumption has been as central to the workings of capital as the time of media production, making a consumer's capacity for absorption and distraction in media events (their attention) a prime commodity (2004: 7–10). Capital extends its own limits, as does DVD culture, and the making-of phenomenon turns the conditions of a commodity's production into an "ever-newer and more abstract commodity" in order to mine consumer desire and attention. In an age of informatics, everything can be translated into audiovisual terms including the mechanisms, techniques and technologies that create the audiovisual event. With the rise of DVD culture we are increasingly being invited to touch the technologies of cinema and to arrest its cinematic flow by pushing the pause button or freeze-framing an image. Our engagement with cinema as a DVD database involve us in a realm of excess information with the capacity to produce new regimes of movement and duration that not only serve a social function (direct social engineering) but provide the necessary conditions for interrupting the regulatory regimes produced by such systems of control. As the ambivalent nature of control systems suggest, we are increasingly involved in regimes of capture where our time and attention can be caught up, coded and regulated by systems of control at the same time as these systems provide the conditions for the production of chaotic and deterritorializing forms of attention.

In audiovisual culture's expanded circuits of production, consumer attention and time become premium values and the site where capital kick-starts the cycle of production again. In relation to the proximity between cinema and capital (cinema *as* capital) Jonathan Beller has argued:

> Technologies such as cinema and television are machines that take the assembly line out of the space of the factory and put it into the home and the theatre and the brain itself, mining the body of the productive value of its time, occupying it on location. The cinema as deterritorialized factory, human attention as deterritorialized labor
>
> (Beller 1998: 92).

Beller's comments emphasize the spatial and temporal dimensions of attention and the house where domestic screens (the television, the computer screen, the gaming console) work to "mine the body of the productive value of its time." The time it takes to view a making-of or director commentary, is time spent giving attention to the conditions of capitalist production. Literally. In the case of *Gangs of New York*, our attention and time, and the playful labor involved in examining the 360 degree tour, hardwires the consumer into the system of exchange value underpinning capitalism. The affects generated by the technological set-up of the DVD, as well as the home entertainment system that accompanies it, intensifies this relay between consumer, media object and the spectacle of capitalist production. The making-ofs, remote control options, and extra-texts invite us *in* to the cinematic image itself, where we can experience the banalities of an age of informatics and communication. While we are spun in an interactive net of instant communication, how do we affirm the creative and resistant potential of DVD cinema? If DVD producers have refined and enhanced techniques of audiovisual control to such a degree that it almost constitutes an art of control, how do the aesthetic dimensions of cinema return in DVD form to produce new forms of freedom and new, chaotic and deterritorialized forms of attention?

Beller makes the claim that attention is a form of labor that can be made amenable to capitalist systems of exchange, quantification and equivalence. But it is also a form of deterritorialized labor that produces intensive loops between the body, image and technological set-up, constituting a rich and complex amplification of the human sensorium. The affects and percepts generated by this relay system defy easy description; these intensities are not easily verifiable, nor can they be completely commodified by the logic of exchange. Accordingly, being "spun" in a net of immediate communication via DVD and home entertainment systems perhaps retools our bodies and their social relationships in a manner that enables the emergence of new modes of subjectivity and new forms of agency.

If DVDs find a way *in* to the image, so much so that we can almost touch the technology that captures our attention, time and labor, we need to assess and investigate the new relations made possible by DVD cinema. While Beller's comments appear to shut down the possibility of some form of action against this process of corporeal mining, he offers a potential remedy when he writes "[b]ut if, for example, we put our eyes elsewhere, or re-channel our viewings into different media, or effect alternate mediations, we create new formations, different machines" (1998: 92). This may be the case. However, Beller appears to privilege the site of sight itself as providing a break with these regimes of capture, and he suggests that we must break with cinema itself, in order to forge other more productive assemblages. Yet, Deleuze's enigmatic comments on the need for an art of control that might take the "battle to the heart of cinema" suggests that we must go *through* cinema to forge these new alliances. It seems to me that DVD versions of cinema directly strike at this notion of an art of control in that this digital technology objectifies, extends, upgrades and subsequently *materializes* the cinematic image. Our augmented powers of manipulation and control given in the DVD, while extending the circuits of capital in ways that enrich the media producer, also invite us to understand cinema (and ourselves) as matter in movement and in stasis. This is where the battle might be waged. It is to the object-status of the DVD that I now turn to consider these issues.

DVDS AND THE "CLUNK" AFFECT

While I have outlined the manner in which capital functions to code, decode and recode attention in order to perpetuate the "mining" or industrialization of the human body, the last part of this discussion focuses on the "supplementary function" of DVD versions of cinema and the pedagogic potential of this medium. That is to say, how might the DVD offer a brief break with an informatics society where thought and attention is regulated and disciplined? How might DVD technologies re-engage our attention in new and critically conscious directions?

Throughout this discussion I have highlighted the DVD's status as not only an older form of media (television and cinema) but also how the DVD contributes to discourses surrounding the "new" of new media. The DVD is a database, it offers pristine digital reproductions of what were once celluloid images. The interactive domains enabled by DVD technologies invite the consumer to playfully engage with their media content in new and novel ways. The special features of the DVD multiply the various entry points that a consumer has to the media content that they consume. This ability echoes Jack Z. Bratich's comments on the audience-producer relationship in RTV as that which "multiplies life's points of contact with networks of power," thus producing "a wired habitat that delivers instructions and takes feedback" (2006: 78). As Brookey and Westerfelhaus' comments on the intratextual nature of the DVD also attests, the DVD is a site that blurs the distinction between primary and secondary texts and it trades on the promise of a closer synergy between producers and consumers. While this discourse is intoxicating to some degree (recall the *Touchstone* promotional text and its breathless and ecstatic tone), the DVD also offers us a sober pause to new media myths of greater freedom and control.

The idea of the DVD as generating greater consumer control is very quickly challenged when one actually goes to play the feature film. Where videotape once allowed the consumer to fast-forward through the piracy warnings, media producers can now prevent such practices from occurring with DVDs. Zoning restrictions also make quick and simple access to some DVD versions of film and television difficult. Thus, while we may delight in the pristine reproduction of the sound and image of the feature film (once we get to it), the DVD also exposes its consumer to the systems of governance surrounding contemporary media culture. Couple this exposure with the rather "clunky" navigational features of the DVD and we might find some pedagogical value to the material dimensions of the DVD.

This notion of a clunky navigational structure relates to the DVD's status as a hybrid medium. While the actual content of the DVD delivers on the promise of improved reproduction (particularly in relation to its now poor cousin, the videotape), accessing this content requires dealing with book-like chapter structures that appear anachronistic in relation to the high-tech promises of DVD Dolby surround-sound and digital imagery. DVD navigational interfaces are not yet intuitive or seamless mechanisms for engaging with the film, even if these interfaces are increasingly incorporated into the "look" and aesthetic world of the film. As such, DVDs act as indexical markers to the conditions of their own production and consumption; the DVD is neither old nor new but an interstitial media that will no doubt be superseded in the years to come. As such, the general hinge condition of the DVD (neither cinema, television nor database but an amalgam of all three) suggests a kind of interruption or time lag in new media's drive towards dematerialization. In this age of continuous variation, augmentation and improvement, the DVD provides a time lag or interruption that derails (if only for a moment) the speed of audiovisual industrial changes. The "clunky" dimension of the DVD acts as a blockage to new media's promises of more efficient and immediate media consumption. It points to the "not yet" of digital technologies and the industrial drive towards newer and improved forms of audiovisual culture even as it demonstrates the refashioning of older versions of cinema. As such, the hybrid nature of the format, its status as an object or "thing" draws attention to the logic of continuous variation that characterizes capitalist creative industries. The "clunk" of the DVD is perhaps that supplementary force of cinema that Deleuze spoke of, a supplement that reminds us of our enmeshment in networks of social power, control and regulation. The "clunk" moment interrupts the drive for information and is a moment where thought is pulled towards the future, with the DVD acting as an indexical marker of more virtual relations. In doing so, the "clunk" of the DVD offers up an interval or an opening in the drive for instantaneous communication through which more creative and resistant forces might emerge. So, counter to dominant new media discourses of dematerialization, perhaps we need to return to the force of "things" that our ludic engagement with DVD cinema reveals so that we can diagnose and interrupt the industrialization and "mining" of audiovision.

The new time and space relations offered by DVD technologies have yet to be classified, mapped or produced. This is the creative task facing media scholars today. In his taxonomy of images in the Cinema books, Deleuze identifies the time-image as disrupting what is seeable and what is sayable, and as opening up an attentive form of recognition that can inspire new modes of thought. As Gregory Flaxman notes, Deleuze readily admits that, "new forces of 'control' will inevitably put these disjunctions to use, forging vast digital archives, dead spaces that swallow so much vision," even as Deleuze's cinema books hold out hope that it can be otherwise (Flaxman, 2000: 26). This is the political dimension of Deleuze's philosophy, which attends to the ways in which cultural change enables new forms of life and new modes of subjectivity to emerge. As Nicholas Thoburn puts it, "[p]olitics for Deleuze is at once a process of the invention of life and an engagement with specifically capitalist relations" (2003: 6). If the informatic dimensions of DVD technologies threaten to overwhelm the creative potentials of cinema, if DVD cinema has set up shop between the seeable and the sayable, providing endless information to produce cinema as a marketable commodity, then it is at this site that we must forge new modes of thought and new forms of critical engagement. One potential method could be to affirm the object-status of the DVD and the techno-ecologies we are caught up in, so that we can consider how the DVD demonstrates Deleuze and Guattari's approach to life as "a single cosmic flow of matter-movement" (Bennett 2004: 347). The "clunk" affect of the DVD, then, might return us to our bodies, to the relations between our bodies and other "things" in the world so that we can create new forms of recognition and new modes of action that can diagnose and act upon the transversal systems of control societies as this age dawns.

NOTES

1. Elsewhere I have argued that the DVD involves a productive oscillation between the two visual practices (televisual and cinematic). See Jo T. Smith (2008).
2. Gareth Palmer makes a similar point when he explores the theme of conduct and governmentality in relation to RTV in 'Big Brother': an Experiment in Governance' (2002).
3. The promise of more interactive television is an increasing feature of contemporary audiovisual culture. James Bennett discusses the emerging category of

the TV "viewer" (a viewer and a user) in his essay "The Public Service Value of Interactive Television" (2006).
4. Lev Manovich's work on the relationship between narrative and database organization could be usefully deployed in relation to DVD technologies (2001).
5. Both John Caldwell in this volume and Craig Hight (2005) situate the "making-of" documentary features of the DVD in relation to earlier industry practices, such as the Electronic Press Kit (EPKs), which extends the promotional discourses of the feature film following a corporate agenda.

BIBLIOGRAPHY

Beller, J. (1998) "Capital/Cinema," in E. Kaufman and K. J. Heller (eds) *Deleuze and Guattari: new mappings in politics, philosophy, and culture*, Minneapolis and London: University of Minnesota Press: 77–95.
Bennett, J. (2006) "The Public Service Value of Interactive Television," in *New Review of Film and Television Studies*, 4(3): 263–285.
Bennett, J. (2004) "The Force of Things: Steps Toward an Ecology of Matter," *Political Theory*, 32(3): 347–372.
Bratich, J. Z. (2006) "Nothing is Left Alone For Too Long," *Journal of Communication Inquiry*, 30 (1): 65–83.
Brookey, R. A. and Westerfelhaus, R. (2002) "Hiding Homoeroticism in Plain View: The *Fight Club* DVD as Digital Closet," *Critical Studies in Mass Communication* 19(1): 21–43.
Busk, M. (2001) "Micropolitics: A Political Philosophy from Marx and Beyond," in P. Pisters (ed.) *Micropolitics of Media Culture: reading the rhizomes of Deleuze and Guattari*, Amsterdam: Amsterdam University Press: 103–124.
Cubitt, S. (2004) *The Cinema Effect,* Cambridge, MA: MIT Press.
Deleuze, G. (1986) *Foucault,* Minneapolis and London: University of Minnesota Press.
———. (1990) *Negotiations,* New York: Columbia University Press.
Deleuze, G. and Guattari, F. (1996) *What is Philosophy?,* New York: Columbia University Press.
Flaxman, G. (ed.) (2000) *The Brain is the Screen,* Minneapolis and London: University of Minnesota Press.
Guins, R. (2001) "Now You're Living: The promise of home theatre and Deleuze's 'New freedoms,'" *Television and New Media*, 2(4): 351–365.
Hight, C. (2005) "Making-of documentaries on DVD: *The Lord of the Rings* trilogy and special editions," *The Velvet Light Trap*, 56: 4–17.
Klinger, B. (2006) *Beyond the Multiplex: cinema, new technologies, and the home,* Berkeley, Los Angeles and London: University of California Press.
Manovich, L. (2001) *The Language of New Media,* Cambridge, Massachusetts: MIT Press.
Moseley, R. (2000) "Makeover Takeover on British Television," *Screen*, 41(3): 299–314.
Mulvey, L. (2006) *Death 24x a Second,* London: Reaktion Books.
Palmer, G. (2002) "*Big Brother*: An Experiment in Governance," *Television & New Media*, 3(3): 295–310.
Smith, Jo. T. (2008) "*Lord of the Rings* in the Living Room: Changing Technologies of Display and Reception," in S. Cubitt, T. Jutel and H. Margolis (eds) *Studying the Event Film: The Lord of the Rings*, Manchester: Manchester University Press: forthcoming.
Thoburn, N. (2003) *Deleuze, Marx and Politics,* London and New York: Routledge.

8 Prefiguring DVD Bonus Tracks

Making-ofs and Behind-the-Scenes as Historic Television Programming Strategies Prototypes

John T. Caldwell

We decided to do it all the best that we can. It's basically the *coup-de-gras* of all of our work (on the TV series) to-date.

Director Rob Bowman, on DVD of *X-Files: The Movie*
(1998[2001])

Much has been made of the big changes underway as new forms of digital media—online user-generated content, mobile media, and the DVD in particular—are popularized. Some political economists, like Daniel Schiller (1999) and Toby Miller, et al. (2005), caution us about the ways new media technologies reinforce existing imbalances in socio-economic power as part of resilient corporate conglomeration strategies. Other cultural theorists, like Lev Manovich (2001) and Henry Jenkins (2006), see recent changes in more benign, and sometimes celebratory terms, as driven by either techno-aesthetic convergence or new forms of collective "transmedia" audience participation and agency. Rob Cover provides a particularly prescient analysis of the DVD as part of the latter trend (2005: 137). Cover connects the explosive popularity of the DVD to a corresponding rise in "peer-to-peer" networking and media de-centralization, going so far as to say that DVDs unsettle the dominant "center-periphery motif" that scholars have simplistically imported from broadcasting studies to understand new media. While Cover rightly underscores the importance of consumer media activities that continue long after the retail sale of DVDs, this view risks understating the continuing importance of audience activity and collective participation as essential parts of *industrial* business plans and media strategies. I would like to complement Cover's account by suggesting two things: first, that decentralized consumer unruliness is also a key to the success of contemporary viral marketing; and second, that the DVD has actually shored up and re-anchored important and long-standing media centers like Hollywood.

Fully understanding this industrial "flip-side" of the DVD as a "cultural technology" means considering the various media prototypes that pre-figured the DVD (like the "EPK," or electronic press kit); and how the new direct-to-consumer imperative of the DVD (which ostensibly cuts out cultural middle-men and gatekeepers) actually uses reflexive critical inter-actions with users to bolster consumer ties and brand loyalty. Industrial pro-totypes for the DVD "bonus track," like behind-the-scenes features, have been widely used in television since the late 1940s. Since that time, behind-the-scenes segments have been integrated across multiple media platforms. For example, when director Rob Bowman, in the epigraph above, touted the *X-Files: The Movie* the "coup-de-gras" of the entire television franchise on the film's DVD, he was kick-starting a profitable chain of events that have come to define media conglomeration: the "synergistic" repurposing of content across film, television, syndication, music, home video, DVD, and merchandising platforms. Far from being novel or innovative, reflexive DVD bonus tracks (or "featurettes") also emulate one of the most basic marketing mechanisms and artifacts deployed profitably by broadcasters for several decades: the moving image iteration of the traditional "press pack," or the EPK. Viewed in terms of institutional logic, rather than via "new media" theory, the hard distinctions that are usually made between analog (or old media) on the one hand, and digital (or new media) seem far less convincing than the hype that greets each new technology.

To address the question of how the DVD has been mainstreamed and disciplined as part of traditional programming and marketing strategies, I would like to consider several problems: the institutional logic of DVDs and bonus-tracks; why the new industrial landscape of corporate, multime-dia conglomeration has facilitated the popularity of the DVD medium; and how the EPK has changed media's critical and gate-keeping functions by animating viewer connoisseurship and critical acumen as direct marketing opportunities. What does it mean that the *viewer* now poses as an indus-trial gatekeeper and operates as a quasi-critic? What implications follow when consumers purchase what are essentially marketing materials for use as consumer entertainment? What industrial purposes do the vast amounts of new "Film Studies-style" behind-the-scenes and backstage knowledge and theorization in film/TV DVDs serve? To address these questions I will consider DVDs broadly, but also closely examine one case study: the "migration" of an originating EPK through three mutating stages of viewer engagement in *X-Files: The Movie*: as a marketing EPK, as a broadcast "making-of," and as a DVD.

EPKs (THE "DEEP" VARIANT AND VIRAL DVD PROTOTYPE)

Making-ofs almost invariably play a part in, result from, or share footage with electronic press kits. EPKs are descendents of traditional print-based press kits, through which public relations officers, publicists and market-ers traditionally provided "useful" background and backstory about films and television programs to influence the trade or popular press. Press kits usually included cast and crew bios, pre-digested angles for stories in short, double-spaced, 1–2 page press-releases, and photographs intended for republication in the trade and journalistic press. While print reviewers and magazine critics still mostly need hard-copy photographs and preview "screeners" (half-inch VHS tapes and then DVDs), broadcast and cable reviewers and on-screen show-biz reports need the higher "broadcast-quality" moving images and sounds that are pre-edited onto EPKs (usually in BetacamSP, DigiBeta, or DVCam formats) since they have much higher resolution than VHS screeners. Now digital and more interactive screeners and EPKs provide a fundamental connection and means of communication between the industry's producing cultures and the audience's consuming cultures. This strategic nexus between producing cultures and consuming cultures traditionally "delegated" and placed the publicist-reviewer relationship at the center of the transaction. As such, their interactions collectively framed most entertainment experiences. EPKs and now DVDs increasingly define this nexus and trigger this framing.

In one sense, video or digital EPKs can be understood as institutionally coded artifacts used to "negotiate" critical reception in culture at large. Fully understanding EPKs would entail more closely studying the day-to-day ways that publicists, journalists, and editors interact to collectively make value judgments and critical distinctions, an ethnographic task beyond the scope of this chapter. Sometimes this interaction is formalized between the networks or studios and the media in the form of network sanctioned set-visits, press-junkets, or the semiannual Television Critics Association meetings in Los Angeles. At other times the interaction is more informal (when publicists conveniently pose in the role of unnamed "sources" for journalists). Whether marketing and publicity departments adopt hard-sell or soft-sell to get their promotional message out on a new film or television show, an EPK is now an obligatory part of this exchange/negotiation aimed at positive critical reception—especially when broadcast and cable coverage are pursued. As a result, understanding on-screen critical activity in the industry, means better understanding the codes, predispositions and formal strategies of the EPK artifact as well. This is because much of the footage that makes its way into broadcast making-ofs, behind-the-scenes documentaries, promos and the like originate in pre-edited EPK videotapes or DVDs.

During the transition from hardcopy to electronic formats, electronic or moving image documentation was usually fairly minimal in EPKs. As late as 1992 the EPK for *Wayne's World 2* (1993), a feature film adapted from television, included only spare two-minute versions of the film's promo, edited back-to-back on a single BetacamSP tape.[1] One version had pre-written critical narration already added (graphically identified on the tape as: "news wrap 1" w. "text"); the other version was without voice-over narration (graphically titled on the tape as: "news wrap 2, no narration"). In short, the visual images, sync sounds, music, and effects are the same in both versions, but the second version—without prerecorded narration—allows the reviewer or "critic" to record and add their own commentary, thus claiming the footage as part of the critic's "personal" take on the movie or show. The first version, pre-digested, pre-edited and narrated, means that even deadline-stressed producers who needed to fill screen time could do so, almost mindlessly, with the EPK. EPKs help fuel the public relations world, and by definition are planned and designed to be "helpfully customizable." Since PR and publicity are forms of marketing that companies do not have to pay for (unlike advertising), studios and networks work out elaborate schemes to make their video EPKs available and attractive to deadline-focused producers and on-screen show-biz reporters at *Access Hollywood* (1996–ongoing), *Entertainment Tonight* (1981–ongoing), *Extra* (1994–ongoing), and the E-Channel!

A 1992 *Roseanne* (1988–1997) EPK was considerably more customizable than the *Wayne's World 2* EPK. Roseanne's EPK opens with an onscreen graphic table of contents that reads:

Electronic Press Kit
Roseanne

1.) Featurette-Short 2:02
2.) Featurette-Long 4:20
3.) Open-Ended Interviews
   A. Roseanne
   B. Roseanne and Tom Arnold
   C. John Goodman
4.) Clips
5.) B-Roll[2]

The two "featurettes" included on this EPK are pre-edited "stories" complete with a scratch-track (an audio recording by a non-professional voice-over narrator) which provides show-biz reporters with suggested, easy-to-use "off-the-shelf" narration. Reviewers who are in a hurry, can simply strip-off the voice-over scratch track, and mouth the same words on tape to "author" the "review" as their own. The menu includes long and short versions to fit the time constraints of EPK end-users. Part three of the EPK consists of "open-ended interviews," which are later graphically introduced as "Sound Bites." Graphic titles precede each open-ended sound-bite, telling reporters how to mouth interview questions in their own voice. This scripted ventriloquism of journalists suggests that even the quasi-comatose can edit together a "story" or review on the series. The EPK's pre-scripted "questions" for the reporter/reviewer include: "Q: What kind of realities does *Roseanne* portray?" This question is "answered" by

Roseanne's video/sound bite paraphrasing the show's pitch: "Well, it's a working class comedy from a woman's point-of-view."[3] Roseanne does not hesitate to historicize her show's importance in the next sound-bite: "I think that she's the first and only three-dimensional female that's been on the small screen." Then, in response to the pre-scripted question that appears as an onscreen graphic, "Do you enjoy the shoots?," Roseanne mouths in a bored monotone her first obvious lie in the EPK: "We all get along great, and in between the takes we have a great time." In the four seasons leading up to the release of this EPK, the *Roseanne* show was notorious in trades and popular press for the tirades and fighting that went on between an "out-of-control" Roseanne Arnold and her producers and writers. The *Roseanne* show chewed-up and spit-out writer-producers at a frantic pace during this period (Wild 1999).

The content and structure of the *Roseanne* EPK can be understood vis-à-vis four institutional activities beyond mere promotion. The EPK functions on one level as "damage control" intended to blunt accusations coming from many quarters in the press at that time. On a second institutional level, Roseanne's EPK served to cross-promote then-husband Tom Arnold's new sitcom the *The Tom Show* (1997–1998). In the EPK's "Roseanne & Tom Arnold" sound bites, the two awkwardly explain how their on-set interactions are constructive in that Tom brings insights to Roseanne's show, and Roseanne brings insights to Tom's show. Yet, the EPK covers over the acutely asymmetrical nature of their relationship, and the fact that Roseanne's show is immensely successful and Tom's is critically panned and low-rated. The EPK also overlooks Tom's opportunistic marriage to Roseanne, which he exploited to launch his show-business career before the couple divorced. Third, the EPK makes concerted attempts to re-connect Roseanne—then the most powerful female figure on- and off-screen in television—with her "working-class" roots. Despite the EPK's repeated assertions of social realism and working-class authenticity in interviews, however, this is not the Roseanne Barr of the late 1980s. The Roseanne appearing in this EPK has clearly benefited from cosmetic surgery, a face-lift, and the fashions and cultural airs that come with wealth and power. The claims of low culture solidarity and authenticity mouthed by Barr in the tape, then, seem suspiciously out of alignment with the star's visage onscreen. Fourth, and finally, the EPK was produced to announce completion of the 100th episode of the *Roseanne* series. Historically, the 100-episode mark has been a crucial goal for all primetime programs since the number guarantees that a show will have a long and profitable life in syndication. The EPK, therefore, provides a valuable opportunity to sum up and overstate the historical and critical importance of the show, and the cultural significance of the star and her social values, through the first four seasons of the series. In effect, the EPK functions to "counter-program" and "negotiate" dissonant buzz about the series and its star's turbulent reputation, by offering less prejudicial interpretive schemes.

To facilitate positive critical reception and constrain open-ended interpretation, the EPK adds "unedited clips" in Part Four, and "B-roll" footage in Part 5 to help the reporter/editor assemble an on-screen story. The unedited shots here either match those in the pre-edited, pre-narrated "featurettes"—or, they helpfully "illustrate" the themes and questions discussed by on-camera interview subjects. The B-roll footage in Part Five of the EPK, by contrast, is narration-less footage shot on video with a handheld camera during the actual production of the show. Even though B-roll footage records some of the same dramatic action as the studio pedestal cameras recording the sitcom for broadcast, B-roll usually is comprised of hand-held "documentary" images. Here, jerky camera movement constantly re-frames images of video-assist monitors, boom mics, studio lights, etc. Such images sell viewers on the sense that we have been given special access to an intense, normally guarded production. Taken as a whole, this repertoire of tactics—pre-scripted questions, pre-recorded voice-over scratch tracks, pre-cut sequences and stories, interview sound-bites, and "ready-to-use" unedited B-roll footage all make this EPK more like a "paint-by-number" art kit for the critics. Effective EPKs likewise predispose end-users to cut stories and critical reviews in ways that are congruent with the critical agenda of producers, rather than with those of consumers or show-business reporters. At least from a marketing or publicist's perspective, an intelligently designed EPK ideally serves as a pre-emptive critical strike, useful in softening up potentially hostile recipients.

If *Roseanne*'s "helpful" EPK emulates a paint-by-number methodology (valuable for rapid editing-to-air and publicity damage control), then a more complicated EPK designed for *X-Files: The Movie* in 1998 closely approximates a different paradigm: a film/video editor's task during non-linear editing. The *X-Files* EPK includes an extensive list of promotional features, variations on those features, interviews, shots, and B-roll footage, just like the *Roseanne* EPK. But the stylistic and editorial choices available for the *X-Files: The Movie*'s entertainment reporter are much vaster. A detailed table of contents is affixed to the EPK's Betacam-SP case. This table is repeated as an on-screen graphic within the EPK's video. The broad segments of the EPK are listed on these printed and video "menus" as follows (where D stands for dialogue, M for music, E for sound effects, and Comp for mixed tracks):

Twentieth Century Fox Film Corporation: The X-Files: The Movie *Electronic Press Kit*

- Trailer-Version #1 (Ch 1 Audio= D/M/E; Ch 2 Audio=Narration) 2:17
- Trailer-Version #2 (Ch 1 Audio= D/E; Ch 2=Music) 2:17
- Featurette (with text) (Ch 1 Audio= D/M/E; Ch 2 Audio=Music) 4:27

- Featurette (without text) (Ch 1 Audio= D/M/E; Ch 2 Audio=Music) 4:27
- Film Clips (unedited) (Ch 1 & 2 Comp)

1. "I Had You"
    1:42
2. "Spooky"
    1:02
3. "Blame Me"
    1:10
4. "Cornfield Chase"
    0:42
5. "The Virus Has Mutated"
    1:12
6. "Somebody's Covering Their Tracks"
    1:10
7. "A Planned Armageddon"
    0:52

- Selected Sound Bites

David Duchovny	5:09
Gillian Anderson	4:20
Martin Landau	2:37
Blythe Danner	0:44
Armin Mueller-Stahl	1:01
William B. Davis	0:51
Mitch Pileggi	1:14
John Neville	0:57
Chris Carter	3:46
Rob Bowman	1:36

- Unedited B-Roll (Ch.1 Prod. Audio * Ch.2 Music) 7:29

**** LOG ****

This graphic menu of featurettes on the *industrial* EPK strongly prefigures the design of bonus featurette menus soon popularized on *consumer* DVDs. The industrial editor's and critic's graphical user interface (GUI), thus evolves into a ubiquitous fan and viewer's graphical user interface. The sequence of features and variations in format in the EPK's menu also gives the end-user (reporter, reviewer, or show-biz program producer) a set of options that allow for "individualized" appropriations of the EPK's footage. For example, segment one can be aired as is (leaving Fox's preemptive voice-over intact for broadcast). Segment two, however, allows reporters to cleanly add their own voice-over to audio channel two (without disrupting the dialogue, music and sound effects pre-recorded on audio channel one).

Without pre-scripted narration, segment two allows greater flexibility in custom assembling discrete elements on the sound track (dialogue and sound effects on one, music on two). Segment three, by contrast, provides a longer form featurette (a mix between a trailer and a making-of) for users and editors to work from (where dialogue from interviews and a narrative text provides "needed" information). Segment four, in turn, provides the same featurette as three, but strips off the verbal text allowing greater customizability. Segment five then starts a lengthy sequence of what the EPK labels as "unedited" clips from the forthcoming film. In fact, the clips are already edited into scenes for the end-user, but these scenes were not subsequently narrated or edited into a trailer or making-of featurette. Segment six includes unincorporated interviews entitled "selected sound bites." Each of the seven minute interview footage chunks here provide lengthier source materials that incorporate the shorter character "sound-bites" chosen for the fully edited segments. Finally, "Unedited B-Roll" (hand-held making-of footage) comprises segment seven on the EPK. This systematically categorized audio, video, and film footage has the appearance and feel of "rough-cut" scenes that typify the latter stages of the non-linear editing process. Not only are potential media stories already roughed-out for the EPK's end-user, but the organization of the material itself is reminiscent of the graphical "bins" and user interfaces typical of the Avid non-linear editing systems used to bang-out show-biz reports at E-Entertainment! and *Access Hollywood* on a nightly basis.

Interestingly, this EPK includes the same basic audio, video, and interview material used in the creation of the hour-long making-of examined in the next section of this chapter, and in the film's eventual DVD as well. In fact, well over half of the footage in Fox Network's subsequent "special" is prepackaged from this EPK tape. Although all of the audible questions are cutout of the sound-bites provided here, the interview chunks left on the tape bear the heavy traces of the kind of reduced "talking points" that the Bush Whitehouse used to master Fox News in the 2004 election.[4] Each of the ten featured interview subjects (crew and actors) are asked the same questions over and over again ("how is this different from producing for television?," "will viewers who are not fans be able to understand the feature movie?" etc.). More importantly, each interviewee responds with a set of very compatible answers. These shared talking points (coached by the marketing department or set-up by the studio interviewer) mean that potential media stories on the film will be easy to edit around a limited cluster of recurring themes. Editing from this EPK is therefore less like post-production on a documentary (with its inordinately high shooting ratios) than it is like editing the fine-cut of a commercial spot from a short script. In effect, the EPK pre-selects and arranges interview themes and footage in a de facto rough-cut, even as the EPK pre-arranges audio, film and video *footage* into identifiable, ready-to-use thematic hierarchies for efficient use in post-production. The reduced set of pre-conceptualized themes in this EPK will eventually dominate the subsequent hour-long Fox making-of "documentary" as well. Gillian Anderson, David Duchovny, and Chris Carter, for example, all echo on camera how the film will simultaneously "reward" the hard-core fan, even as it introduces newcomers to the *X-Files* (1993–2002) world. In clichéd making-of fashion, director Rob Bowman underscores the physical hardships of working long hours alternating between "freezing sound-stages" and "106-degree desert heat" where the "crew was dropping like flies." EPK statements about the many physical hardships that Duchovny and Anderson faced on the set and in stunts, prefigures the broadcast making-of's tired (and almost always false) assertion "that the stars did many of their own stunts." Martin Landau at one point sketches out the narrative arc of the film ("Mulder doesn't believe him; he begins to believe him; he finally believes him; then he doesn't believe him, again"), along with the back-story needed to understand the two-hour plot. A close comparison of the Fox Studio EPK, the Fox broadcast making-of, and the subsequent Fox DVD shows how tightly contemporary multimedia marketing campaigns are woven into productions. EPKs merit attention because they integrate and encode—in tight, clustered moving image artifacts—a studio or network's preemptive theoretical conception of each film and series. These encodings quickly find their way into other formats as well, like making-ofs.

MAKING-OFS (THE NEGOTIATED VERSION AND PROTOTYPE)

One behind-the-scenes programming genre—the making-of—is an obligatory part of almost all feature film and television development and marketing initiatives today. Whereas behind-the-scenes documentaries reflect topically on production knowledge, lives, and behavior off-camera, making-ofs usually document a specific film/television production from start to finish.[5] Some, like HBO/Miramax's *Project Greenlight* (2001) and Dreamworks' *On The Lot* (2007) are programmed for viewers in weekly primetime installments intended as "appointment television." Still others, like Pixar's, Dreamworks, or LucasFilm's making-ofs about each studio's feature film releases, provide niche-appropriate content for cable networks like The Sci-Fi Channel, Fox Movie Channel, HBO, or Tech-TV. As a dominant variant of the "bonus-track," making-ofs are also prerequisite, significantly budgeted categories in DVD production. Making-ofs, though, are not simply relegated to niche cable nets or DVDs as background material. The genre is also regularly programmed as "specials" on network television as well.

Fox's making-of, *X-Files: The Movie*, for example, hyped itself as important, breaking, movie news, but also displayed an acute level of industrial incestuousness and self-dealing. Broadcast June 15, 1998, *X-Files: The Movie*, posed as a making-of about the feature film *The X-Files* which was scheduled to premiere worldwide a few days later. Yet the actual contents of the hour-long special proved that it was far more. The special included extensive footage of production sets, studios, stunts, problems, and inter-actions between cast and crew, along with repetitive footage of the stars running, falling, reacting, and emoting. Intercut throughout this documen-tary field footage are interviews with all of the chief figures on the cre-ative team: executive producer Chris Carter, stars Gillian Anderson and David Duchovny, director Rob Bowman, writer and co-executive producer Frank Spotnitz and others. Like most making-ofs, this one betrays a sense of its own self-importance. Using the movie to help re-launch his aging, stalled career, on-camera host Martin Landau somberly asks "big" intel-lectual questions after ad breaks at the start of each segment of the special ("What *are* the basic human fears that audiences relate to in the *X-Files*?"). The special then loads up the hour with an extensive list of "scientific" and quasi-scientific experts to explain altered state phenomenon. Dr. Peter Panzarino, "Chairman of Psychiatry at Cedar-Sinai" hospital explains the basis for the show: "If you look at the history of paranoid psychopathology, you will find the newest technological advances to be a part of paranoia." "Psychotherapist" Steven Zucker describes how we are "alienated from ourselves," then explains the existence of "aliens within us," and public-intellectuals and authors Whitley Streiber and Matt Roush weigh in on the universal importance of the *X-File* themes to humanity. Literary "cyber-punk" patriarch William Gibson defines paranoia and shares the series' anxiety when he asserts: "What we are worried about now, is that we are becoming post-human. We are the aliens." This posture of intellectualism is answered by a long list of pop culture celebrities who appear on camera "because they love the show," including: Cher, Melissa Etheridge, NHL hockey star Luc Robataille, rock star Dave Grohl of the Foo-Fighters, LA Doger first-basemen Eric Karros, and many others. Best-selling novelist Stephen King sums up the sentiments of the group on camera: "I loved the show so much, I got in touch with *them*." Another segment includes a clip montage of dubbed foreign language versions of the film (in Spanish, Japa-nese, French, German) along with actor interviews describing the *X-Files* as a cult hit (in England and Milan).

Apparently, the entire world somehow yearns for the *X-Files* phenom-enon and waits desperately for the pending release of the feature film. Yet the special's over-earnest efforts to discuss many important off-screen issues ultimately raises suspicions that this making-of is neither fully about the film being made, nor about the intellectual ideas and social themes that inform the show. Landau states, "I can offer this exclusive clip" and then shows a leaked movie scene days before the public will "get" to see it on the big screen. Yet the making-of ends up being more about the television series and *X-Files* franchise as a whole rather than a singular cinema event. Numerous interviewees talk about information from the television series that you will either know—or not need to know—to appreciate the film.

Practitioners theorize extensively about how this film production experience compares to their years of work on the *X-Files* TV production. Commercial breaks insert Fox network promos previewing upcoming episodes of the current season's *X-Files* television series, along with local affiliate promos for *Fox News* (1987–ongoing) at 10 p.m. that promised: "secrets revealed about the *X-Files* . . . at 10." The special also includes a segment (now obligatory in making-ofs) about how the film's special effects were created.

But the segment on the film's music betrayed a much broader set of institutional forces at work in the special. The musical score making-of segment celebrates lone-synthesizer/composer Mark Snow crossing-over to conduct an 85-piece orchestra as it greatly expands and heightens the *X-Files: The Movie* sound "experience." The segment, however, also extensively describes the *X-Files* CD—which will be simultaneously released with the movie and includes "original interpretations" of the *X-Files* theme music by dozens of famous rock bands and musicians: Tonic, Foo-Fighters, Better Than Ezra, X, Ray Manzarek of the Doors, Bjork, and Sting, among others. By the end of the hour making-of broadcast, it is clear that well over half of the international stars who appeared as "fans of the show" are also *profit participants* in the multi-media release of *X-Files: The Movie* or in the franchise as a whole. Most of the effusive rock-star interviews were filmed when the musicians simply showed up to record their tracks for the *X-Files* CD. The making-of TV special also includes an embedded *music video making-of* produced for cable for one of the *X-Files* songs, and a full performance "from England" of Sting's performance-based music video. Even the intellects behind the franchise—William Gibson and Stephen King—doubly function not just as devoted fans but as screenwriters for episodes of the *X-Files* as well (although this admission of "commercial interest" is not disclosed to viewers). *The X-Files: The Movie* making-of, therefore, functioned as a full-blown multimedia exercise in cross-promotion. The film's release and making-of were less about film than they were about television, music, and the financial fortunes of the *X-Files* franchise as a whole.

DVDS AND BONUS TRACKS (THE DISCIPLINED VARIANT)

While considerable trade and popular attention is paid to online, user-generated interactivity, the DVD may emerge as a more popular, and far less radical, form of digital convergence. The film and television industries in Hollywood certainly share this view. The DVD, after all, fits within the consumer electronic product model of technical convergence favored by home entertainment manufacturers and studios without broadcast or cable networks, like Sony. Unlike amorphous Newscorp/MySpace, Google/YouTube, DEN and WebTV convergence schemes (which seek to harness the work of fans through online crowd-sourcing to expand interactive multimedia entertainment on the World Wide Web), the DVD exists on a more identifiable and ostensibly locatable scale. Since DVDs are hand-holdable and not networked as part of the World Wide Web, they follow the more humble tradition of home video (VHS) and consumer audio (the CD and Walkman). In fact, whereas new media apologists and cyber-prophets frequently theorized online experience and culture in futuristic, utopian, and metaphysical terms, the DVD can easily be theorized within the logic of a fairly traditional Hollywood studio distribution window. No need for McLuhan, Negroponte, or Virilio here. Fox set the standard for its DVDs in the Hollywood studio paradigm, and Blockbuster updated this for the age of home video. The major studios/networks persistently strategize DVDs within the decades-old paradigm of motion-picture distribution. They now also strategize its release in terms of merchandising and "shelf-space" at its key retailers, like Wal-Mart. Yet despite this traditional studio distribution practice and new discount retailing scheme, the DVD has also stimulated new forms of theorizing and critical reflexivity by those same studios/ networks. In addition to providing a manageable distribution window, that is, DVDs epitomize striking innovations in the ways that industry re-presents itself to viewers and the ways audiences engage Hollywood's self-representations as part of viral marketing.

One of the DVD's chief innovations has been its ability to provide a cultural interface in which critical discourses in making-ofs, bonus tracks, and director's commentary (aesthetic analysis, knowledge about production technologies, working methods, and behind-the-scenes infor-mation) can be directly discussed and negotiated with audiences and users without the burden of critical/cultural middlemen. Some produc-tion knowledge has always percolated up through studio/network mar-keting and promotions for almost a century. Yet studios have aimed such knowledge mostly at cultural intermediaries, handlers, and gatekeepers (trade editors, distributors, exhibitors, theater owners, journalists, fan publications, reviewers, critics). These sanctioned intermediaries would then "translate" and sometimes "dumb-down" the critical and produc-tion knowledge from publicists for the audience and lay reader. As the preceding section of this chapter indicated, the EPK evolved through this historical process as a way to preemptively embed a rich mix of criti-cal analysis and on-screen theorizing through cultural intermediaries (through production bios, making-ofs, behind-the-scenes looks, director interviews, and the like). DVDs continue this preemptive analysis but do so by making secondary promotional material a direct part of the viewers primary onscreen experience. In many ways, therefore, DVDs are merely redirected and "repurposed" EPKs. The DVD "bonus tracks" and "fea-turettes" that home viewers click on are almost exactly like the features on BetacamSP EPKs disseminated en masse to press and broadcasters in the 1980s and 1990s. As a result, the change in technical format, from analog video (on the EPK) to digital video (on the DVD) is rather inconsequential, whereas the viewing context has changed considerably.

From the perspective of its prototypes, DVDs now aim marketing directly at the viewer/buyer, not at an intermediate cultural handler who stands in for and negotiates or processes marketing information for the viewer. Of far greater consequence than technical change has been the gradual elimination of key cultural middlemen from the traditional equation: the editors, reviewers, and journalists in the trade and popular press who used to handle and interpret via EPKs. Endless pages have been published about how the internet and digital will "cut out" the old media gatekeepers so that individual Web surfers at home can access any information at any time they want. What no cyber visionary seems to address, however, is that while the old studios and networks may have lost control in the face of a vast, new "digital democracy," the same studios and networks have figured out ways to create digital and new media content that can be "managed" on (their own) more traditional terms. The DVD serves just such a *management-of-navigation* function, and it does so in four ways. First, although the online user ostensibly cuts out the network gatekeepers, those same gatekeepers cut out the traditional "representatives and advocates" of the mass audience through the DVD—the critical and popular press. This "short-cut" to the viewer aligns cleanly with the increasingly popular tactic of releasing lowbrow features directly to theaters without preview screenings for critics. Disregarding the popular critical press in these ways ostensibly allows studios/networks to talk "directly" with the audience about artistry, quality, and cultural significance. Second, studio/networks now circumvent the "dumbing-down" role of the popular press, and incorporate their critical activities *within* the industry's producing organizations proper. Reviewers and critics become superfluous in this scheme, for the DVD system pre-authors and provides critical analysis as primary onscreen content. The resulting "dumbing-up" rewards distinction in viewers who fancy themselves discriminating, culturally knowledgeable, relatively sophisticated fans.

Third, the DVD "hardens" the entertainment experience into a saleable consumer product. This is no small accomplishment, since the first decade of online entertainment proved to be an unpredictable and extremely difficult world from which to economically harvest viewer dollars and distribution profits. Fourth, and finally, the DVD greatly tamed and constrained the original god of the cyber-visionaries: "interactivity." Interactive DVDs today provide menus to choose from, but little else, even compared to fairly rudimentary websites, which at least allow for fan interactions, bulletin boards, contests, feedback, and the like. At least with these greatly controlled online old media websites, users were always only one click away from going somewhere else, and thus creating their own "unruly" migration or "flow" across the Web. In addition, even though television (in particular) has usually posed as an entertainment provider, the medium has always also been about merchandizing, with ads, sponsorships, and product placement encouraging viewers to buy other consumer products. Now, however, the onscreen DVD experience *is* the primary consumer product. No sleight-of-hand (narrative experiences masking an underlying advertising and merchandising function) is even needed. In effect, the DVD rewards consumer impulse and the possibilities of cultural gratification and distinction through a package of "featurettes" and bonus-tracks that are also hold-able and collectible.

The "bonus tracks" alone on DVDs are worth considering as a pervasive critical industrial preoccupation. Bonus tracks are sometimes deployed as part of two antithetical strategies. Some DVDs, first of all, are loaded with bonuses. The *Lord of the Rings: The Fellowship of the Ring (LOTR)* DVD (2001[2002]), for example, includes 23 bonuses: the film-related music video "May it Be" by Enya; a preview of the video game "The Two Towers" by Electronic Arts; a "behind the scenes preview of the yet-to-be released second installment of the trilogy (*LOTR: The Two Towers* [2002]); a short preview of the special DVD extended version of the film; 15 featurettes of interviews with cast members, as well as documentary explorations of the geography of Tolkien's "Middle-Earth" (which were repurposed from the franchise website www.lordoftherings. net); three longer documentaries about the secrets "behind" the production taken from other sources (The Sci-Fi Channel, the FBC Network, and "in-store" documentaries distributed originally to bookstores by Houghton Mifflin); and special "live" online content available to DVD users on set dates. By contrast, other DVDs have almost no bonuses, like Quentin Tarantino's initial *Kill Bill-Vol.1* (2003[2004])—though Miramax has the resources to jam its other DVDs with *LOTR*-quantity and -quality featurettes. Business logic drives both of these antithetical DVD strategies. The bonus overload in *LOTR*, for example, fits both the "total merchandizing" requirement of contemporary blockbuster films and the goal of "building" a comprehensive fan community capable of growing over the life of the franchise's three features. Miramax's sparse bonus menu strategy, by contrast, cultivates an existing Tarantino fan-base niche in a different way. As an art-house film, Miramax forces Tarantino's junkie-like fans to buy an initial stripped-down version, in order to subsequently sell them a second and (possibly third) extended version as well. This is the approach mastered by LucasFilms for the *Star Wars* franchise, where "special" reiterations of the same films will appear endlessly, for purchase by the same buyers. Many films, by contrast, do not have the Tarantino-Miramax luxury of a committed, pre-existing niche fan-base and the guaranteed first and second DVD sales that usually come with it. Instead, less stellar efforts load up even box-office duds with extensive bonus materials, based on the sometimes desperate assumption that more icing makes a better DVD cake.

A brief survey of 45 DVDs released in 2002–2004 shows the wide-ranging ways that bonus tracks function institutionally and industrially, even as they update and deploy the viral marketing tactics of EPKs in DVD form. DVDs like *The Stepford Wives* (2004[2004]), *Hollywood Homicide* (2003[2003]), *Pinnochio* (2002[2003]) and direct-to-video animated films like *Batman: The Mystery of Batwoman* (2003), all feature bonus tracks that address the first industrial function: to *"resuscitate"* box-office duds and financial failures. Sometimes this resuscitation works, as when the martial arts film *Jing Wu Men/Chinese Connection* (1972[2002]) was re-dubbed with contemporary slang and hip-hop music to update it for a new market and generation; or when Roger Ebert provided advocacy and a film appreciation lecture for the European film *Dekalog / The Decalogue* (1989[2002]) in order to save the film from relative obscurity in the US. Sometimes, studios will actually savagely ridicule their own failed film in order to "recreate" it as an "intentional" camp or cult classic. Because Director Paul Verhoeven refused to participate in the DVD production, for example, MGM hired writer David Schamer to provide commentary on the critically reviled, disastrous MGM film *Showgirl VIP Limited Edition* (1995[2004]). At one point Schamer mocks: "Showgirls triumphs in that every single person involved in the making of the film is making the worst possible decision at every possible time." On another DVD bonus track, "Heather" (termed an "exotic" dancer) teaches a "10-step lap dance tutorial lesson" for women DVD viewers at home: "You tease him—don't let him touch. . . . Your partner will find it sexy if you spank yourself." MGM works overtime in these bonus tracks to create camp, as well as a "second shift" opportunity (media engaged activities after the "first shift" viewing of the primary text) that allows DVD viewers to emulate the film's onscreen erotic action in their living rooms. In less demeaning ways, many DVDs, like *Predator: The Collector's Edition* (1987, 1990[2004]), *Alien: Quadrilogy* (1979, 1986, 1992, 1997[2003]), *Girl With a Pearl Earring* (2003[2004]) and *CBS Sneak Peak* (a compilation promotional DVD [2004]) shamelessly *"cross-promote"* other entertainment properties (music videos, other films or sequels in the franchise, upcoming network seasons, or other television series on the same network) via their respective bonus tracks. The nature of media conglomeration makes this kind of cross-promotion almost obligatory. While resuscitation and cross-promotion can be understood as rather direct attempts to add economic value to films or series at the DVD stage, two other broad groups of bonus track functions can be identified in DVD design: first, appeals aimed at canonizing films or series, and second, appeals aimed at direct rhetorical or physical interaction with other parties.

Aesthetic canonizing functions as a DVD industrial strategy which cultivates explicit consciousness of aesthetic distinction by critically analyzing four different issues: control, virtuosity, authenticity and cultural influence. A resilient way to aesthetically elevate a film involves documenting a high degree of *"authorial control"* on a production. *Panic Room* (2002[2002]) and *Russian Ark* (2002[2003]) both dramatize complete directorial control through pre-visualization via exacting storyboard-to-scene comparisons and footage of excessive pre-planning respectively. Other DVDs, like *The Cooler* (2002[2004]) and box sets for *Curb Your Enthusiasm* (2000–2005[2004–2006]), show the importance of the quality-via-control ethos by mocking authorship through disclaimers and disinterest on the part of participants. Meanwhile *Once Upon a time in Mexico* (2003[2004]) showcases the obsessive involvement of zealous director Robert Rodriguez through three different production documentaries made for the same DVD. Another set of DVDs artistically "canonize" films as works of *"intelligence and virtuosity"* by documenting examples of profound quality (via complex analyses of cinematography and sound design in *The Godfather* [1972{2004}]); profound intellect (via director interviews by figures like Salman Rushdie and footage of manic behavior in *Lost in La Mancha* [2002{2003}]); and artistic genius (via a composite reel of the "early" music videos that prefigured the eventual accomplishment of feature directors in *The Work of Directors Spike Jonze, Chris Cunningham, Michael Gondry Box Set* [2004]). A slightly different means of canonization comes when bonus tracks seek to establish the *"cultural influence,"* or significance of a film or series. Some DVDs do this via historical juxtaposition (the 1964 anti-Nuke "Daisy Girl" ad in *Fog of War* [2003{2004}], and the montage of interview footage with Kennedy and Goldwater in the *Jack Paar Collection* [1962 {2004}]). Others simply reappropriate media coverage by other organizations as forms of self-proof (the Sundance channel documentary in *Girl With A Pearl Earring* and the E! Channel promotional teasers in the *Anna Nicole Show* [2002–2004{2003}]). These examples use juxtaposition to establish cultural significance, but other DVDs canonize themselves by underscoring *"legacy and authenticity"* in more direct ways. *Beyond Borders* (2003[2004]) cites UN Secretary Kofe Annan's endorsement of authenticity in the film to tame its melodrama. This approach emulates the DVD-prefiguring design of various Criterion Collection Laser Discs, like *Bram Stoker's Dracula* (1992, which was subsequently re-released on DVD by Sony Home Entertainment [2007])[6]. Both versions parade Coppola's memorabilia and photos for production design to highlight its substance and origins. And *The Dick Van Dyke Show* (1961–1966[2003]) provides an orgy of retrospection alongside the unearthing of the "lost" failed series pilot, all as evidence of cultural standing and America's heritage. Finally, one of the now-standard clichés of bonus track and making-of stories is the *"against-all-odds"* mythology. *Searching for Paradise* (2002[2003]) shows early and rough glimpses of scenes from the indie film via "workshops" at the Sundance Institute four years before the production had the resources to commence; *Finding Nemo* (2003[2003]) includes the hackneyed trope of cadres of dedicated technicians struggling to overcome a mountain of detail through human artistry and dedication; while low-budget *Dopamine* (2003[2004]) documents the frantic pace of production necessitated by an abrupt loss-of-funding during the shoot. For centuries, the trope of the suffering artist, persisting against all odds, has been a staple part of aesthetic canonizing. Trade EPKs and now DVDs employ the mythology now for profitable ends.

A final set of institutional appeals and functions depend less on the traditional thematic motifs described in the preceding paragraph, than on direct address, interaction, or contestation between the producers of the DVD and other parties. For example, some DVD bonus tracks serve as overt *"rebuttals"* against detractors or adversaries of the production. Yanked from the broadcast by CBS because of right-wing political pressures, then dumped onto Showtime, *The Reagans* (2003[2004]) restores censored scenes and overt anti-right politic speech on its DVD in a slap back at Viacom and its attackers. Michael Moore includes a defensive, 15-minute speech justifying his anti-Bush Oscar speech on the *Bowling for Columbine* (2002[2003]) DVD. The *Magdalene Sisters* (2002[2004]) includes a "serious" history of asylums and interviews with actual abuse victims to "prove" its case against critics. *Capturing the Friedman's* (2003[2004]) defensively fires back at skeptics by including two hours of never before seen "evidence" about the crime, while the star of *King of Queens* (1998-ongoing[2004-ongoing]) mocks NBC for rejecting the show as "stupid" before it became a hit on CBS. Actually getting a film or television production to the screen is sometimes an arduous and warlike task, and fall-out from this contention regularly seeps via bonus tracks like these into public consciousness. A less strident form of direct interaction comes in the form of DVD features that allow users an experience in *"virtual filmmaking."* *Men in Black* (1997[2002]), like the *Bram Stoker's Dracula* laser disc provides viewers with an interactive editing workshop which allows them to choose alternate takes or shots of scenes in the film. This essentially allows the viewer to not only imagine "cutting" his or her own film version but to over-identify and masquerade as a filmmaker as well. Interactive or virtual filmmaking is one of the few actual DVD functions that fits the emancipatory rhetoric that once dominated discussions and theories of new media. Many more bonus tracks serve to exploit fan relationships by offering featurettes that function as "fan barter." Such tracks usually include extensive background information and minutiae about the series. *The Godfather DVD Collection* (2001) includes a detailed "Corleone Family Tree" and timeline for the entire franchise. *Buffy the Vampire Slayer* (1997–2003) Season Five, DVD box set (2001) includes an extended examination of non-supernatural death on the series. *The X-Files* ninth season DVD box set (2002), includes two documentaries on the series made six-seven years earlier; and *Final*

Destination 2 (2003[2003]) includes "Pop-Up Video" screens that give DVD users links detailing "secrets" behind the production. All of these examples overload the viewer-user with extensive detail that would not normally be available at the time of the viewing. In effect, these functions directly address an implied fan base capable of constructing a narratological timeline over the nine years of the *X-Files* series, or the three installments of *The Godfather* (1972, 1974, 1990). Such DVDs seek to animate fan interaction by performing minute details that may or may not be known widely. Finally, some DVDs have what might be termed "unruly bonuses," or featurettes that directly exacerbate relations or tensions operative on the industrial side of the DVD equation. The best example of this is probably the *Three Kings* (1999[2000 re-release]), whose original 33-minute anti-war bonus documentary entitled *Soldiers' Pay* (2004) was cut from the original DVD by Warner due to political pressure. Director David Russell went on to screen and broadcast the documentary elsewhere, and the negative publicity that erupted around Warner's decision to censor was disruptive in ways that Warner Bros. had not wanted.[7]

Interestingly, DVDs of television series (not just films) are among the hottest and most lucrative areas of the home entertainment industry. This is somewhat surprising, because unlike film, old television series are always available (somewhere) in broadcast or cable syndication. This suggests, in part, that DVDs are bought not to screen content that is unavailable otherwise, but rather as collectibles capable of memorializing some earlier, personal film/TV experience in the life of the viewer/user. Unexceptional and mostly forgotten shows like 1978's *Battlestar Galactica* (2004) almost immediately sold 150,000 copies at $110 each for Universal, while limited-run 1980s series like *Sledgehammer* (1986–1988[2004]) have sold 100,000 copies (Taylor 2004: E1, E2). With 24 and 41 episodes respectively, neither show was around long enough to even go into broadcast syndication. The pervasiveness of DVD hits made from old, failed TV shows suggests that mediated experiences may serve as popular ways to mark one's individual biographies. Even more recent financial failures, like the critically lauded *Boomtown* (2002–2003[2004]) on NBC and *Arrested Development* (2003–2006[2004–2006]) on Fox, have rushed the DVD component of each series to the market after only one full season. Both of these latter efforts (the first unsuccessful in earning broadcast renewal, the second successful) aimed to keep a struggling series alive and profitable. In these two recent series, fan communities are solicited, created, rewarded, and addressed in "real-time" via DVD. In both historical contexts—shows lost in the archives that are reborn as DVD hits (like *Battlestar* and *Sledgehammer*) and current shows that are rescued and sustained by DVDs (*Boomtown* and *Arrested Development*)—the interactive DVD and its bonus tracks have proven to be strategic ways that producers can reverse their fortunes.

The DVD offers some interesting permutations for flow and second shift theories.[8] On the one hand DVDs are inert consumer artifacts that seem to exist as very bounded experiences when compared to online entertainment sites. That is, DVDs can be viewed as first-shift experiences, since interactivity and navigation are severely limited. On the other hand, the wild success of "old" TV shows as DVD hits suggests that DVDs are used differently than other forms of home video or first-shift media. Research by Universal Home Video shows that 85 per cent of TV-on-DVD buyers have already seen the shows that they buy, which contrasts dramatically with film-on-DVD buyers of whom only 45 per cent have usually seen the film they are buying on DVD (Taylor, 2004, E1, E2). Most TV-on-DVDs are purchased to allow for repeated viewings and opportunities to think through the complicated fictional worlds of multi-year television series that are narratively far more massive than a mere two-hour film. In these ways, even the DVD employs a second-shift tactic, since DVD developers now build the potentially endless "re-viewing" of episodes and bonus tracks into the very function and logic of the DVD format. From the audience side of the equation, by comparison, DVDs allow new relationships with film and television, first, as collectibles, and second, as ways to "memorialize" ones personal history. New activities and relationships like these suggest that scholars would do well to emphasize not just user-generated content, but the ways industry generates user activities as well.

CONCLUSION

Mainstream television, unlike the "legitimate" modern arts, tends to take reflexivity, intertextuality, and deconstruction to the bank in very visible ways. Unlike the exceptional cultural status that critics and theorists have granted reflexivity in cinema, "radical" stylistic strategies in television, and now the DVD, have typically represented dominant industrial tendencies (marketing, promotion, ancillary distribution, branding).[9] As such, these strategies can be understood as rather direct expressions of capitalist economic and industrial practices as well. That is, television and DVD reflexivity are not merely the result of postmodernism, "late capitalism" or the de-centered subject. Instead, radical stylistic methods—like those found nightly on show-biz reports, making-ofs, and DVD bonus tracks and featurettes—have set-up, referenced, or fractured commercial television programs in clockwork-like fashion for decades as cross-promotion and marketing. The artifacts and practices studied in this chapter—which migrate from television and cross multimedia platforms in the *X-Files* franchise—show just how extensive and complicated the cultural reach of even one EPK can be in the multi-media landscape. EPKs function virally, like migrating semiotic cluster-bombs, since they essentially provide user-friendly spin-fodder that can be cut, copied, re-cut, customized and forwarded in potentially endless ways. Hollywood used EPKs to do this long before "mashers" did this on YouTube. A schematic map of the migration of spin-fodder that made up the *X-Files: The Movie* marketing campaign would go something like this:[10]

Transmedia viral marketing: mutating critical analysis and industrial reflexivity as business plans

Audience Model	Economic Model	Model of Interactivity
1.) DEEP VERSION (EPK)		
critics as surrogate viewers	affiliation-driven, user-friendly	most-open, interactive
pre-scripted analysis	soft-sell, risk-aversion	most-customizable
2.) NEGOTIATED VERSION (Broadcast Making-of)		
migratory viewer flow	conglomerate repurposing	multi-tasking
manufactured news/event	hard-sell, risk mitigation	herding/push-tactics
3.) STUNTED VERSION (Theatrical Film)		
self-segregated viewers	loss-leader, trailer, preview	textual activity
1st-shift management	commercial agit-prop	gazing, hallucination
4.) VALUE-ADDED VERSION (Website)		
unruly/ stealth viewers	ancillary promotions	rhizomatic navigation
2nd-shift management	soft-sell, branding	grazing, pull-tactics
5.) DISCIPLINED VERSION (DVD)		
viewers as quasi-critics	rationalized, merchandizing	locked-down interactivity
viewers faux-gatekeepers	risk management	least open, revenue harvesting

Successful film/television content development today means setting in motion pre-scripted chunks of critical analysis (production backstory), and facilitating their migration and mutation across as many different multi-media platforms as possible. Ironically the original genetic code built into the EPK's marketing virus (the first format) poses as the most open, most customizable of the four media mutations analyzed here. Reviewers, editors, and critics can ostensibly copy, rearrange, and individuate raw and rough-edited footage on these reels in order to recast the material as part of their uniquely "original" story. The second and fourth intermediate formats (the broadcast making-of and the website tie-in) morph in complexity, but take as their common goals the management of viewer migration. When producer Chris Carter states in the broadcast making-of: "At the end of five years, we wanted a big [film] event to celebrate and reward the [television] fans," he is actually spiking interest and boosting the value of the franchise in ancillary electronic media (television syndication, home video, DVD, music CDs and merchandise). This "negotiated version" of the marketing virus in broadcast mitigates economic risk via hard-sell methods: manufacturing news events ("a motion picture event"), herding viewer flow, repurposing content, and using programming tactics to "push" content at the inattentive, multi-tasking viewer at home.

The other intermediary digital form, the "value-added" online website, necessarily deploys softer-sell methods than the broadcast making-of: ancillary marketing, third-party affiliations and promotions, branding, and "pull-tactics" to more loosely orient the unpredictable rhizomatic navigations of users in the second-shift (when viewers leave the "off-line" first-shifts of film/television for flipside interactions in "online" second-shift forms). These online variants of the marketing virus, by contrast to the DVD, typically only add value to the existing brand, rather than harvest revenue, since websites seldom return enough revenue to pay for their development and maintenance. The *X-Files: The Movie* making-of and DVD examined in this chapter both repeat the same boast: "a certain amount of secrecy was involved . . . scripts were printed on colored pages so they couldn't be copied . . . disinformation was leaked all year long." This disclosure by an insider underscores how the studio used websites as calculated security counter-measures to playfully interact with (and thus brand) unruly fans on the franchise's websites.[11] Finally, the idealized end-state of the viral migration/mutation is the DVD and the target market it represents: the DVD fan. The DVD is the most disciplined and least open of any of the four main bodies that give life support to the virus. The DVD's interactivity is locked down, content migration is brought to a material conclusion, and revenue is harvested via the new economy of scale that mass merchandizing and Wal-Mart bring. Even though we marvel at all of the quasi-critical and theoretical functions that DVDs now embody, we must recognize that these film-studies activities are also among the most effective forms of consumer marketing available.

The practices examined here—how the EPK, television making-ofs, and viral marketing prefigure DVDs as prototypes—should change the way we think about media's "center-periphery" relations. But not just in the ways that Cover argues. Yes, DVD use by fans (repeated viewing, collecting, exchanging, ritualizing) adds a peer-to-peer dimension that scholars must account for, and makes the consumer's periphery far more important than it once was when "broadcasting" ruled media studies questions. I would argue, however, that while the model of national broadcasting as a center may have faded in importance, the sites of high-production value film and television—the studios that produce quality television and feature films—have actually increased the importance of studio brands as centers of media culture. Online unruliness and new forms of audience migration and flow may have eclipsed the centrality that NBC, CBS, BBC, ARD, and RAI may once have had. But the explosive popularization of the DVD has made audience interactions with the long-time corporate partners of those same centers—Paramount, Fox, Columbia, Universal, Disney—more important than ever. DVD fan activities represent ideal conditions within which the studios can stimulate the kind of loyal crowd-sourcing that is the key to viral marketing. The new, revived entertainment brands succeed precisely to the extent they can develop decentralized psychological and affective relations within the ubiquitous new worlds on the home entertainment peripheries. In effect, the profitable, stealthy collusion between studio/publicist-and-reviewer/gatekeeper in the era of the EPK has morphed into the stealthy, viral collusion between the studio/marketers-and-fans/users in the era of the DVD. In this way, the studios have learned their lessons well. After all, the DVD may well represent the final collapse of significant distinctions between marketing and onscreen entertainment. Such a conflation represents an ideal "endgame" for today's media conglomerates.

NOTES

1. See *Wayne's World 2*, "Electronic Press Kit," for the feature film, Paramount Pictures, 1992. UCLA Film and Television Archives, inventory number VA-20047M.
2. See *Roseanne*: "Electronic Press Kit," for primetime series, Fall 1992, 36:15 min., UCLA Film and Television Archives, inventory number 200043t.
3. After the scripted question "How are you similar to your character, and how are you different?" Roseanne replies: "She is part of me, but she's not all of me . . . she's a character of mine, but not that far from me."
4. Various critics of the Bush administration decried the incestuous relations between the Whitehouse and Fox News, where a series of daily "bulleted points" were almost immediately translated into editorial policy by the Fox News conglomerate. See especially the documentary feature film *Outfoxed* (2004[2004]) for an account of this relationship.
5. Some making-ofs offer freestanding theatrical experiences without the obvious taint of cross-promotion, like Chris Marker's film *AK* (1986) about legendary Japanese director Akira Kurosawa; or Les Blank's *Burden of Dreams* (1982) about legendary German director Werner Herzog.
6. The Criterion Collection Laser Disc version of Coppola's 1992 feature film is indexed as "spine number 183." The title is no longer available from Criterion, but was released by Sony Home Entertainment as both a DVD and Blu-Ray Disc in October 2007.
7. The documentary short, originally planned as a DVD bonus track by Warner Bros., was subsequently released on DVD by itself by the studio Cinema Libre.

8. For a discussion of "second shift" theory in the age of new media (how studios and networks "program" viewers' time outside of the primary onscreen entertainment experience through multimedia and repurposing), see Caldwell 2003.
9. Since film is fast approaching the sensory and cognitive experience of television (in technology, multiplexing, narrowcasting, booking, advertising, home video, DVD design and viewing scale), cinema theorists would do well to consider the history of both television and marketing not just as precursors to the DVD, but as possible prototypes for the contemporary cinematic experience as well.
10. This model and table of "Viral Marketing" is elaborated in my forthcoming book (Caldwell 2008).
11. The actors who narrate and re-narrate the same "making-of" (Mitch Pileggi and Martin Landau) both mouth these same lines (the latter in the broadcast making-of, the former in the DVD version of the making-of).

BIBLIOGRAPHY

Caldwell, J. (2003) "Second Shift Aesthetics: Programming, Interactivity and User Flows," in A. Everett and J.T. Caldwell (eds) *New media: theories and practices of digitextuality*, New York: Routledge: 127–144.

———. (2008) *Production Culture: industrial reflexivity and critical practice in film/television*, Durham, NC: Duke University Press.

Cover, R. (2005) "DVD Time: Temporality, Audience Engagement, and the New TV Culture of Digital Video," *Media International Australia*, 117: 137–147.

Jenkins, H. (2006) *Convergence Culture*, New York: NYU Press.

Manovich, L. (2001) *The Language of New Media*, Cambridge, MA: MIT Press.

Miller, T. et al. (2005) *Global Hollywood 2*, London: BFI Press.

Schiller, D. (1999) *Digital Capitalism*, Cambridge, MA: MIT Press.

Taylor, J. (2004, August 16) "Duds Find New Life in a Box," *Los Angeles Times*: E1, E12.

Wild, D. (1999) *The Showrunner,* New York: Harper Collins.

9 The Last Format War
Launching the High-Definition DVD

William Boddy

By the end of 2007, many observers of the US consumer electronics industry were showing signs of fatigue with what already felt like an endless marketing war around competing formats for the high definition heir to the wildly successful DVD. As early as 2002, when Toshiba pitched an abortive red-laser system against a new generation blue-laser player supported by Sony, one financial analyst complained that "the DVD format battle is horrible. It will continue until I die" (Gartner Dataquest analyst Mary Craig quoted in Ross 2002: C2). The subsequent competition between Toshiba's HD-DVD and Sony's Blu-ray formats for high-definition optical discs, battling over what Microsoft founder Bill Gates has called "the last physical format there will ever be," can illuminate the complex mix of players, economic calculation, and consumer desire which governs the process of innovation in the consumer electronics industry (Sethi 2005).

Unpacking the fierce public disputes and shifting alliances of advocates of the rival technological platforms for high-definition DVDs must include an appreciation of the challenges facing the contemporary Hollywood film industry, the shifting profiles of the traditional television set, the personal computer, and video game system, and the imponderable judgments of consumers regarding issues of image quality, interactivity, and the appeal of acquiring and collecting moving image texts in the form of physical artifacts. The emerging scholarly literature on the ongoing format war and the situation of the contemporary moving image industries, notably work by Robert Alan Brookey (2007) and Paul McDonald (2007), respectively, has helpfully set up the stakes in the battle between rival high-definition DVD formats. Prospects for the eventual success of either the HD-DVD or Blu-ray formats, as well as for the viability of the entire optical storage product category, are linked to a dizzying array of factors within and beyond the consumer electronics industry, including the diffusion of HDTV receivers and broadband internet access, the market primacy of competing game systems, the allegiances of the porn industry, and the licensing commitments of the Hollywood studios. The cacophony of divergent self-interests and competing claims of consumer satisfaction, which have marked a tortured transition to the high-definition DVD, should underscore for media scholars the radical non-autonomy of technological innovation in the media industry. In the following, I detail the competing factors that position the battle between HD-DVD and Blu-ray as simultaneously both the next generation DVD standard, as well as the "last format war" in physical media. In so doing, I highlight how the battle over the high-definition DVD questions the seemingly inexorable drive towards digitalization and de-materialization in the media industries.

LAUNCHING THE HIGH-DEFINITION DVD

Among the plethora of new digital media technologies marketed to US households in the 1990s—from laserdiscs and D-VHS tapes to digital satellite systems, high-definition television sets, Web-TV devices, digital video recorders, and home media servers—the DVD stands as the consumer electronics industry's conspicuous success story. In the closing six months of 1997, the year of its commercial release, twenty manufacturers were selling DVD players (some for as little as $500) and consumers purchased 5.5 million discs, and by 2007, DVD players could be found in 80 per cent of US homes (Koseluk 2007: 1). The DVD's rapid success reflected its duel paths into the home, via the platforms of both the personal computer and the television set. Indeed, one journalist argued in 1998 that "the real engine that will drive the DVD revolution is the use of DVD drives in computers," noting the prevailing industry expectations that PC-based DVD drives would far exceed DVD player sales that year and that over half of all desktop computers sold by year's end would ship with a DVD drive (Heiss 1998). The DVD's duel status across the two devices, each associated with distinct viewing protocols and cultural positions, presented unique challenges and opportunities for hardware and software firms promoting the DVD. The marketing of the first generation of DVD devices, capable of playback only of standard-definition video content, presented the new device as a technologically-enhanced and more convenient way to deliver Hollywood filmmaking to the home, replacing the dominant application of the traditional VCR, then at saturation levels in the domestic market.[1]

In many ways, the marketing of the DVD was made easier by its essentially conservative nature in regard to prevailing models of consumer behavior and industry economics. Contrary to other contemporaneous domestic digital devices, including Microsoft's Web-TV, the integrated TV-PC appliance, the digital video recorder, and the home media server, whose novel functions proved both difficult to encapsulate in brief marketing messages and potentially disruptive to traditional viewing and industry economic practices, the DVD was largely promoted on the promise of a more sensually-engaging and convenient delivery vehicle for traditional Hollywood products. While the success of the DVD, along with the concurrent marketing of home theatre audio systems and large-screen TV sets, undoubtedly introduced new viewing protocols, architectural imperatives, and masculine associations of technophilia and connaisseurship into the social practices of domestic television consumption (Klinger 2006), as one industry consultant pointed out in 2000:

> People talk about DVD's fantastic growth rates. . . . But the reality is that VHS created the mold, set the pattern. . . . DVD's fast growth rate is due in part because it's building on what VHS created—ownership of home video. In the early days [of VHS], a player cost $1000 and tapes cost $60. . . . With DVD, the player costs dropped to below $250 within a year and the discs cost about $20. You can see the effect that VHS had on how DVD developed. And it would have that same effect on any new physical media
> (Industry Consultant Doug Booth quoted in Daley 2000: 26).

As another industry insider, Ed Havens, observed in 2000: "DVD . . . even though it is new technology and offers unique advantages, is not an entirely new product category. . . . The basic idea is a refinement on what came before, and in its present form, a limited one at that." Havens went on to draw a contrast from "the early days of VHS [as] a revolution" that DVD would merely profit from: "DVD will reap the benefits of the road that VHS pioneered, but will never compare with its history" (SKC Director of Global Media Business, Ed Havens, quoted in Daley 2000: 26). Seen in a broader frame, the DVD represents another instantiation of the transition from analog to digital recording and display devices across a series of consumer artifacts following the launch of the Philips-Sony CD audio format in 1982, from the digital camera and camcorder to digital satellite service (leaving aside for the moment the failed innovations of the digital audio cassette, CD-interactive, the video CD, and the laserdisc). Nevertheless, while early estimates predicted that the DVD would take ten years to achieve the consumer penetration of the VCR, by 1999 the laserdisc was dead, and by the end of 2001, DVD players were outselling VCRs (Block 2002: 25).

The DVD's late-1990s success came at the expense of D-VHS, a tape-based high-definition digital VCR format announced in 1995 and marketed in 1998 by JVC and Thomson/RCA; the $1000 recorder's single application was to time-shift RCA's digital satellite programming, and the February 2002 D-VHS trade announcement promising a scattering of prerecorded films from four Hollywood studios for the high-definition digital tape format was seen by some in the industry as the provocation for the first public announcement from the Blu-ray consortium, which was staged despite the absence of a Blu-ray product or even prototype at that point (Frankel 2002: 4). Notably absent from the list of Hollywood studios supporting D-VHS were Warner Bros. and Columbia TriStar (which was owned by Sony); according to press accounts at the time, Warner Bros.

was part of a group of six companies which received DVD royalties of 7.5 cents a disc (a Sony, Philips, and Pioneer patent pool divided royalties of 5 cents a disc) (Prange and Hunt 2002: 1). Perhaps not coincidently, a Warner Bros. executive denounced the D-VHS format at the time: "Warner is not planning on releasing titles in this format. It doesn't have a chance of success. It doesn't have the kind of functionality of DVD," and the President of Columbia TriStar called D-VHS "a really dumb idea" (quoted in Prange and Hunt 2002: 1). A month later, a trade publication quoted a video duplicator who was a supporter of D-VHS complaining that the format was "not even a blip on the radar screen. There's no push. Customers don't know anything about it. The industry has made itself absolutely clear: it wants DVD and it will have DVD" (Resolution President Bill Schubart, quoted in Block 2002: 25). As *Variety* explained in 2000:

> Though D-VHS has been on the drawing boards for years, hardware makers have been reluctant to introduce it for fear of a backlash from studios and other copyright owners, many of whom are reluctant to arm consumers with digital recording capability. And with DVD taking off—at least in the US—many have doubted the need for another digital format
>
> (Sweeting 2000: 18).

The historically-forgotten misadventures of D-VHS provide a preview of the tangled interests and alliances between consumer electronics manufacturers and the Hollywood studios that have obsessed contemporary observers of the ongoing battles between HD-DVD and Blu-ray partisans for control of the nascent high-definition DVD market. Indeed, the fearful and inconsistent attitudes of the Hollywood studios over the past decade concerning digital recording and storage technologies in the home have been striking. On the one hand, in 2002 industry veteran Bill Mechanic could reflect with equanimity on the long-term impact of the VCR-fueled emerging home film culture upon the business of feature filmmaking:

> From a "creative" plane, video—combined with pay TV—has fostered an interest in film that is more robust than at any time since the advent of TV, which severely cut into moviegoing. What video did was turn the movie business from purely moviegoing to movie-watching, and this watching "rekindled" the consumer interest in film—sometimes the interest taking the form of going to the theaters and sometimes of watching at home
>
> (*Video Business* 2002: 1).

While the film industry's accommodation of the shift from public movie-going to domestic movie-watching since the introduction of the VCR had not been without trauma (MPAA [Motion Picture Association of America] President

Jack Valenti famously told a Congressional committee in 1982 that "the VCR is to the American film producer and the American public as the Boston strangler is to the woman home alone" [Valenti 1982]), by 2007 Paramount Pictures Chair and CEO Brad Grey could explain his studio's move from support of both HD optical disc formats to an 18-month commitment to release exclusively on the HD-DVD format merely as "part of our vision . . . to aggressively extend our movies beyond the theater and deliver the quality and features that appeal to our audience" (Netherby and Ault 2007: 5). Notwithstanding the equanimity of Hollywood CEOs in the face of the declining role of the theatrical box office, anxieties within Hollywood's creative community over the shift from public to domestic reception sites have recently become more heartfelt. Director M. Night Shyamalan told *The Hollywood Reporter* in October 2005 that "if you tell audiences there's no difference between a theatrical experience and a DVD, then that's it, game's over, and that whole art form is going to go away slowly . . . I'm going to stop making movies if they end the cinema experience" (Mehta 2006). Similarly, director James Cameron made a plea at the 2006 Digital Cinema Summit for a 3D digital theatrical exhibition format, rallying his audience: "It can get people off their butts and out of their homes, away from their portable devices and back in the theatres where they belong . . . Who's with me, damnit?" (Williams 2006). While the prospect of the permanent decline of the public cinema as an exhibition venue in favor of the living room HDTV, the computer screen and the mobile phone, has provoked apocalyptic lamentations from some prominent Hollywood directors, the studios themselves are eager to capture the proliferating revenue windows represented by various forms of non-theatrical digital delivery. Indeed, if Hollywood's ever-present anxieties over piracy could somehow be assuaged, the prospect of windfall revenues from new sales of Hollywood product, new and old, in the form of high-definition DVDs, or anything else, would be welcome without hesitation.

Capturing the potential revenues from high-definition DVDs has taken on greater urgency for the Hollywood studios since 2005, as standard-definition DVD sales have stagnated, broadcast license fees have declined, and new challenges have emerged in foreign markets, all in the face of faltering blockbuster franchises, relentlessly rising production and marketing costs, and the specter of widening video piracy (Sabbagh 2007: 65). As the editors of this collection note in the introduction, the current strike of US film and TV writers reflects the determination of the union to redress the disastrous 1996 DVD royalty agreement, which exempted 80 per cent of studio DVD revenues from royalties (which were set between 1.8 per cent and 5.4 per cent of the remaining 20 per cent) (Johnson 2004). Over the past several box-office seasons, studios have become increasingly dependent upon the windfall of DVD revenues; as an unnamed Warner Bros. executive explained to the *New York Times* in 2004: "Sixty per cent of studio films never, ever, recoup their cost. . . . We need the huge profits of some of the money makers to cover the losers" (Johnson 2004).

As movie sales in the standard-definition DVD market falter (one journalist noted in mid-2007 that "with DVD hardware penetration at more than 80 per cent in the US, the disc gold rush days are long past"), the appeal of high-definition optical formats is starker than ever (Ault 2007b). While the studios were reluctant to support competing formats like D-VHS and the high-definition DVD in the midst of the explosive growth of the standard-definition DVD market, they may have underestimated how quickly that market would reach saturation. A journalist quoted an industry observer in 2002 who predicted that any high-definition DVD market was 10 to 15 years away, arguing that "none of the studios are going to want to cannibalize DVD. . . . It's making too much money for them" (The Digital Bits website owner and editor Bill Hunt quoted in Rivero 2002: 1). However, by the end of 2007, *Variety* was grimly concluding that "ten years in, the DVD format appears to have peaked and its successors remain more murky than ever," and cited trade predictions of a decline in DVD revenues between three and five per cent in 2008 (Garrett 2007: 9). The trade paper also noted that "uncertainty about the future of Hollywood's cash cow hasn't escaped Wall Street's notice. Several analysts have downgraded the entire entertainment sector due in part to these concerns," and cited one Wall Street estimate of annual declines in DVD revenues between three and five per cent over the next five years (Garrett 2007: 13). Another analyst warned "the decline of the DVD market will accelerate in 2008 and beyond" (Ibid).

Meanwhile, there was also growing concern within the consumer electronics industry over the declining market for DVD players. In August 2007, the British magazine *Marketing* reported that the saturated DVD hardware sector had become a commodity market; price, not technical features, was of chief concern to consumers, and 50 per cent of the players sold were low-cost store brands. The entire market for DVD players, recorders, and home theatre systems had declined 14 per cent in the UK since 2005, the magazine reported (Bainbridge 2007: 28). Furthermore, the rapidly declining prices for high-definition LCD displays also meant falling profit margins for electronics retailers, who increasingly viewed the high-definition DVD player as the industry's next big product category. In September 2007, a Warner Home Video executive explained the predicament of retailers: "Flat-panel prices have come down so much, they have to do more than just sell flat-panels to grow. They have to sell audio systems and players to keep comps up" (Warner Home Video Senior Vice President Worldwide for High-definition Steve Nickerson, quoted in Netherby 2007b: 4).

In the face of falling sales of standard-definition DVDs and players, the continued stalemate between the two rival HD optical disc formats has served to suppress consumer interest in the entire product category. Industry efforts in early 2005 to seek a compromise around a single high-definition DVD format failed, and the subsequent HD-DVD versus Blu-ray battle has continued undiminished (Shim 2005). The unprecedented 2002 coalition of nine consumer electronics manufacturers which split from the DVD Forum to form the Blu-ray group was led by Sony and Philips, and their plans for the new format reflected the lessons of previous format wars and careful calculation about the potential benefits of what Philips CEO Gerald Kleisterlee in 2002 called "co-opetition," or cooperative competition, "in order to start a marketplace in the first place" (Jones 2002: 4B). The same year Sony CEO Kunitake Ando confessed to an Australian journalist: "We are so bad at making a family. That's the reason we lost the VHS/Betamax war," and touted Sony's new cooperative efforts with traditional rivals Panasonic and Microsoft in developing the Blu-ray format (Thom 2002: C6). Indeed, the former president of Warner Home Video was so troubled by the joint efforts by traditional rivals Sony, Panasonic, and Philips that he requested that his firm's outside antitrust counsel explore ways to encourage the US Department of Justice to launch an antitrust enquiry aimed at the Blu-ray alliance (Warren Liebenfarb quoted in Kirsner 2007: A12). However, despite the proclaimed fidelity to the virtues of cooperation and unified standards within the industry, as one executive pointed out, the industry's fixation on the substantial royalty revenues earned by Philips from the original VHS format inevitably encouraged the development of proprietary standards which could be licensed to rival manufacturers and video duplicators; "patents, and not the sales of boxes, are where the money is made," he argued (Yamaha Product Manager Paul Astbury quoted in Leung 2002: 1).

The most significant strategic lesson Sony took from its failed Betamax experience of the 1980s was the importance of securing exclusive home video rights to Hollywood feature films, leading to its subsequent acquisition of the Columbia TriStar studio and its current aggressive courting of the other major studios on behalf of Blu-ray. Sony's efforts initially seemed to give the Blu-ray format a stronger hand, despite HD-DVD's lower disc duplication and player costs. A Sony Pictures Home Entertainment executive told *Video Business* in June 2007 that such studio exclusivity deals were:

> [T]he most powerful tool that we have. . . . .This is not like the game business, where the consumer can have a format but have certain content available but not others. Consumers in this business expect to have a movie playback machine and expect it to play everything. Blu-ray is the closest to having that
> (Sony Pictures Home Entertainment President David Bishop quoted in Netherby 2007a: 8).

Indeed, despite the August 2007 surprise announcement that Paramount Pictures and DreamWorks Animation would release exclusively on HD-DVD for the next 18 months, the next month Sony CEO Howard Stringer was still confidently telling *The Economist* magazine: "I think the war is virtually over" (*Economist* 2007: 8). Some Blu-ray partisans even argued that the Paramount-DreamWorks defection was in fact a sign of desperation on the part of the HD-DVD camp, pointing to a reported $150 million payment by Toshiba to the studios; the headline in *US News.com* read "HD-DVD Buys a Victory" (LaGesse 2007).

By the end of 2007, industry speculation centered on intense efforts by both camps to woo Warner Bros. into an exclusive licensing deal before the January 2008 Consumer Electronics Show; a victory for Sony would give Blu-ray an estimated 70 per cent of the feature market, leading *Business Week* to speculate that "the Blu-ray team is so determined to win that it will throw hundreds of millions of dollars of marketing support behind Blu-ray equipment if Warner gets on board" (Grover and Edwards 2007: 28). As 2007 ended, however, Sony CEO Howard Stringer, near completion of a three-year reorganization of the faltering Japanese consumer electronics giant (including shutting down manufacturing plants, dropping unprofitable businesses, and shedding 10,000 workers), was expressing new anxieties about the high-definition DVD format battle. Stringer was reported in *Business Week* as telling a New York City audience in November 2007: "We have a sort of stalemate at the moment. We have four studios, and they have two or three studios. . . . It's a difficult fight" (Anon 2007). A blogger for *Arstechnica.com* commented upon Stringer's public remarks:

> the high-profile CEO is showing signs of wear. . . . He candidly indicated that the war mostly came down to bragging rights over who was winning, and said that the two camps could have collaborated better in the past to develop one format. Stringer even said that he wished he could go back in time to make that possible—is that the smell of regret floating in the air?
>
> (Cheng 2007).

Describing the HD-DVD-Blu-ray rivalry the next month, Stringer told the Associated Press: "We have momentum. . . . But that's all we have at the moment" (Kageyama 2007).

Meanwhile, studios, hardware manufacturers, and retailers all lamented the slow roll-out of the high-definition DVD devices; "this has been a very, very ugly market," complained one Forrester analyst in October 2007 (J.P. Gowner quoted in Bray 2007: A13). Earlier that year the CEO of the consumer electronics retailer Best Buy told the trade association's magazine that "the damage the industry does to itself by not choosing a format is enormous. . . . Two incompatible formats is as much a nightmare as you can make for consumers" (*CE Vision Magazine* 2007). In June 2007, Toshiba estimated that North American sales of HD-DVD players had fallen by 44 per cent, from 1.8 million to 1 million units (Ault 2007a: 6). Many observers argued that the Paramount-Dreamworks exclusivity agreement with HD-DVD would serve to prolong the stalemate between the rival formats. One industry publication noted in September 2007 that the "Hollywood studios are becoming increasingly divided over which high-definition technology will replace the DVD, increasing prospects that it will be years before next-generation players become standard equipment in US households" (*ExtremeTech.com* 2007). By the second half of 2007, financial analysts were also becoming more cautious about the prospects for quick resolution of the format war; for example, PriceWaterhouseCoopers' *Global Entertainment and Media Outlook: 2007–2011* predicted that it would take several years for a winner to emerge, finally providing US consumers with confidence to purchase either format (*ExtremeTech.com* 2007). In October 2007, UK research firm Screen Digest concluded that both formats were likely to coexist "for the foreseeable future" in the US and Western Europe. Forrester Research, which had earlier predicted the supremacy of Blu-ray, was now predicting that the Paramount/Dreamworks-HD-DVD deal and the falling prices of HD-DVD players would result in at least 18 months of continued stalemate (Sweeting 2007b: 6). By the end of 2007, the *New York Times* wondered: "What if nobody wins the high-definition DVD format wars? That increasingly looks to be the situation" (Taub 2007: C1).

The history of the marketing efforts of manufacturers of both high-definition DVD formats reflect the slow maturation of the market. Until the second half of 2007, marketing campaigns for the sponsors of two competing formats were relatively modest and narrowly targeted. For example, in July 2007 Sony hosted a Blu-ray Experience Booth at the science-fiction fan exposition Comic-Con in San Diego, and a Sony marketing executive explained that:

> [T]his is our first big show where we are really focusing in on the consumer. . . . It's the perfect event to showcase Blu-ray, because you're attracting a perfect demographic. These people love films, they love gaming and they love new technology
> (Sony Vice President of New Business Development Rich Marty quoted in Ault 2007c: 8).

Reflecting the early focus on gamers and science fiction fans as early high-definition DVD adopters, Paramount Home Entertainment enlisted the son of *Star Trek* creator Gene Roddenberry to announce the launch of the original TV series on HD-DVD at the same event. Warner Bros. President Ron Sanders described the fan convention as "the perfect venue to marry the intensity of passion from the fans and next-generation formats. . . . The average Comic-Con attendee is so into these properties, they are perfect to adopt [high-definition]" (Ault 2007c: 8). Continuing to tap the presumed affinity of science fiction fans with the high-definition format, a few months later Toshiba announced that consumers who purchased the *Star Trek* first season boxed set along with a HD-DVD player would be given a free remote control in the shape of a *Star Trek* phaser (along with five free HD-DVD movies) (Hachman 2007b).

The second half of 2007, however, witnessed obvious efforts by both camps to widen the target demographic for high-definition DVD marketing; in August, Disney launched an 18-mall tour of a 40-foot model of Disneyland's Sleeping Castle featuring a high-definition mini-theatre and 14 interactive kiosks, part of the "Magical Blu-ray Tour" underwritten by Panasonic (Jaffee 2007: 14). A Disney executive explained: "Our goal with the Disney Magical Blu-Ray Tour is to reach as many people as possible and help educate consumers across all demographics" (President of Walt Disney Studios Home Entertainment Bob Chapek quoted in *Extreme-Tech.com* 2007). At the same time, in an effort to reach internet-oriented technophiles beyond the science fiction fan community, Sony enlisted the marketing firm that had helped create the successful multimedia campaign for Sony's Bravia line of LCD televisions a few years earlier. The viral campaign invited web visitors to make use of exclusive video footage, teasers, and behind-the-scenes footage, as well as "online widgets, interactive infographics, images, videos, online PR and a branded Flash player." Sony's marketing consultant explained: "With Bravia the campaign picked up on a consumer interest in an event as the spectacle; with Blu-ray the spectacle is the technology" (*New Media Age* 2007: 4). Moving in another distinct marketing direction, this time evoking the themes of technologically-enhanced domesticity which accompanied the original launch of postwar television in the US, Panasonic launched a TV spot and print campaign in October 2007 around the theme "Bring Back Family Time." Inspired by proprietary polling data which indicated that 63 per cent of US respondents said they'd be willing to spend more money on technology if it increased family time, Panasonic's campaign supplemented the firm's "'Living in HD' tour of four tricked-out trucks traveling the country to offer the hands-on Panasonic HD experience." One industry analyst explained the company's marketing aims:

> In trying to re-establish the primacy of TV—and the stack of equipment around it—as a central gathering point for family . . . they are more focused on an almost anti-technology theme and more about what these products can do for you
> (NPD Group analyst Steve Baker quoted in Bulik 2007: 4).

The widely varying promotional messages and demographic targets in the current high-definition DVD marketing wars suggest a high degree of uncertainty about the state of the current market for the devices.

The diverse marketing efforts of high-definition DVD manufacturers are complicated by several wider constraints; beyond the obvious deleterious consequences of the prolonged format war, they include wider consumer confusion about high-definition equipment, the slow uptake of high-definition TVs, and high-definition DVD's dependence upon the success of competing video game and PC platforms which can also serve as high-definition DVD players. Consumer confusion around all matters pertaining to high-definition television concerned many in the industry. A 2007 consumer survey by consumer electronics retailer Best Buy that reported that 90 per cent of American respondents confessed a lack of complete understanding of HDTV, with nearly half seriously underestimating the costs associated with high-definition equipment (Sweeting 2007b: 6). One research firm reported that 10 per cent of HDTV owners thought they owned a high-definition DVD player, even though only one per cent actually did (Netherby 2007b: 4). Reinforcing consumer confusion about the status of high-definition DVD were marketing efforts from manufacturers and retailers on behalf of so-called "upconverting" standard DVD players, which interpolate and insert missing lines of resolution to high-definition TV receivers. One manufacturer's website explained:

> As your video display moves into the High Definition era, don't leave your DVD collection behind. Even while looking forward to a future with more High Definition content availability, we must not forget the great wealth of material already available on the DVD format. A DVD collection can represent a sizable investment, both financially and emotionally, in our favorite content
>
> (Oppodigital.com 2007).

Defending the upconverting standard DVD player against the new high-definition DVD systems, a *Washington Post* reporter argued in May 2006 that while "videophiles may scoff at this trickery. . . . upconverting can work pretty well. It can help a well-produced DVD look almost as fantastic as an HD-DVD—especially to a viewer not looking for that difference in the first place" (Pegoraro 2006: F6). However, if some retailers and manufacturers had an interest in promoting upconverting DVD players, the Hollywood studios would gain no benefit in extending the life of consumers' standard-definition DVD collections. As one journalist noted:

> the studios get nothing out of the upconverter business. It gives consumers no incentive to replace their current DVD library, it does nothing to lift new release prices and has no need for enhanced copy protection. It provides none of the benefits the studios are hoping to reap from the transition to high-def
>
> (Sweeting 2007a: 4).

Reporting on research indicating that 66 per cent of respondents said they were not likely to purchase a high-definition player in the next six months, an industry analyst told a trade group in October 2007: "Unfortunately, we developed the perfect product (with the DVD). . . . We've got to overcome the fact that we're competing against a wonderful product that's in 80 per cent of households" (NPD Group analyst Russ Crupnick quoted in Ogg

2007). According to a December 2007 report in the *New York Times*, only 11 per cent of US consumers strongly intended to purchase a high-definition DVD player in the following quarter, and almost three-quarters of respondents said they were satisfied with standard-definition DVDs (Taub 2007: C1). The paper quoted an industry analyst who warned that the device "may emerge as a premium, luxury item, not a successor to DVD" (NPD Director for industry analysis Ross Rubin quoted in Taub 2007: C1).

Beyond the challenges of consumer confusion over high-definition storage and display technologies, the success of any high-definition optical disk depends on an installed base of high-definition television receivers, and while the standard-definition DVD market was exploding in the late 1990s, most national markets (with the exception of Japan) for HDTV sets were growing slowly. In 2001, for example, 12.7 million DVD players were sold in the US, adding up to a cumulative installed total of 32 million units, while the total number of all HDTV-related products sold that year was only 1.5 million, reaching a cumulative 2.5 million devices. As one journalist reported in 2002, "if anything, it's HD that needs DVD—or at least some form of physical carrier that can broaden HD's appeal by extending its reach beyond broadcasting" (DeLancie 2002: 24). However, if the market for high-definition receivers languished for several years, there are recent signs that the diffusion of HDTVs has accelerated. In October 2007, one research firm estimated that 35 per cent of US homes would be equipped with HDTV sets by the end of the year (up from 28.6 per cent the previous year [Adams Media Research, Inc quoted in Bray 2007: A13]) and another research firm predicted that a majority of US homes would be HDTV equipped by the end of 2008 (Understanding and Solutions director Jim Bottoms quoted in Ault 2007b). At the same time, Forrester Research estimated that less than ten per cent of HDTV homes had a high-definition DVD player, suggesting a great deal of room for expansion of high- definition DVD sales within an expanding market (Forrester Research quoted in Bray 2007: A13).

Besides its dependence upon the diffusion of high-definition TV receivers, the success of the high-definition DVD is also tied to the alternative platforms of the personal computer and game console. In mid-2007, Toshiba announced it would bundle HD-DVD drives as standard on its notebook PCs by 2008 (Akass 2007), and in November it predicted that five million HD-DVD-equipped laptops would be sold in 2008, more than twice the number sold in the previous year (Sanchanta 2007: 15). According to the *Financial Times,* "many industry observers say the format that becomes standard in PCs could ultimately become the victor" of the wider multiplatform HD format war (quoted in Sanchanta 2007: 15). Meanwhile Sony announced two new Blu-ray computer devices: a Blu-ray equipped Media Jukebox/Server operating on a branded version of the Windows Home Server operating system (Hachman 2007a), and a $2900 PC/TV equipped with a Blu-ray player and wall-mountable wireless 22-inch LCD display (Carroll 2007).

If the computer platform has been a relatively little-noted battleground for the rival high -definition DVD formats, the video game platform was central to Sony's plans for Blu-ray since the launch of the format. Indeed, it was expectations that Sony's PlayStation 3 would dominate the three-firm rivalry between Sony, Microsoft and Nintendo as its previous PlayStation 2 had dominated the previous generation of game platforms, which led many observers to give Blu-ray the edge over HD-DVD. However, the delayed launch and sluggish initial sales of the PS3 frustrated Sony's plans to deliver millions of Blu-ray DVD players in the guise of a video game console.

Sony's willingness to sell the PS3 at a substantial loss on each unit in order to seed the profitable game software business and boost the Blu-ray format meant that, until recently, 95 per cent of Blu-ray players were game consoles, not stand-alone devices. (In 2007, Microsoft released an add-on HD-DVD player to its XBox 360 console, though it sold only 300,000 of these compared to 3.4 million PS3s sold through March 2007 [Taub 2007: C1]). While boosting the installed base of potential high-definition DVD players, Sony's dependence upon the game platform made the success of its high-definition DVD format dependent upon the vagaries of the game market, itself dominated by the appeal of blockbuster game titles. Moreover, the so-called "attach rate" (the number of high-definition DVD discs purchased for each player sold) starkly differs between the game platform and stand-alone high-definition DVD player. As a result of Sony's dependence upon the PS3 as a platform for bringing Blu-ray playback into the home, the attach rate for the entire Blu-ray format was a modest 0.6 DVD discs per unit, compared to a rate of four discs per unit for–HD-DVD (Carroll 2007).

The intimate involvement of the high-definition DVD format with the video game platform links its fortunes to a wider shift in the marketing and social position of gaming as a leisure activity. The remarkable success of Nintendo's Wii platform has called into question conventional wisdom about the users and appeal of video games, and as game consoles have been transformed into internet entertainment portals and high-definition DVD players, their manufacturers have adjusted marketing campaigns to move beyond the core gaming audience of young males. As *PR Week* explained in September 2007, both Sony and Microsoft were attempting to reposition the traditional image of the device, away from an association with the solitary gamer toward more social contexts, emphasizing interactive web features, karaoke, and fitness games. Microsoft's fall 2007 London launch of the blockbuster game *Halo 3* was modeled after a film premiere, not a game release ("We want to take it away from gaming reference points and position it within popular culture," a Microsoft executive explained), and Sony's 2007 UK introduction of the PS3 was linked to a season of promotional events partnered with elite cultural institutions like the Sadler's Well, Gateshead's Baltic Centre for Contemporary Art, the Victoria and Albert Museum, the English National Opera, and the British Film Institute.[2] As the Sony PR flack explained, "The subtext was: 'we're part of the cultural and entertainment landscape.' . . . The PlayStation proposition needs changing" (Xbox European PR director Paul Fox and director of UK PR for Sony Computer Entertainment Europe David Wilson quoted in *PR Week* 2007: 22). As *PR Week* described the two formats' strategy, "a gaming audience made up mainly of young men has limited potential for growth. Tap into the hearts, minds and wallets of 'non-traditional' audiences, however, and the revenue opportunities increase dramatically." However, as the unexpected success of Nintendo's technologically impoverished Wii game system suggests, whether and in what manner consumers choose to take up the distinct technological capabilities of any particular media device are difficult to predict.

Beyond the importance of content deals with Hollywood studios and success upon the personal computer and gaming platforms, the fortunes of the emerging high-definition DVD formats also depend on highly changeable relationships with video duplicators, video rental firms like Blockbuster and Netflix, and consumer electronics retailers like Wal-Mart, Amazon, Target, and Best Buy. However, a less obvious industry sector has also been nominated by some observers as the possible arbitrator of success of the rival high-definition DVD formats: the adult film market, which has been credited with helping to determine the victory of VHS over the Betamax videotape format in the 1980s and with fueling the growth of the DVD in the 1990s. "As was the case with VHS, pornography is one of the driving forces behind DVD," the trade journal *Tape-Disc Business* reported in 2002 (Block 2002: 25). An April 2007 article in the tech journal *EWeek*, "Porn Could be the Key to the Next-Generation DVD War," quoted a Forrester analyst who argued that "if the porn industry wanted to break the logjam of HD-DVD and Blu-ray, it could. . . . If they said 'We are going to go with HD-DVD' you would see a few million homes immediately go out and buy HD-DVD players. They have that power" (Forrester analyst James McQuivey quoted in *EWeek.com* 2007). Other observers wondered if the added visual resolution of the high-definition formats would be of much utility or appeal in the porn industry: "Is an HD picture that reveals blemishes and imperfections that would not be apparent in a standard-definition picture necessarily a good thing for the genre?" and quoted an industry executive who argued that "the HD format sometimes provides too much detail. . . . .Less is better in some instances" (In-Stat analyst Michael Paxton quoted in Clark 2007: 15) A more substantial and evocative objection to the notion of pornography as key to the fortunes of the high-definition DVD was voiced by another Forrester analyst: "Today, if you're into porn, you have it in front of you 24–7 on the Internet" (Forrester Research Vice President James McQuivey quoted in Walsh 2007). The suggestion here of a more general shift from moving image texts as physical artifacts to ephemeral appearances conjured up from the web haunts the overall prospects for the high-definition DVD or indeed any optical, magnetic, or holographic storage medium, as we shall see. A writer of a May 2007 article in *Billboard* convincingly concluded: "despite published reports suggesting otherwise, don't look for porn—which is credited with helping decide the Betamax vs. VHS battle in the early '80s—to be the determining factor in this format war" (Walsh 2007).

CONCLUSION: THE LAST FORMAT WAR?

Despite the seemingly irresistible journalistic comparisons to the Betamax-VHS format war of the 1980s, the current battle between HD-DVD and Blu-ray hardly represents a replay of history. For a start, it is likely that no single contemporary device will combine the VCR's distinct functions of time shifting, archiving, and playing Hollywood films. Instead these separate functions are increasingly taken up by the set top digital video recorder, the DVD recorder, and the DVD player or video on demand or internet downloads or streams. Indeed, the standard-definition DVD player's lack of recording capability (a limitation shared by both rival high-definition players on the market) made it more palatable to the Hollywood studios. In any event, the worlds of consumer electronics, computing, and telephony has been transformed since the introduction of both the VCR and the standard-definition DVD, and any new physical storage medium must find its place in a new world of nascent technologies and services—from Netflix and video on demand to internet streaming and downloading—delivered to a bewildering array of screens in and out of the home.

In addition, powerful new economic actors have entered the world of domestic film entertainment since the DVD's introduction, and Hollywood has reacted fearfully to the outsiders represented by figures like Steve Jobs, Bill Gates and Mark Cuban. The expressions of agency under siege recur in recent Hollywood rhetoric. "We know that Apple has destroyed the music business, in terms of pricing, and if we don't take control they'll do the same thing on the video side," NBC Universal chief Jeff Zucker told a 2007 US college audience (Edwards 2007: 54). Striking out in another direction, blockbuster director Michael Bay warned on his official website in December 2007 that "Microsoft wants both formats to fail so they can be heroes and make the world move to digital downloads. That is the dirty secret no one is talking about" (Kingsley-Hughes 2007). To some degree, the high-definition player has become merely one part of a larger battle over control of the long-anticipated entertainment and information gateway and repository in the home. The appeal of the new attributes and capabilities of the high-definition DVD, including enhanced visual quality, online premium content, and interactive menus, all remain untested beyond the current anomalous market of early adopters.

However, the cloud of uncertainty most troubling to the would-be architects of the competing high-definition optical storage media involves the untested question of whether consumers will continue to covet and collect moving images in the form of physical artifacts of any sort. As Microsoft CEO Bill Gates told his 2005 Princeton University audience in response to a question about the high-definition DVD format war: "For us it's not the physical format. Understand that this is the last physical format there will ever be. Everything's going to be streamed directly or on a hard disk. So, in this way, it's even unclear how much this one counts" (Sethi 2005). Gates's ambivalence about the future role of any physical storage medium for high-definition video content has been expressed across the electronic moving image economy. As one professional videographer explained in 2006: "HD delivery on optical discs may soon become last year's news—or news that never even happened. If they don't figure out HD-DVD/Blu-ray soon, we may just skip it altogether and deliver our finished programs via the Internet" (Burokas 2006: 35). An extensive survey in mid-2007 by the trade magazine *Video Business* of public libraries in North America regarding the acquisition of high-definition DVDs quoted a library direc-tor in Toronto, Canada explaining that "downloading is kind of our holy grail because, of course, it means not having to handle any kind of artifact at all" (Koseluk 2007: 1). The high-definition DVD market is still quite immature; within a year of the high-definition DVD's launch, each format had sold a total of one million discs each, compared with 5.5 million DVDs sold within its first year; meanwhile, the bestselling standard-definition DVD of 2006 sold 5 million copies in a single day (Koseluk 2007: 1). Given the immaturity of the high-definition DVD market, it's unclear whether any physical storage medium will assume the importance of the VHS tape or the DVD enjoyed during their reign. As one analyst told *Daily Variety* in April 2007: "The longer these guys battle now, the more that Bill Gates, networked media, personal video recorders and satellite become the rival format to high-definition DVD. . . . Hard disc drives and fast network con-nections win in that scenario, not HD-DVD or Blu-ray" (Invisoneering Group's senior analyst Richard Doherty quoted in Kirsner 2007: A12). In late 2007 a Forrester analyst warned leaders of the high-definition DVD industry that in the face of the growing popularity of Internet downloading of feature films, "it's possible this market might never actually take off at all" (Forrester analyst J.P. Gowner quoted in Bray 2007: A13).

At the same time, the commitment of the Hollywood studios to any particular exhibition venue, revenue window, or physical format is no more permanent than any historically-specific calculation of their economic inter-est. From the point of view of motion picture producers, the high-definition DVD is merely another in a long string of so-called "packaged media" for-mats for non-theatrical distribution of Hollywood filmmaking. A Disney executive told an October 2007 HDTV industry conference in Hollywood that "mainstream Americans are buying (content) in the digital world for immediate need, not for long-term collectability to watch over and over," while admitting that packaged media would continue to play a role over the next decade (Executive Vice President of Distribution and Marketing for

Walt Disney Home Entertainment Patrick Fitzgerald quoted in Ogg 2007). Analogizing high-definition packaged media as "a sort of training wheels for digital downloads," in the words of a journalist covering the event, a Warner Bros. vice president told his audience: "We can use HD discs to train consumers to move into digital, but it's a transition," said Dan Silverberg, vice president of high-definition media development at Warner Bros. "Downloaded content will come, but the consumer will get quicker tutorial into video-on-demand, etc. by owning a Blu-ray player or HD DVD" (Warner Bros. Vice President of High Definition Media Development Dan Silverberg quoted in Ogg 2007).

The debate over the future appeal of any physical storage medium for moving images centers upon judgments regarding the psychic investment consumers may have in acquiring and collecting media texts in hard copies. In 2002, David Cox, writing in the *New Statesman*, argued that the slow UK uptake of the digital video recorder and broadband downloading and the spectacular success of the standard DVD format suggested that:

> [W]e are reinforcing our archaic habit of squirrelling away physical copies of conventionally constructed artifacts. . . . [I]t is the physicality itself of DVDs that seems to attract us. Because the discs come in neat and colourful boxes (unlike data down a wire), we can display them in collections expressing our tastes, just as our parents displayed their vinyl LP collections. So it is, unfortunately, the very virtuality of the revolutionary approach that we are rejecting
>
> (Cox 2002).

Telling his readers that "we can congratulate ourselves on our unexpected triumph over technological determinism," Cox concluded that "the people, it seems, have spoken. The global communications revolution is not, it seems, compatible with human behavior. We are going to continue entertaining and informing ourselves much as we always have done, because that's the way we like it" (Cox 2002).

However, by 2007, in the face of the sluggish adoption of either of the rival high-definition DVD formats, skepticism about consumer interest in collecting another generation of physical artifacts seemed to be growing. A *PC Magazine* article in June 2007, headlined "Format War? Who Cares?; Once this format war is over, the industry will come to a sad realization: Most people will never buy high-definition movies on disc," suggested that:

> [N]o matter how you dress up a disc, it's still a physical entity that needs to be mastered, packed, shipped, sold, and stored on a shelf—and that's not what consumers want. They just want the movie. They just want the media file. They just want the bits. And when it comes to moving bits, packaged media just doesn't make sense
>
> (Costa 2007).

Surveying the ongoing high-definition format battle, Costa concluded that "by the time the whole thing is resolved, watching HD movies will involve nothing more than pointing and clicking. That makes this format war, like most wars, pretty pointless" (Costa 2007). Skeptics of future optical storage formats point to the shift in the music business from the sale of physical CDs to the downloading of individual songs via Apple's iTunes or to a number of competing subscription-based music services. Pointing to a future of ubiquitous streaming of media texts, free of both physical media and downloaded files, one venture capitalist argued: "once we have true mobile broadband, the streaming model is going to take off. Then there's never really going to be a need to own files at all. It'll all just be there in the cloud" (New York venture capitalist Fred Wilson quoted in Heilemann 2007). While Steve Jobs described his company's first television-based product, Apple TV, as merely "a hobby" to a May 2007 industry audience, one journalist noted that the new media server signaled that "the company has invaded the sanctum of living-room entertainment," with potentially significant implications for the industry (Heilemann 2007). Describing Apple TV as "a DVD player for this new internet age," Jobs described the shift from the more limited set top box model to the goal of digital moving image gateway to the home. Observers cited iTunes movie download deals with Disney and MGM (and an announced plan to make 20th Century Fox titles available for rental), along with its 2007 agreement link between Apple TV and Google's YouTube as a sign of their future ambitions (Heilemann 2007: Richtel, Stone and Holson 2007: C1). In addition, studio concerns over digital rights management and the disruptive threat of the iTunes music model was also slowing the move to digital downloads. At the end of 2007 the *New York Times* explained that, unlike the US TV networks who have quickly moved into a number of experiments in online distribution, "movie studios . . . have been more cautious in their approach, particularly when dealing with Steven P. Jobs . . . the fear was that Mr. Jobs would undermine studio's traditional DVD business in a bid to sell more iPods" (Richtel, Stone and Holson 2007: C1).

If Apple has been typically unforthcoming about its video delivery plans, Netflix, another recent entrant in the business of video delivery, was less shy about its long-term goals. In January 2007, the company, which boasts seven million mail-delivery DVD subscribers, made 5,000 of its 85,000 video titles available online. While Netflix's download business is small compared to its traditional service of mailing DVDs (40,000 downloads versus 1.6 million DVDs shipped in October 2007), the company's long-term goal is to move away from the exchange of physical media altogether. If act one for Netflix, according to the *Washington Post*, "was getting people used to renting DVDs over the Internet" and the second act experimenting in digital downloads, Act three is, in the words of a Netflix executive, "no more DVDs and everything . . . online" (Netflix Vice President of Corporate Communication Steve Swasey quoted in Musgrove 2007: F1). A November 2007 survey indicated that 16 per cent of Americans with web access watched full-length TV broadcasts online (double the per centage of the previous year) and in other parts of the world the rate was much higher (a reported 60 per cent of Hong Kong households, for example [Edwards 2007: 54]). However, the widely-expected long term transition from physical media to the artifact-free universe of downloads and streaming is currently beset with so many technological, competitive, and consumer uncertainties as to make the current troubled transition from standard-definition to high-definition DVD straightforward in contrast. For example, in December 2007 giant US retailer Wal-Mart quietly pulled the plug on a movie download business it had launched a year earlier with computer giant Hewlett-Packard. In its announcement, HP noted that "the market for paid video downloads has not performed as expected, and the broader Internet video space continues to remain highly dynamic and uncertain," evidence, according to the *New York Times*, "of the ho-hum reaction by many consumers to the download-able movie concept" (Richtel, Stone and Holson 2007: C1).

The wider uncertainty about the continued commitment of consumers in the US and elsewhere to so-called packaged media may have contributed to a prevalent tone of ill temper and impatience among observers of the current high-definition DVD format war. One of the striking aspects of the fierce disputes between Blu-ray and HD-DVD supporters is the relative lack of sub-stantive discussion of the technical or aesthetic advantages of either format. Instead, the diverse discourses around the ongoing format war, from tech-nophile blogs to the mainstream media, are marked by a scarcely concealed tone of resentment and antipathy aimed at the entire corporate community of would-be architects of domestic film culture. For example, after suggesting readers either purchase an upconverting standard-definition DVD player or order an HD-capable digital video recorder from the local cable company, a columnist for the *Washington Post* concluded: "Neither of those options comes close to being perfect. But they're a lot smarter than risking hundreds of dollars in the hope that the ego-driven, self-destructive greed of the movie and electronics industries will somehow work out in your favor" (Pegoraro: 2006: F6). A columnist for *ExtremeTech.com* in August 2007 wrote: "How can I not care about which storage format wins in the end? Simple. I don't want to use either of them. Period. They're both garbage and they're both indicative of 90's [sic] era thinking that has to be gotten past" (Lynch 2007). Another *ExtremeTech* blogger argued:

> [T]here's just so much convenience and safety involved with download-ing your movie and TV content. Why would any of us opt to go the Blu-ray or HD-DVD route instead? It's a scam, designed to get you to buy all the stuff you already bought on DVD again. Don't fall for it. Stand your ground and wait for downloadable HD movies and TV shows and then store it all on a portable hard disk or two (or right on your computer).
>
> (Case 2007)

A respondent to *Gismodo*'s blog covering the format wars declared: "Personally, I'm not buying either one. I want to be able to rip my DVDs to my home server, make my own backup copies, move the movies to my PSP or whatever. Until these new formats allow me to do that, why would I switch from normal old DVD? It's still the same bad Hollywood [sic] crap, no matter what format it's in. :-)" (ImThe King 2007). As techno-skeptic David Cox argued in the *New Statesman* in January 2002, after witnessing the bursting of the high-tech financial bubble of the late 1990s:

> Entertainment moguls readily acknowledge that, when it comes to the software of their business, "nobody knows anything." Perhaps, after this great disaster of misplaced certainty, everyone will also acknowledge that, until the free will of humanity has been factored in, this goes for the hardware, too
>
> (Cox 2002).

With such constraints in mind, the current outpouring of intemperate commentary directed at the rival corporate architects of the high-definition DVD suggests both the psychic investment and lingering antipathies of consumers in our brave new digital world. The undercurrent of unfocused consumer resentment suggests the need for caution among all those who enter the thicket of speculation over the future formats and uses of electronic media in the home.

NOTES

1. By early 2000, the VCR was found in 93 per cent of US homes, and 53 per cent of US homes had more than one (O'Reilly 2000: 10).
2. *PR Week* described Sony's PS3 strategy: "November 2006–March 2007: PlayStation Season. Five well-known cultural institutions were approached to partner with PS3. Sadler's Wells hosted a weekend event called Sampled, showcasing different types of dance. The Baltic created an animated artwork, the V&A produced a light sculpture entitled Volume, the English National Opera offered an interactive website, Inside Out, which offered a behind-the-scenes view of the London Coliseum, and the British Film Institute hosted the Optronica festival" (2007: 22).

BIBLIOGRAPHY

Akass, C (2007, 12 July) "Toshiba Raises HD Ante as Blu-ray Inches Ahead," *Personal Computer World*: np.

Anon (2007, 26 November) "Sir Howard on Recharging Sony," *Business Week*: np.

Ault, S (2007a, 18 June) "Price Drops Boost High-def Hardware," *Video Business*: 6.

———. (2007b, 25 June) "Forecast: DVD Flat to Down This Year: High-def Momentum Will Make the Difference," *Video Business*: np.

————. (2007c, 6 August) "Comic-Con Draws on High-def," *Video Business*: 8.

Bainbridge, J. (2007, 22 August) "DVD Players: Confusion Slows Sales," *Marketing*: 28.

Block, D.G (2002, 1 March) "DVD Still Shines, But Other Technologies on the Horizon," *Tape-Disc Business*: 25.

Bray, H. (2007, 30 October) "Battle Rages for HD Movie Supremacy, But Costs, Incompatibility Keeping Consumers Away," *Boston Globe*: A13.

Brookey, R. (2007) "The Format Wars: Drawing the Battle Lines for the Next DVD," *Convergence*, 13(2): 199–211.

Bulik, B. S. (2007, 8 October) "Panasonic: We Bring Households Together," *Advertising Age*: 4.

Burokas, A. (2006, 1 January) "Happy New Year: HD Today," *EventDV*: 35.

Carroll, J. (2007) "HD DVD vs. Blu-ray ad Nauseam," ZDNet Blogs. Online. Available HTTP: <http://blogs.zdnet.com/carroll/?p=177> (accessed 28 December 2007).

Case, L. (2007, 15 August) "Counterpoint," *ExtremeTech.com*: np.

CE Vision Magazine. (2007, January/February) "Dueling Formats: Blu-ray vs. HD-DVD," *CE Vision Magazine*. Online. Available HTTP: <http://www.ce.org/Press/Vision/1520_1854.asp> (accessed 28 December 2007).

Cheng, J. (2007, November 10) "Sony CEO Wants to go Back in Time, Avert High-def Format War," *Arstechnica.com*. Online. Available HTTP: <http://arstechnica.com/news.ars/post/20071110-sony-ceo-wants-to-go-back-in-time-avert-high-def-format-war.html> (accessed 28 December 2007).

Clark, T. (2007, 6 August) "Programmers Weigh Format Costs, Demand," *Multichannel News*: 15.

Costa, D. (2007, 26 June) "Format war? Who Cares?," *PC Magazine*: np.

Cox, D. (2002, 21 January) "The Future Has Been Cancelled," *New Statesman*: np.

Daley, D. (2000, 1 December) "VHS: Yesterday, Today, and Tomorrow," *Tape-Disc Business*: 26.

DeLancie, P. (2002, 1 June) "High Definition on Digital Versatile Disk: Natural Match or Dangerous Diversion?," *EMedia Magazine*: 24.

Economist. (2007, 8 September) "And in the Blu Corner . . . ," *The Economist*: np.

Edwards, C. (2007, 19 November) "I Want my ITV," *Business Week*: 54.

EWeek.com. (2007, 6 April) "Porn Could be Key to Next-Generation DVD War," *EWeek.com*. Online. Available HTTP: <http://www.eweek.com/article2/0,1759,1437823,00.asp> (accessed 27 December 2007).

ExtremeTech.com.(2007, 27 August) "Sony Adds Blu-ray to All-in-One PC," *ExtremeTech.com*. Online. Available HTTP: <http://www.extremetech.com/article2/0,1558,2126924,00.asp> (accessed 27 December 2007).

ExtremeTech.com. (2007, 3 September) "Lines are Drawn in Next-Gen DVD Race," *ExtremeTech.com*. Online. Available HTTP: <http://www.extremetech.com/article2/0,1558,1733057,00.asp> (accessed 27 December 2007).

Frankel, D. (2002, 25 February) "DVD Faction Responds to D-VHS: Nine Companies Agree on Sharper-Looking Format," *Video Business*: 4.

Garrett, D. (2007, 17–23 December) "Disc Biz Seeks New Spin in '08," *Variety*: 9, 13.

Grover, R. and Edwards, C. (2007, 17 December) "Next-Gen DVDs: Advantage Sony," *Business Week*: 28.

Hachman, M. (2007a, 6 September) "Sony Announces Blu-ray Media Jukebox/Server," *PC Magazine.com*: np.

————. (2007b, 6 September) "Toshiba Pushing Freebies to Lure HD DVD Buyers," *ExtremeTech.com*: np.

Heilemann, J. (2007, 25 June) "Steve Jobs in a Box," *New York Magazine*: np.

Heiss, M. (1998, June) "DVD: The First Stop of the Digital Revolution," *Video Systems*: np.

ImTheKing (2007) Gizmodo.com. Online. Available HTTP: <http://gizmodo.com/gadgets/format-war/businessweek-says-blu+ray-ahead-analysts-predict-hd-dvd-ftw-332434.php> (accessed 28 December 2007).

Jaffee, L. (2007, 1 September) "Seeing is Believing," *Promo*: 14.

Johnson, R. (2004, 13 December) "Sales Are Soaring and Hollywood is Split Over Dividing Profits," *New York Times*: np.

Jones, D. (2002, 19 November) "Philips CEO Expects Spirit of Cooperation to Pay Off," *USA Today*: 4B.

Kageyama, Y. (2007, 11 December) "CEO Says Sony Aims for Reviving the 'Wow' Factor with Game Console, TV, Other Innovations," *Associated Press Financial Wire*: np.

Kingsley-Hughes, A. (2007) "Michael Bay Blames Microsoft for HD DVD/Blu-ray War," ZDNet Blogs. Online. Available HTTP: <http://blogs.zdnet.com/hardware/?p=1019> (accessed 28 December 2007).

Kirsner, S. (2007, 24 April) "Don of DVD's Peace Plan Unheeded by Warring Format Clans," *Daily Variety*: A12.

Klinger, B. (2006) *Beyond the Multiplex: cinema, new technologies, and the home*, Berkeley: University of California Press.

Koseluk, C. (2007, 14 May) "High-def on the Horizon," *Video Business*: 1.

LaGesse, D. (2007, 21 August) "HD DVD Buys a Victory," *US News.com*. Online. Available HTTP: <http://www.usnews.com/blogs/daves-download/2007/08/21/hd-dvd-buys-a-victory.html> (accessed 3 January 2008).

Leung, C. (2002, 12 December) "Format Fights," *The Age (Melbourne)*: 1.

Lynch, J. (2007, 15 August) "Who Cares About Blu-ray and HD DVD,?" *ExtremeTech*: np.

McDonald, P. (2007) *Video and DVD Industries*, London: BFI Publishing.

Mehta, M. (2006, 27 January) "Bursting Hollywood's 'Bubble,'" *Media Culture*: np.

Musgrove, M. (2007, 28 October) "Waiting to Netflix's Plot to Advance," *Washington Post*: F1.

Netherby, J. (2007a, 16 July) "Format War Rages On," *Video Business*: 8.

———. (2007b, 3 September) "Heading Mainstream: Studios, Retailers Plan Broader Promo Push for High-def in Fourth Quarter," *Video Business*: 4.

Netherby J. and Ault, S. (2007, 27 August) "Studios Step up for High-def: Paramount, DreamWorks Choose HD DVD," *Video Business*: 5.

New Media Age. (2007, 30 August) "Sony Attempts to Recreate Bravia Success for Blu-ray Player Launch," *New Media Age*: 3.

Ogg, E. (2007,10 October) "Blu-ray vs. HD-DVD: War Without End," ZDNet News. Online. Available HTTP: <http://news.zdnet.com/2100–9584_22–6212782.html> (accessed 27 December 2007).

Oppodigital.com. (2007) "Getting the Most out of DVD on a HDTV Display," Oppodigital. Online. Available HTTP: <http://www.oppodigital.com/Getting-Most-out-of-DVD-on-HDTV-Display.html> (accessed 28 December 2007).

O'Reilly, T. (2000, 1 April) "Staying Alive: Videotape Industry is Still Alive," *Tape-Disc Business*: 10.

Pegoraro, R (2006, 28 May) "Two Movie Formats, Heading for a High-def Collision," *Washington Post*: F6.

PR Week. (2007, 28 September) "Playtime is Over," *PR Week*: 22.

Prange, S. and Hunt, B. (2002, 3 February) "Four Studios to Issue Titles on Digital VHS," *Video Store*: 1.

Richtel, M. Stone, B. and Holson, L. M. (2007, 29 December) "Wal-Mart Pulls Plug on Movies Via the Web," *New York Times*: C1.

Rivero, E. (2002, 24 February) "New High-Def Disc on Tap: Blu-ray Disc Used by Nine Hardware Manufacturers," *Video Store*: 1.

Ross. R. (2002, 10 March) "Showing Their Colours," *Toronto Star*: C2.

Sabbagh, D. (2007, 16 November) "Film Industry Faces a Whole Series of Epic Battles," *London Times*: 65.

Sanchanta, M. (2007, 1 November) "Toshiba Dims View of DVD Recorder Sales," *Financial Times*: 15.

Sethi, C. (2005, 14 October) "A Conversation with Bill Gates," Daily Princetonian.com. Online. Available HTTP: <http://www.dailyprincetonian.com/archives/2005/10/14/news/13474.shtml> (accessed 28 December 2007).

Shim, R. (2005, April 21) "Unified Next-gen DVD Format in the Works," C/Net New.com, NewsBlog. Online. Available HTTP: <http://www.news.com/8301-10784_3-5680095-7.html?tag=txt> (accessed 28 December 2007).

Sweeting, P. (2000, 17 April) "The Backend," *Variety*: 18.

———. (2007a, 3 September) "High-def Light," *Video Business*: 4.

———. (2007b, 1 October) "No High-def Tipping Point," *Video Business*: 6.

Thom, G. (2002, 20 November) "Sony Joins in at Playground," *Melbourne Herald Sun*: C6.

Taub, E. A. (2007, 31 December) "In the DVD War Over High Definition, Most Buyers are Sitting It Out," *New York Times*: C1.

Valenti, J. (1982) Congressional testimony. Online. Available HTTP: <http://cryptome.org/hrcw-hear.htm> (Accessed 28 December 2007).

Video Business. (2002, 9 September) "Mechanic: Engine is Video: Without it, Studios Could Not Absorb Increases in Production, Marketing Costs," *Video Business*: 1.

Walsh, C. M. (2007, 26 May) "High Noon for High Def," *Billboard*: np.

Williams, F. (2006, 1 June) "4K rules, OK," *Encore Magazine*: np

Yoshida, J. (1997) "Consumer electronics firms await verdict on satellite receivers, digital cameras and DVD—What's under the tree for holiday shoppers?," *Electronic Engineering Times*: np.

Contributors

James Bennett is Senior Lecturer in Media Studies at London Metropolitan University and is the author of a number of articles on digital, interactive television in the UK. His work has been published in *Convergence*, *Screen*, *New Review of Film and Television Studies*, *Media International Australia* and a number of edited collections.

William Boddy is a professor in the Department of Communication Studies at Batuch College and in the Film Studies Certificate Program at the Graduate Center, both of the City University of New York. He is the author of *Fifties Television: the industry and its critics* (University of Illinois Press) and *New Media and Popular Imagination: launching radio, television, and digital media in the united states* (Oxford University Press).

Tom Brown is a Lecturer in Film at the University of Reading where, amongst other topics, he lectures on the relationship between film style and technology. Tom is currently developing a long-standing research interest in the history and function of "direct address" in the cinema. He has also published on the relationship between French and American "classical" film industries.

John T. Caldwell, a media studies scholar and filmmaker, is Professor and Chair of Cinema and Media Studies in the UCLA Department of Film, Television, and Digital Media. Caldwell has authored and edited several books, including *Televisuality: style, crisis and authority in american Television* (1995), *Electronic Media and Technoculture* (ed., 2000), *New Media: digitextual theories and practices* (ed., 2003), and *Production Culture: industrial reflexivity and critical practice in film and television* (Duke UP, 2008). He is also the producer/director of the award winning feature documentaries *Freak Street to Goa: immigrants on the Rajpath* (1989) and *Rancho California (por favour)*, which premiered at the Sundance Film Festival in 2002

Glyn Davis is Academic Coordinator of Postgraduate Studies at Glasgow School of Art. He is the author of monographs on *Queer as Folk* (BFI,

2007) and *Superstar: The Karen Carpenter Story* (Wallflower, 2008), and the co-editor of *Queer TV* (Routledge, 2008).

Catherine Grant is Senior Lecturer in Film Studies at the University of Kent, where she researches questions of film authorship and world cinema. She recently co-edited *Screening world cinema: a Screen reader* (Routledge, 2006), with Annette Kuhn, and is completing a book called *Directing cinema: the new auteurism* that will be published by Manchester University Press.

Barbara Klinger is a Professor in the Department of Communication and Culture at Indiana University in Bloomington, Indiana, where she teaches film and media studies. Her research focuses on reception studies, fan studies, and cinema's relationship to new media. Along with numerous articles, she is author of *Melodrama and Meaning: history, culture, and the films of Douglas Sirk* (Indiana University Press, 1994) and *Beyond the Multiplex: cinema, new technologies, and the home* (University of California Press, 2006).

Caroline Millar is a DVD Producer at the British Film Institute. She was worked on the production of over 40 DVDs on the BFIs DVD list.

Jo T. Smith researches in the area of postcolonial media theory and new media studies, with a particular interest in the interplay between political and aesthetic economies. She has published work on DVD technologies, New Zealand postcolonial politics and Maori Television. Her most current project examines the politics of New Zealand cultural production and is entitled "Unsettled States: settler-native-migrant media in Aotearoa/New Zealand". This project is funded by a Fast Start Marsden grant (2008-2009).

Ginette Vincendeau is Professor of Film Studies and Director of the Film Studies Department at King's College, London. She is the editor of *The Encyclopedia of European Cinema* (1995) and *Film/Literature/Heritage* (2001). She is the author of, among others, *Pépé le Moko* (1998), *Stars and Stardom in French Cinema* (2000), *Jean-Pierre Melville, An American in Paris* (2003) and *La Haine* (2005).

James Walters is Lecturer in Film and Television Studies at the University of Birmingham, having previously taught at the universities of Warwick and Westminster. His written work has appeared in refereed journals including *Screen, Journal of Film and Video, Journal of British Cinema and Television* and *Critical Survey*. He has contributed a chapter to the collection *Violating Time: History, Memory and Nostalgia in Cinema* (Continuum, 2008) and is the author of the monograph *Alternative Worlds in Hollywood Cinema: Resonance Between Realms* (Intellect, 2008).

Index

For the sake of manageability, the index does not include critic names.